MEAT.

How to choose, cook and eat it

Adrian Richardson with Lucy Malouf

Photography by Dean Cambray

Enjoy Your MEAT !

Adrian

Hardie Grant Books

MELBOURNE · LONDON

To Michelle, Rex, Rudi and Roman.

This paperback edition published in 2009
First published in 2008 by
Hardie Grant Books
85 High Street
Prahran, Victoria, 3181, Australia
www.hardiegrant.com.au
www.hardiegrant.co.uk

Cataloguing-in-Publication data is available from the
National Library of Australia.

ISBN 978 1 74066 806 4

Co-authored, edited and indexed by Lucy Malouf
Design by Dominic Hofstede, Hofstede Design
Styling by Caroline Velik
Photography by Dean Cambray
Colour reproduction by Splitting Image Colour Studio
Printed and bound in China by C & C Offset Printing

The publisher would like to thank the following for their
generosity in supplying props for this book:
Bliink Interiors, Market Import, Minimax, and Safari Living.

Contents

Introduction

For a man who was raised as a vegetarian in his early childhood, it's interesting to see where I've ended up! It's no secret that I have a passion for meat. I love to eat it in all its many forms, and I love to prepare and cook it. In fact my Melbourne restaurant, La Luna Bistro, has earned a fair whack of its reputation because of the quality of the meat we serve. But before you start thinking of me as some sort of carnivorous macho-man who's writing a manifesto for the Australian meat industry, you should know that I also love the animals that provide us with our meat. And this is one of the main reasons I wanted to write this book.

For most of us, the knowledge that a living, breathing animal has had to lose its life so that we can eat dinner is something we prefer not to think about. But for me, a love of the meat on my plate sparked a burning need to understand how it got there. During the twenty-odd years I've spent working in restaurants, it's probably true to say that I've been just as interested in what goes on outside the kitchen, as inside it.

This interest has led me on a fascinating journey, and along the way I've met the farmers who raise the animals, the slaughtermen who have the unenviable job of dispatching them and the butchers and small-goods manufacturers who process their meat for our enjoyment. I've learnt that each of these stages makes a vital contribution to the quality of the end result.

As most of us know, there are blindingly obvious differences in the way meat looks, smells, feels and tastes, depending on where you buy it and how much you pay for it. The sad truth is that all meat is not equal because all animals are not treated equally well, and I'll tell you more about this in Chapter 1.

I've also discovered that the more one thinks about and understands the way animals live – and die – to feed us, the more it's natural to want to give them back some sort of dignity. For me, this is not just about ethical farming practices and ensuring that animals have happy lives, but it's also about valuing the animal by using its meat to the fullest extent you can. I'm a big fan of this 'nose-to-tail' philosophy, which has been brilliantly expounded by legendary English chef, Fergus Henderson, among others.

It saddens me that here in the affluent West, we seem only to value or want to use the obvious easy-to-cook cuts of meat, such as steaks, chops and roasts. This is incredibly wasteful when you think that these expensive cuts make up such a small percentage of the overall carcass. I think it is essential to do away with this idea that there is some sort of hierarchy in meat: that price equates to taste and to how we value it. In my view the tougher, more challenging cuts of meat – which, let's face it, make up the bulk of the

beast – can produce far more creative and rewarding meals than the top-dollar cuts: it's all in the way you cook them. So in Chapter 2 I'll explain a little bit more about the differences between tender and tough cuts, and the best ways to cook them, and I'll give you some tips about the equipment you'll need in your kitchen to make the job easier.

Then follow chapters that will give you more specific information and delicious recipes for each animal – beef, veal, lamb, pork, game and poultry. There is a chapter about offal, a chapter about making meat go further by processing or preserving it (which includes some of my favourite charcuterie and sausage recipes) and an entire chapter devoted to pies. And because man (and woman) really can't live on meat alone, there are three final chapters about the other things you'll want to complete your meal, such as side dishes, sauces and condiments.

In the course of writing this book I've cooked and tasted several hundred recipes, and I've selected my favourites to share with you here. You'll find all the classic meat dishes, as well as some old family recipes and some La Luna Bistro specialties. I hope that I can inspire you to try them and that you'll love them as much as I do.

So, in a nutshell, this book is a celebration of every aspect of meat, from the living animal to the recipe you cook for dinner. It's not about trying to persuade you to eat more meat, but I do want to try to convince you to eat *better* meat. And along the way, I also hope to persuade you to expand your meat repertoire to embrace the tougher, more challenging cuts as well as the tender familiar favourites. It's definitely going to mean a shift in focus from quantity to quality – but in the end, don't we owe it to our animals, as well as ourselves, to try to get the absolute most out of our meat?

Adrian Richardson
November 2008

GETTING TO KNOW MEAT

"ONCE YOU'VE FOUND A BUTCHER YOU LIKE, NEVER LET HIM GO!"

Getting to know meat

In wealthy western countries we take meat for granted. Most of us eat it every day because it tastes great and because we know that it is a good and easy source of nutrients. While some of us might have the odd twinge of conscience about eating warm-blooded animals that once frolicked in the fields, the reality is that we humans seem to be hard-wired to eat and enjoy meat.

Like it or not, animals and their meat have played a major role in our development as a species. Archaeological evidence suggests that we have been hunting animals for hundreds of thousands of years and that it was our need to band together to form hunting groups that led to the earliest communities – the start of civilisation itself. These primitive societies soon realised that they could herd animals together and farm them, so as to ensure a more reliable supply of food. A better diet led to improved health, a longer lifespan and bigger brains. Many historians go as far as to suggest that a carnivorous diet is directly responsible for the great evolutionary leaps that mark our progress down through the ages.

It's a very different world today, of course, and the relationship we have with our animals has changed too – and not always for the better. In times past we placed a far greater value on livestock. For the most part households raised their own animals close to home and because they were valuable, they were only slaughtered seasonally, as needed. Once slaughtered, every single part of the animal was used, either to provide an immediate source of fresh meat, or to be preserved to last through the long winter months. Meat was a scarce foodstuff, and something to be saved for special occasions.

With the industrial revolution everything changed. Mechanisation led to large-scale farming, faster transport and refrigeration, which meant that fresh produce could be delivered to the marketplace without spoiling. For the first time, the general population had access to an abundance of meat.

With the evolution of intensive farming came the commoditisation of livestock, to the point that we humans really began to lose touch with our animals. And this has led, inexorably, to today's world, where our children think of meat as something that comes pre-portioned in plastic-wrapped trays, as widely available – and as insignificant – as a fast-food burger. Isn't this a sad dissociation of our bellies from our minds and our hearts?

And it's not just our kids that are confused. Even though we are eating more meat than ever before and we live in an age of information overload, the irony is that we know less and less about it. It seems that every day we are being bombarded with conflicting dietary advice. Some doctors tell us to eat less meat; they say it is loaded with saturated fats that will give us a heart attack. Other contradictory reports tell us that lean meat is relatively low in saturated fats and, better still, it is a good source of omega-3 fatty acids, the 'healthy fats'. We read scary newspaper articles about chickens being pumped full of hormones and cattle being forced to eat their own dead cousins. In the supermarket we hover indecisively between a pricey organic pork roast and bargain-priced barbecue chops, and then decide that we don't have the time or energy to cook, and plump for a Kentucky Fried takeaway instead.

I think the time has come for us to try to get to know our meat again.

FROM THE FARM TO THE FORK

This is the story of the people and places that feature in the journey of meat. These are my people – the folk I like to hang out with given half a chance – and these are the places that I choose to visit when I've got a day off from the restaurant. So to begin at the beginning, the journey of meat starts with the farmers.

The farmers

In the early days of La Luna Bistro I made the decision to bypass the large commercial meat suppliers and go straight to the source: the farmer. I've never regretted this decision and as a result, I've made some great mates, who are as passionate about their animals and food as I am.

The first thing to say is that, in general, Australian livestock farms, whatever their size, are some of the best in the world. We have an enviable reputation for animal husbandry and because it is an island, Australia remains free from many of the cattle, sheep, pork and poultry diseases that beset other countries.

Broadly speaking, livestock farming in Australia can be divided into two types. The majority are intensive, large-scale farms, where the emphasis is on high yields and consistent returns for the operators. These farms have evolved to supply the massive consumer demand for cheap, abundant meat. While Australian farms stack up pretty well against their American and European counterparts, they are definitely all about delivering a product. On these farms there is little attention given to the animal itself, and its living environment and diet are designed with the express aim of bringing it to market size as quickly and as inexpensively as possible.

At the other end of the scale are small farmers, who often have a particular interest in rare breeds, and these are the people that, in the main, I want to give my business to. On this sort of farm the animals are free to roam and they are fed as natural a diet as possible. There is far more emphasis on the animal's welfare, and on bringing it to market in the best possible condition. Don't misunderstand me, it's not that these farmers are sentimental fools; they are fully aware that they are raising animals for eating. It's just that they feel a sense of responsibility about giving the animal a good life while it is alive. As one of my farmer friends says, 'A happy animal is a tasty animal'.

The abattoir

There is nothing pretty about abattoirs, or about the slaughtermen (and they are mainly men) who work there, but they are an essential part of the journey. I've spent a fair amount of time in these places, and I can honestly say that after each visit I come away feeling an overwhelming sense of gratitude and admiration for the people who work there. I'm not denying it's a confronting and even a brutal experience, but slaughtermen are skilled professionals and I've always been impressed by the pains that they take to give the animal as stress-free and comfortable a death as possible. It certainly seems no worse a way to go than any other more 'natural' end.

The whole process is also surprisingly quick, taking perhaps 45 minutes from beginning to end. If you are squeamish, you might want to skip the next paragraph, but for those who are interested, or who wish to try to come to terms with the fact that there can be no meat without the death of an animal, here's what happens.

The animals are received into holding pens at the abattoir a day or two ahead of time, to give them time to settle. When the time comes, they are herded, single file, through a corral. At the end of the line each animal enters a small restraining pen, screened from the animal behind it. Its head is held firm and the 'knocker' holds a bolt gun to the forehead, which stuns and kills the animal instantaneously. It then drops through a trapdoor to the floor below where it is hung upside down by one of the hind legs onto the processing line. Next comes the most dangerous, and perhaps the most confronting stage of the process: the main arteries in the animal's throat are cut and in some slaughterhouses an electrical current is applied which forces the muscles to pump and hasten exsanguination. As a result, the animal's limbs kick and jerk frantically, and you do have to remind yourself that these are not death-throes, and that the animal is already dead. Next, it is skinned and the head, hooves and internal organs are removed. Each of these parts is despatched on its own conveyor belt for various uses: the hides are sent for tanning, heads and guts are processed for fertiliser or pet food, the hooves might be sent for use as bait in the crayfish industry. The carcass itself is split in half and sent to the blast-chiller. Twenty-four hours later the carcass goes to an off-site processor or to the abattoir's own boning room, where it is broken down to varying degrees, boxed up and despatched.

The wholesale butchers and processors

These processors specialise in bulk supply to the hospitality industry and to hospitals, schools, caterers, independent supermarkets and retail butchers.

The retailers

In Australia, we eat around 36 kilograms of beef, 14 kilograms of lamb (and mutton), 23 kilograms of pork and 35 kilograms of poultry every year. So where are we buying all this meat from? Well, if you're anything like the majority of Australian shoppers, you'll be buying most of your fresh meat at the supermarket – which means from Safeway/Woolworths, Coles/Bi-Lo and other independent supermarkets. Supermarkets now account for around 65 per cent of fresh meat sales, which doesn't leave much for the local butcher, fresh produce markets and farmers' markets.

It's a great shame, really, because although there is nothing actually *wrong* with supermarket meat, it's just that meat can and should be so much better. The supermarkets are where most of our intensively farmed meat ends up. It comes from grain-fed animals that have been rushed to the supermarket without the benefits of dry-aging. It is cut into small family-friendly portions, bunged on a polystyrene tray and wrapped in plastic. You'll usually find an absorbent pad underneath the meat to mop up the blood, but more often than not, plastic-wrapped meat will be wet and will have a strong smell from the oxidised blood that leaches out of the meat. What you won't find on supermarket meat is any sort of meaningful information about the meat's provenance.

In my opinion, the worst thing about supermarkets is not that they supply us with ordinary meat, but that they have bamboozled us into thinking that this is the way meat *should* be. So most of us have come to believe that our beef or lamb is best if it is a vivid red (accentuated by the cunning in-store lighting); that it should be lean; that any fat (when it hasn't been trimmed off) should be a pure white; and above all, that it should be super-fresh. And we've grown so used to seeing this sort of product, that now we seem unable to recognise the good stuff any more.

And you are far more likely to find the good stuff at an independent butcher or your local market. Yes. These are the guys who I hope will become your heroes. They are at the frontline of the industry; they are the true experts and your link to quality. If you take only one message away after reading this book, it is to make friends with your butcher. At the very least make sure you know his name, and that he knows yours. And ask him questions. With a good butcher, you'll find that the more you ask, the more interesting you'll become to him, and the more effort he'll take to find you a good bit of meat. And more often than not he'll give you plenty of advice about how to prepare and cook it, too.

Once you start looking, you'll find that there are all kinds of different butchers out there, many of whom have distinct areas of expertise, in addition to the more usual meat offerings. In different neighbourhoods in your town you might find Eastern European butchers specialising in smoked and cured smallgoods, or Italian butchers, famous for their veal, salamis and sausages. Elsewhere there might be Chinese butchers who excel with pork, British butchers offering gammon, black and white puddings and haggis, or French butchers selling offal and homemade terrines and confits. It's a whole new world of meat-adventure to explore out there.

Seriously, butcher's shops are fun places – and most butchers are fun blokes! And at the very least you know that they are passionate about their meat – they have to be to have survived the onslaught of supermarkets. Sure, there is always going to be the odd shifty one around, the guy who trades on price and whose meat looks like it's been sitting there for a while. But the majority of independent butchers are dedicated to their trade and are interested in making you, the customer, happy. So it's really worth taking the time to find a butcher you like. And once you've found him, never let him go!

The language of meat

People often tell me that they feel overwhelmed, intimidated and bewildered by the array of meat on display in supermarkets and butchers' shops. So this is why, time after time, they'll go for the same old pork chops or chicken breasts. And I agree; the language of meat can be difficult to learn. It is confusing the way the same cut sometimes has different names in different shops or cities or states. And then there are all the marketing terms that have crept in to try and entice us to buy the 'new white meat', 'heartsmart' lamb racks, a 'New York steak' or 'chemical-free' chicken.

In my opinion, this is yet another good reason to make friends with a good butcher. He's the man to help you learn the language of meat and before long you'll be chatting away happily.

You'll find more information about specific animals in individual chapters, but here are a few basics to get you started.

FARMERS' MARKETS
I do realise that it is not as easy for you to buy your meat straight from the source as it is for me, as a restaurateur. But if you are interested in buying direct from the farmer, then farmers' markets are a great place to start. You'll find a limited selection of different types of meat, but these are the people who are perhaps most passionate of all about their product. Remember, though, that these people are farmers, not retailers. They won't have the same broad knowledge base about meat as your butcher, although they will know everything you ever wanted to know about their own particular animals' lifestyle and diet – especially if it's a rare breed.

When an animal is butchered, its carcass is broken down into large sections known as the *primal cuts*. These in turn are broken down by your butcher into smaller portions, such as steaks, cutlets, leg roasts and so on, for retail sale. There are plenty of charts (available on-line or at your local butcher) which will give you a visual guide to all these primal and retail cuts, but as a shopper and cook, what you really need to know is a bit of basic anatomy.

Meat is muscle, and common sense will tell you that the muscles in different parts of an animal will do more – or less – work. And the amount of work a muscle does will make it more – or less – tender. In the language of meat, the tender muscles are often called the prime cuts and they are more expensive – you might like to think of them as 'tender-and-top-dollar'. The secondary cuts are less expensive and can be characterised as 'tough-but-tasty'.

For all four-legged animals, the tenderest cuts come from the back, where the muscles do little work in moving the animal around. The back section of the animal includes the rib and loin, which are broken down into smaller pieces to produce tender steaks and roasts. Lower on the tenderness scale, as you move down the back, comes the rump. Then come the large leg muscles, which do plenty of work, making them tasty, but a bit tough. Muscles from the shoulder, neck, forequarter and belly are long and layered with plenty of interconnective tissue, so they are the toughest of all, but yielding and juicy when cooked long and slowly.

And then there is offal, the 'yucky' parts of the animal that many people don't even want to think about, let alone eat. Offal includes the animal's head (and everything within), its innards, internal organs, glands and tail.

Every single cut of meat can make a delicious meal. As I've said before, it's all about the way you cook it. In the next chapter we'll learn a bit more about the best ways to cook the different cuts of meat.

A few useful definitions

Feedlot farms are concentrated feeding operations where animals are confined to a small area and fed a controlled diet. Sometimes animals enter a feedlot prior to slaughter and are fed energy-dense food to encourage fat or marbling. Feedlot farming has become more common in Australia, especially in drought-affected areas. Animals fed from feedlot operations are sold as **grain-fed** meat.

On certified **organic farms** animals are free to roam and graze on pastures that are completely clean of synthetic chemicals, herbicides and pesticides. They are not fed hormones or antibiotics.

Free-range means slightly different things, depending on the industry group, but in general, free-range animals shouldn't be closely confined and must have access to outside areas, as well as to shelter.

Many people wonder about the difference between **grass-fed** and **grain-fed** animals. Historically, all beef cattle were grass-fed because they were raised on pastures, and as ruminants, this sort of grazing was their natural diet. On a natural grass diet cattle take much longer to mature and fatten, which doesn't suit many of today's intensive farming businesses. Increasingly, many beef cattle are moved in to feedlot operations, where they are fed a diet of grains (corn, barley, soy and sorghum) to fatten them up quickly for slaughter.

These different diets result in very different meat. The first giveaway is the colour of the fat, which is various shades of creamy yellow for grass-fed beef and a purer white for grain-fed beef. The texture of the meat differs too, with grass-fed beef being leaner and grain-fed more marbled with fat. The ultimate grain-fed beef is Wagyu beef, which is called Kobe beef when it is raised in Japan.

Dry-aging is also known as hanging meat, and it is one of my passions. If you walk into the cool-room in my restaurant on any day of the week you'll see a row of beef carcasses hanging from the ceiling, at various degrees of aging. In my view, this is one of the most important things I can do to improve the flavour, tenderness and moistness of meat I serve up to my customers. So what does it mean, and why is it so hard to find these days?

First, it is important to understand that not all meats are suited to aging – immature, fresh meats, such as veal, lamb, pork and chicken shouldn't be aged – but beef and game benefit enormously from this process. When butchers (and the odd crazy chef) dry-age meat (which doesn't just mean that they let it get old), it dramatically affects both the texture and flavour. During the dry-aging process the natural enzymes in the meat start to act upon the muscle fibres, making them softer and more tender. Some of the moisture in the meat evaporates, so the flavour becomes much more concentrated. This drying out of the flesh also means that it cooks much better than fresh wet meat.

Because it takes time, and because there is some weight loss, dry-aging is a costly process, which is the main reason fewer and fewer butchers think it worthwhile. And you'll never see dry-aged meat in supermarkets because avoiding weight loss is vital for the maximisation of returns.

Ironically, though, big meat processors and supermarkets do see a benefit in prolonging the lifespan of meat, which has led to a big increase in **wet-aged** or vacuum-packed meat. Wrapping meat in plastic prevents moisture loss through evaporation (which is why it is popular), but it does mean that the meat will sit in a bath of its own blood for a few weeks. In my view this does nothing to improve the quality of the meat, and worse still, when you open the bag, it can really pong.

Just a word of caution about dry-aging: this is not something to try at home. It has to be done under very controlled conditions, at the correct temperature (between 0 and 2°C) and humidity (around 90 per cent). If the temperature is too low, then the enzymes won't activate; if it is too high, there's a risk of harmful bacteria spoiling the meat. If the humidity is too dry, then the meat will lose too much moisture; if the air is too damp, then the meat risks becoming mouldy.

WAYS TO COOK MEAT

"SEASON, SEAR, COOK, REST, CARVE & EAT."

Ways to cook meat

SALT BEFORE YOU COOK
I always salt my meat liberally just before I cook it. Forget the dire warnings that salt will draw out the juices from your meat and leave it dry and tough. This is nonsense. Salting before you cook is not only essential to bring out the intrinsic flavour of your meat, but it also actually helps to brown it. (See Searing, page 14.)

In some countries they like to eat raw meat – think of French steak tartare, or its Middle Eastern equivalent, kibbeh nayee. But on the whole, most of us prefer to cook our meat before eating it.

Heat transforms meat: not only does it kill off any 'nasties', but it makes the meat more tender and develops its flavour. Historians tell us that our desire to 'cook' meat even predated the discovery of fire. Apparently ancient man's first efforts at cooking involved using hot stones and water from naturally occurring hot springs. With fire came our early experiments with grilling and roasting. And once we'd worked out how to make cooking pots, these primitive techniques developed into a much more sophisticated art.

I will discuss the various cooking methods a little further on, but no matter which cut of meat you buy or which dish you cook there are five simple steps that I always like to follow: season, sear, cook, rest, carve...and then eat!

SEASON
All meat needs to be seasoned to some degree. It's the first critical stage of the cooking process, and is all about bringing out the inherent flavour of your meat.

Salt
The simplest and most effective seasoning of all is salt. You probably don't realise it, but the reason food in restaurants tastes so good is because chefs salt the living daylights out of it. And this is not something that should scare you. If you are concerned about excessive salt consumption for health reasons, then my advice is not to stop salting your food, but to stop eating salty food, by which I mean most processed and pre-packaged foodstuffs that are loaded with the stuff.

Salt is an essential mineral for the human body. Simply put, without it, we die. But salt also acts as an important trigger to the production of saliva in our mouths and the gastric juices in our stomachs. While good-quality salt is flavour-neutral, it is the ultimate flavour enhancer. If you don't believe me, try cooking two steaks. Salt one before you cook it, but leave the other unseasoned. You'll quickly realise how the salt heightens the meaty flavour of the one, while the other tastes bland and unpalatable. I like to use unrefined salt flakes, such as Australia's very own Murray River Salt Flakes. Other great salts you might like to try are the English Maldon Sea Salt and Fleur de Sel from Brittany.

Brining is another way of using salt, albeit in a liquid form. Brining is a traditional method of preserving meat by curing (pickling) it. As well as extending its lifespan, brines enhance the texture and colour of meat, and flavoured brines penetrate deep within the meat and change its flavour.

Pepper
If salt is the first step in seasoning meat, then for me, spicing it up with a good grind of pepper comes a close second. I mainly use freshly ground black pepper at home and in the restaurant kitchen because I prefer its flavour to white pepper. But both act to enliven and heighten the flavour of meat, and they add their own unique sharpness and heat to a dish.

Strangely, both salt and pepper seem to have different effects on meat depending on whether they are added before or after you cook it. So I always season twice. And the key rule here is to taste-season-taste again.

Spices

These are the aromatic berries, buds, bark, seeds, fruit and roots of edible plants, and they usually come from faraway exotic places. They are used in many different ethnic cuisines to enliven and enhance the flavour of a dish. They can be added whole (a stick of cinnamon, a sprinkling of allspice berries or a star anise will jazz up a casserole or soup beautifully) or ground to a powder for marinades or dry rubs that are sprinkled onto meat before cooking and left for anything up to a day or two. The longer the meat is exposed to the spices, the more they will infuse it with their flavour.

I often dry-roast spices before grinding them, which brings out their flavour even more.

Herbs

These are the edible stalks and leaves of aromatic plants and they can be used in all sorts of ways to add flavour to meat. I use a bucket-load of herbs at La Luna Bistro – so much so, that I even planted a herb garden on the nature strip outside the front entrance (in consultation with the local council, of course).

You can divide herbs into hard and soft and each type has a purpose. Hard herbs, such as thyme, rosemary and bay leaves are best added at the start of cooking as they impart their flavour over time. Think of a bouquet garni – the bundle of aromatic herbs used for flavouring stocks, soups and braises. Soft herbs, like mint, chervil, basil, chives and so on, are best used raw, or added to dishes at the end of the cooking time. All herbs can be pounded into wet pastes or blended with oil to marinate meat before cooking.

Incidentally, I'm not a big fan of dried herbs, as they're usually a bit old and dusty. The only exception is oregano, which I dry myself – something I learned from my nonno.

Aromatics

These are what I think of as the foundations of many cooked meat dishes, and include garlic, ginger, fresh chilli, onions, celery, leeks and carrots. These last four vegetables are often diced together to form a mirepoix, which is used to enhance the flavour of stocks, stews, soups and sauces.

Fat

Strangely enough, one of the best flavour enhancers is actually part of the meat itself. Yes, it's the fat that marbles the flesh or covers the surface of a piece of meat. In our health-obsessed modern world we have focused on breeding our animals lean and with trimming off every visible skerrick of fat from our meat before we cook it. And the result is a real diminishment of flavour. As most chefs will tell you, it really is important to have some fat in our meat. Fat is tasty in its own right, but it also acts to enhance the intrinsic 'meatiness' of meats. Fat has the added benefit of keeping meat moist as you cook it. This means that you actually need to add fat when you cook with very lean cuts – either in the form of olive oil or butter, or if you're feeling very naughty, pork back fat or lard.

SEAR

After seasoning, the very first step of the cooking process involves searing the meat on all sides over a high heat. Why do we do this? Well, because searing adds colour – in recipes it's often described as 'browning' the meat – and it adds an intense layer of flavour.

The reason for this is that the high heat used in searing causes the juices in the meat to rush to the surface (and generous salting encourages this). These juices contain natural sugars and proteins and, as they are heated, they interact with each other to form new aromas and flavours. The technical name for this effect is the Maillard reaction – but it's simpler to think of it in terms of caramelisation.

COOK

It's vitally important to choose the appropriate cooking method for each particular cut of meat. Get this bit right, and you'll be well on the road to a delicious meal.

As I outlined in Chapter 1, all meat is muscle, but not all muscles in the animal's body are the same. Tender cuts of meat (the ones that have led an easy life) have little in the way of connective tissue, and are best for dry-cook methods, such as roasting, and quick-cook methods like grilling, barbecuing or frying.

Tougher cuts (the muscles that have done lots of work) have bigger fibres and contain a lot of connective tissue, so they need to be cooked by long, slow methods with liquid. Slow-roasting, stewing and braising are all brilliant for tougher cuts, as they gently soften and melt the connective tissue, transforming it to juicy, flavourful gelatine.

So here's a quick run-through of the various methods of cooking meats, matched to the various cuts of meat.

Roasting

Is there anyone who doesn't love a roast? They're usually the meal of choice for family get-togethers and celebrations, and thankfully, roasting is one of the simplest cooking methods of all.

Simply put, roasting involves cooking a large piece of meat by exposing it to a flame (when it's called spit-roasting) or to the radiant heat of an oven. Before you even begin cooking, you should bring your meat to room temperature. If the meat is cold, it may initially steam, rather than roast, and it will take longer to cook, too. Don't forget to preheat your oven to the appropriate temperature either.

Having seasoned your meat (as discussed above) you will sometimes want to sear it in the roasting tin on your stovetop, but otherwise an initial fierce blast of heat in the oven will also cause the inherent sugars to caramelise, and the surface of the meat to brown.

I recommend sitting your meat on a roasting rack set inside a heavy-based roasting tin. This allows the hot air to circulate around the meat, which helps it to cook and colour evenly. As the meat cooks you might like to baste it from time to time with the juices that drip into the base of the tray. Not only does this help to keep the roast lovely and moist, but it adds colour and flavour.

The trickiest thing about roasting is knowing when the meat is cooked to your liking. But all this anxiety can be done away with if you use a meat thermometer (see page 17). Remember that meat roasted on the bone will be sweeter and tastier, but will also take a bit longer to cook.

Grilling and barbecuing

These quick-cook methods use fierce heat to caramelise and brown the meat's surface. Because they use high heat, they are best suited to small, tender cuts of meat, such as steaks, cutlets or chicken breasts, that don't have as much tough connective tissue. More often than not, these cuts of meat are bred with minimal fat, to appeal to the health-conscious. This means that you have to be careful not to let them dry out by cooking them for too long. You should always moisten the meat with a little oil or butter before you cook it. Marinating it before cooking will help too.

Technically speaking, we 'grill' meat by exposing it to radiant heat. The heat source may be below, as when we barbecue over flames, or on a cast-iron grill plate. Overhead grills (which are called salamanders in restaurant kitchens) cook the meat from above. All grilling involves some involvement from the cook. You will need to move it closer to, or further away from the heat source, to control the temperature and cooking speed.

Always keep your grill or barbecue clean so that old burnt flavours don't taint your food. And always, always preheat it, so that it is hot before you start to cook.

Frying

Frying is called sautéing in French, which refers to the way the food 'jumps' in the pan as it is tossed around. Like grilling, it is a quick-cook method of cooking small, tender pieces of meat and needs oil or butter added so that the meat can brown.

There are several different ways of frying, such as shallow-frying or deep-frying, which relate to the quantity of oil or fat that is used. Shallow-frying uses a small layer of oil on the base of the pan, whereas deep-frying requires the food to be immersed in a much larger amount of oil. Deep-fried foods often benefit from being coated in a protective layer of batter or crumbs, which are crunchy and delicious, but also act to seal in the juices and prevent the meat drying out.

Another type of frying is stir-frying, which depends on all the ingredients being prepared to a uniform size, and having them ready to be cooked together over a high heat. Stir-fried foods can be cooked very quickly in a small amount of oil.

With all frying, the type of oil or fat used will affect the end result. Duck fat, lard or dripping, butter, olive oil or flavoured oils all impart their own distinctive flavour to the meat, while vegetable oils tend to be very mild in flavour. Fats also vary in their smoking points, (butter and olive oil both have low smoking points), so you need to watch them carefully so they don't burn and spoil the flavour of your meal.

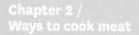

Braising, pot-roasting and stewing

These are all long, slow, gentle methods of cooking meat with vegetables and aromatics in varying amounts of tasty liquid. They are ideal for tougher cuts that tend to be layered with lots of connective tissue, sinews and fat. These don't sound immediately appealing, it's true, but during the long, gentle cooking the texture of the meat softens to fall-apart tenderness and the connective tissues release wonderful gelatinous juices to create a rich, deep-flavoured gravy.

In a braise the meat tends to be cut into large pieces – a pot-roast uses a whole joint – which are first seared (see page 14) to colour the surface a lovely golden brown, and then cooked with aromatic herbs and vegetables in a small amount of liquid. Because braises are cooked in a tightly covered casserole dish, as the meat cooks, the liquid creates a fragrant stream which condenses and is reabsorbed back into the meat. The less liquid used, the more intensely flavoured the sauce will be.

In a stew, the same principles apply, but the meat is cut into smaller pieces, which are completely immersed in a larger amount of cooking liquid. Because they use more liquid, stews are often cooked uncovered, so that the liquid can evaporate to create a thick sauce.

These are three of my all-time favourite cooking methods – and they're some of the most economical, as they use the less popular inexpensive cuts. You can choose anything from the cheeks, neck or shoulder, to the breast, belly, shanks, or tail. Use a heavy-based ovenproof casserole dish with a tight-fitting lid. Older recipes will often suggest dusting the pieces of meat in flour before browning, which helps to thicken the sauce. I'm not wild about using flour in my cooking, so if necessary I prefer to lift out the meat and reduce the sauce over a high heat until it reaches the consistency I like. Although these dishes do take a long time to cook – sometimes several hours – they are certainly not difficult. Once you've put the casserole dish in the oven you can leave it alone and do the gardening, read the paper or help the kids with their homework. This makes them the perfect dinner party dish as you do all the preparation and cooking ahead of time, and simply reheat them in time to serve your friends.

REST

I can't stress how important it is to rest your meat after cooking it. This is essential, especially after all high-heat methods of cooking, from grilling, barbecuing and frying to roasting. Think of a steak for instance. It's been flipped over and over on a hot griddle pan, which causes the muscle to contract and tighten in reaction to the heat – clench your fist, and you'll get the idea. Now imagine cutting into that tight, hard piece of meat. It's easy to see that with all that tension and pressure, the lovely juices are going to burst out. The point of resting is that it gives your meat time to recover from the ordeal of cooking. That clenched fist gradually relaxes, until it is soft and pliable again. All the juices settle back into the meat, and when you cut into it, they will stay right where they are.

As a general rule of thumb I recommend that you rest your meat for at least half the cooking time. Let me say that again: *rest it for half the cooking time*. I know it seems like a lot – especially if your chook has been roasting for over an hour – but believe me, if you follow this rule you will always end up with delicious, juicy and tender meat.

Don't stress too much about the meat getting cold; you'll be surprised how much heat is retained inside. Just make sure that you rest the meat in a warmish place – on the counter next to the oven or on the stovetop is perfect. Cover it loosely with a big sheet of foil or a tea towel and just leave it alone. And, of course, if you are really concerned, then by all means pop it back into a hot oven for few minutes before carving. The added bonus of resting your meat is that it gives you time to get the rest of the meal together, or to set the table, have a few drinks, put on your make-up or read the kids a bedtime story.

CARVE

If you've rested your meat properly, then carving it should be easy. Don't get yourself all worked up about it either. To be honest, I think it's often more about a bit of ceremony, especially when it comes to carving up big impressive roasts at the table.

The basics of carving are simple, and they apply to everything from a big roast to a piece of steak. First, use a sharp knife. Second, use a carving fork to hold the meat steady (resist the temptation to spear the meat with the fork, though). Third, and this is the most technical I'm going to get, cut the meat across the grain of the muscle. Fourth, remember that even if you think you're doing it 'wrong', it's not going to ruin your dinner!

EQUIPMENT

You could probably fill your kitchen five times over with all the stuff that food magazines and fancy cookware shops tell you that you can't live without. But my motto with kitchen equipment is 'beware of gadgets'. The truth is that you don't need a whole set of special equipment for cooking meat. In fact you'll probably find that you already have most of the essentials.

I'm going to assume that you have a stovetop and oven, and the usual array of wooden spoons, spatulas, whisks, measuring cups, scales and so on. So here's a quick run-down of the kitchen tools that I think are essential for successful and happy meat cookery:

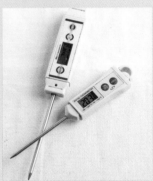

Meat thermometer

If you are really serious about cooking meat then I think it is essential to invest in a good-quality digital meat thermometer. It's the best way I know to eliminate any worries you might have about doneness and all the chefs in my kitchen use them. Many people will be familiar with the old-fashioned style of dial thermometer that you jam into the meat before sticking it in the oven. In my view these are not as accurate or as precise as modern digital models, and nor are they much help with cooking thinner cuts, such as steaks and chops.

My advice is to get yourself a battery-powered instant-read digital thermometer. They will give you an accurate reading when the tip is inserted into a piece of meat, making them ideal for steaks, burgers and chops. They range in price, but all are accurate and reliable to within a few degrees. The most sophisticated versions can be left in the meat while the digital readout sits on your work surface, allowing you to monitor the cooking progress without opening the oven door. These thermometers usually have an alarm that buzzes when the meat reaches your pre-determined temperature.

Tongs

The most inexpensive item is one of the most invaluable. You'll find that you use tongs all the time, for turning big pieces of meat in a roasting tin, for flipping burgers on the barbecue, for moving steaks around on the griddle pan and so on. Tongs are cheap, so it's worth buying a long set, as well as a couple of shorter ones. The best ones have a catch that keeps the arms together when not in use.

Knives, steels and stones

You don't need an entire set of knives for most meat cookery. I recommend that you invest in a good-quality 25 cm cook's knife for chopping, slicing, dicing and carving, and a small sharp paring knife for peeling vegetables and for more delicate work. If you're going to start doing a bit more adventurous meat cookery, then you will also need a 12–14 cm boning knife. There are many good-quality knife brands to choose from, but the main criteria are design and material. The blade should be forged from a single piece of steel that extends the length of the handle. The handle should be made from a durable material, such as wood, stainless steel or a quality plastic or rubber compound.

A top-quality knife will be expensive so, for goodness sake, look after it. This means keeping it sharp (you are more likely to cut yourself on a blunt knife than on a sharp one). Either have your knives sharpened regularly by a professional (your butcher will help you find a good knife sharpener) or learn how to put an edge on a knife yourself using a stone and how to maintain the edge using a steel.

Carving fork

A good-quality fork is not just useful for carving, but also for general manoeuvring of your meat. The best forks are expensive, but they will last you a lifetime.

Ladles

These are indispensable for skimming away any scum and fat from stocks and sauces. They are also handy for serving soups, stews and casseroles. Choose good-quality stainless steel ladles rather than cheap plastic ones.

Roasting tins

It is very important to have a tin that is the appropriate size for the piece of meat, so it makes good sense to have several roasting tins of varying sizes, but at the very least, a large one and a medium-sized one. Make sure they are good-quality, heavy-based tins that you can use on the stovetop as well as in the oven. You want to be able to make your gravy without the tin warping from the intense heat.

Roasting rack

I like to sit meat on a rack that fits inside a roasting tin, rather than plonking it on the bottom of the tin. This allows the hot air to circulate around the meat, and it cooks more evenly. The best racks are sturdy, with handles, so you can easily transfer the cooked meat to a board for carving.

Casserole dishes

These are deep dishes with ovenproof handles and lids that are used for wet-cook methods, such as braising, stewing and pot-roasting. The best ones are made out of a heavy material, such as enamelled cast-iron, earthenware or stainless steel. Casserole dishes should be heavy-based so that you can use them to brown meat on the stovetop before transferring the dish to the oven.

Saucepans and stockpots

You'll need a small, medium and large saucepan – and again, invest in the best quality you can afford. These days it probably goes without saying that you should avoid aluminium pots, not just because of the associated health risks, but because aluminium reacts with acidic ingredients (such as tomatoes, lemon and vinegar) and will taint the flavour of your food. If you're going to make your own stocks, then you'll need a stockpot. There's no getting away from the fact that stockpots are big, because really, there's no point in making small amounts of stock. Choose the largest one you can accommodate in your kitchen.

Griddle pans

I love griddle pans. They are flat heavy pans with raised edges that leave characteristic striped markings on food – mimicking the charring of barbecued food. The best griddle pans are made from cast iron and can be heated to high temperatures on your stovetop. If you can, choose a griddle pan that has a metal handle, rather than wood or plastic, so you can stick it in the oven.

Frying pans

Ideally you should have a large frying pan, and a smaller one, but do try to choose frying pans that are ovenproof, so you can transfer a browned piece of meat to the oven to finish cooking. The best frying pans are heavy-based so they conduct heat efficiently and evenly, but the design and material are often down to personal preference. Some cooks prefer cast-iron pans, other stainless steel or copper. Each has its own benefits and drawbacks. I am also quite fond of my heavy-based non-stick frying pan, which makes things really easy and does mean you can cut down on the amount of fat you use.

Sieves and colanders

These are useful for straining stocks and sauces. They come in various sizes and in varying degrees of fineness, the priciest being a fine conical strainer (a chinois). They need to be durable, so I'd choose metal, rather than plastic.

Secret men's business – the barbecue

You could happily spend all your dosh on a barbecue and barbecue paraphernalia – and in my opinion it would be money well spent! I think most of us blokes feel that there is something in our blood that draws us to cooking outdoors on barbies – it probably dates back to our cavemen days when we would throw a mammoth steak onto the camp fire.

These days, as you'll probably know, there are many different barbecue options to choose from. The most popular are the hooded gas-fired barbecues or solid fuel kettle style (such as a Weber). Both will give you hours of fun, but the main difference is that gas barbies cook at a lower temperature than wood, charcoal or briquettes. Barbecue fanatics will also say that wood and charcoal add an incomparable flavour to your food. But on the the other hand, most of us find gas barbies are easier to clean and look after – they're certainly more suited to spur-of-the moment fits of barbecue enthusiasm as you can crank them up and use them within minutes.

As well as the barbecue itself, you're going to need fuel – a gas bottle, charcoal or briquettes, as appropriate. Try experimenting with woodchips (hickory, mesquite, oak and so on) to add flavour, too. These days there are all manner of different types available that are particularly good if you want to add a smoky American-style flavour to your food.

Additionally, you'll want a few pairs of long-handled tongs, a carving fork, an oven mitt, a selection of metal or wooden skewers, foil drip trays, a heavy-duty wire brush for cleaning and a fire extinguisher in case it all goes horribly wrong!

BEEF

THE KING
OF MEAT

Beef

For much of my life I've been having a not-so-secret love affair with beef. It all began when I was a young apprentice working in the kitchens of a big function centre. Butchery is an important part of a chef's training, and it turned out to be something I was good at and really enjoyed. So by my fourth year of training I was running the entire butchery section, responsible for preparing the meat, poultry, fish and charcuterie for 2000 meals every day.

Years later, when I opened my own restaurant, La Luna Bistro, in Melbourne's North Carlton, budgets were tight. On top of that, I was constantly disappointed by the quality of the beef that was being delivered. Before long, I decided to take matters into my own hands. After a bit of research I took a big step and invested some of our hard-earned profits into buying a whole steer carcass to hang in the restaurant's cool-room. It turned out to be a great move. Because of my butchery skills I was able to break down and use the whole animal, which was far more cost-effective than buying in only the prime cuts that we needed. We had to be really creative in finding delicious ways of using all the tougher, more challenging cuts, and the customers loved the old-fashioned braises and pot-roasts we put on the menu. Even better, they started raving about the taste and texture of our steaks, which reaffirmed my belief in the benefits of dry-aging.

I'm not alone in my love for beef. Ancient European cave paintings of wild oxen show that we humans have been eating beef for many thousands of years, as well as using cattle for their milk and pulling power. Today there are hundreds of different breeds and cross-breeds, all of which are descended from these early wild oxen (*Bos primigenius*). Although they were slower to be domesticated than the more biddable sheep and pigs, nowadays beef is one of the most widely consumed meats around the world.

AUSTRALIAN BEEF

Cattle were first brought to Australia in 1788 with the First Fleet. Five cows and two bulls were taken on board at Cape Town, and brought over for breeding in the new colony. The early attempts at farming were not exactly a resounding success, as all but one of the small herd escaped into the wilderness of the Australian bush. But a few years later a herd of 61 cattle was discovered in pasture land 70 kilometres away from the original settlement. Fifty years later their numbers had swelled to 54,000, by the middle of the 19th century there were 400,000 and today there are close to 29 million cattle in Australia.

Cattle breeders in Australia have adapted their stock – whether dairy or beef cattle – to suit the varying climatic zones here, which range from temperate to tropical. Unlike other parts of the world, our beef industry is quite independent from the dairy industry, which means that we enjoy eating meat from breeds specifically raised for meat, rather than milk. The best known of these are the Brahman, Poll Hereford, Shorthorn, Limousin, Charolais, Aberdeen Angus, and our very own Murray Grey.

Nearly all Australian beef cattle are raised on vast broadacre farms in our northern states. The remainder are raised on small-scale and 'hobby' farms, which tend to be located in the southern states. Although they only make up around 10 per cent of the industry, there are a large number of these small producers, many of whom have a passion for rare and old-fashioned breeds. There has even been a little burst of production of the Japanese Wagyu recently, and you'll see it on the menus of fashionable restaurants all around the country.

Beef is big business in Australia; in fact it's the biggest agricultural enterprise we have, with a gross value of production of over $7 billion. We are the second largest exporter of beef in the world, and in recent years demand for our beef has been driven by bans on meat from other countries relating to BSE (bovine spongiform encephalopathy, or 'mad cow' disease). Thankfully, our beef enjoys an enviable reputation for quality. Our government and the industry itself have done a great job at keeping our farming ethical and our meat products free from disease.

Grass versus grain

It seems obvious that an animal's diet will affect the flavour of its meat, and this is no less true for beef cattle than for any other beast. Historically, most Australian beef cattle roamed free on vast tracts of pasture land grazing on grass and hay. Grass-fed cattle take up to three years to grow to size and their meat is lean and is a deeper red, and has an earthier more gamey flavour.

However, Australian farmers often have to contend with severe drought conditions, which makes it hard to ensure reliable pasture land for our herds. These days, farming is big business, and the focus is on bringing cattle to market as quickly as possible. As a result, there has been a big move towards a more controlled, sustainable and nutrient-dense diet of grains, which allows farmers to take their cattle to market within 18 to 24 months.

Most Australian cattle do still spend at least part of their lives on pasture, but many of them are moved into feedlot operations to fatten them up quickly for slaughter. Because these grain-fed cattle spend less time roaming over pasture all day, their meat has a more consistent texture, while their high-kilojoule diet means that their flesh has a higher fat content, too. The ultimate grain-fed beef is the Japanese Wagyu breed, which is fed a very specific grain diet, resulting in intensely fat-marbled flesh.

In the end, it probably comes down to personal preference. Do you like your meat to be soft and juicy, but at some cost to flavour? Or do you prefer to treat your taste buds to a more intensely beefy flavour?

One final factor to consider is that grass-fed beef has a different nutritional profile to grain-fed beef. Grass-fed beef has a higher proportion of desirable omega-3 fatty acids, while grain-fed beef has a higher proportion of the less desirable omega-6 fatty acids. Grass-fed beef is also higher in vitamin E and in CLA (conjugated linoleic acid), which is linked with boosting immunity and inhibiting certain cancers and diabetes.

BEEF AND NUTRITION

Although roughly two-thirds of our beef goes to exports – mainly to the USA and to Japan – we also eat a fair amount of it ourselves. While we don't match the Argentineans' appetite for beef, each one of us eats around 36 kilograms a year. Our enjoyment of beef has been affected in recent decades by health concerns about its fat content, so the industry has spent a lot of time and money on developing leaner animals. The current view is that we shouldn't be too worried about our red meat consumption. First of all, lean beef is actually lower in fat than lamb, chicken and fish. Furthermore, half the fatty acids in beef are the 'good fats' – monounsaturated, like those in olive oil – while a third of the saturated fats are stearic acid, which studies show have a neutral effect on cholesterol. It is also a great source of protein and a rich source of iron, zinc and vitamin B12.

HOW AND WHERE TO BUY BEEF

In general, the vast majority of the beef we buy in Australia is yearling beef, which means it is slaughtered between 10 and 18 months old. Some butchers will offer young prime (slaughtered between 18 and 24 months old) or prime beef (between two and three years old), which are a specialist – and therefore more expensive – type of beef. True aficionados will also hunt out mature ox, which is three years or older, and has a much stronger flavour as well as a darker flesh. And of course there is also veal (see Chapter 4), which is very young beef, between 3 and 16 weeks old.

Customers will probably be unaware that their beef comes from either steer (which are neutered male cattle) or heifers (females that have not calved). I often ask my farmer friends to supply me with heifers, as I find their flesh a bit sweeter. As I've touched on previously (page 23), you can also choose between beef that has been grain-fed or grass-fed, and yet another aspect to consider is how it is aged.

I have talked about my passion for dry-aged beef in Chapter 1 (see page 9), and this is definitely something you're going to have to seek out – and be prepared to pay a premium for. Most butchers will tell you that all beef is aged to some degree, but the critical thing to find out is whether it has been wet-aged (in vacuum packs) or whether it has been dry-aged. If you can find a butcher who hangs his own meat in the cool-room at the back of his shop – which he will probably do for a nearby restaurant – then you should thank your lucky stars.

And as to the best place to buy your beef, well I've discussed this at some length in Chapter 1. To recap, I urge you to expand your horizons when it comes to buying your meat. I know that supermarkets are convenient, and that their beef is often advantageously priced, but you will find much better quality beef at a good butcher. Just as importantly, a good butcher will be able to answer your questions and give you the appropriate cut of beef for the dish you want to cook.

If you are in a position to buy two similar cuts – a porterhouse steak, say – from a supermarket and from a butcher, take them home and look at them. What you'll see is that the supermarket steak is much brighter red, and is very fresh looking – you might even think it looks a bit wet. The layer of fat will be a pale creamy white. The steak itself will be sitting in a polystyrene tray and it will be covered with a tight layer of plastic wrap. The steak you buy from your butcher will probably come wrapped in a loose piece of plastic wrap, and then a sheet of butcher's paper. It may have a thicker layer of darker fat, and the meat itself will be a deeper, darker burgundy colour and may even look a bit drier than its supermarket cousin.

WHICH CUT TO BUY

As you can see from the drawing opposite, beef cattle are big animals and their muscles can be broken down into lots of individual cuts. As I explained in Chapter 1 (page 8–9), these muscles can be divided into two general types: the prime cuts, which we think of as being tender-and-top-dollar, or the secondary cuts, which are tough-but-tasty. Each type suits different cooking methods, so you do need to understand the differences and choose carefully.

A: Leg
This is also sometimes called the hock, and is cut from the top of the hindquarter legs. It is a lean and rather tough cut that is best for slow-cooked dishes, such as stews.

STORING BEEF

- Vacuum-packed beef should be left in its wrapping until you are ready to cook it. It will keep for up to two weeks in the coldest part of your fridge. When you open the package, you will need to mop up any blood sitting on the surface of the meat. Any odour should disappear after a few minutes.
- Unwrap and refrigerate all other beef immediately.
- Store it in a Tupperware container, or sit it on a rack on a plate and cover it with a tea towel.
- Large joints will keep up to five days.
- Steaks should be used within three days.
- For most cuts, if you rub them with a bit of olive oil, or even cover them in a marinade they will keep a bit longer as it delays the oxidisation process.
- Cubed or minced beef should be used within two days.

Beef cuts

A. leg / B. silverside and topside
C. knuckle / D. rump / E. tenderloin
F. flank and skirt / G. striploin / H. cube roll
I. blade, chuck, neck and bolar
J. brisket / K. shin

THINGS THAT LOVE BEEF
Anchovies, bacon, brandy,
carrots, chilli, garlic,
horseradish, kidneys, leeks,
mushrooms, mustard, olive
oil, paprika, pepper, potatoes,
red wine, rosemary, salt,
shallots, sour cream, thyme.

B: Silverside and Topside

Both these cuts come from the huge thigh of the cow. The silverside is made up of two overlapping muscles and gets its name from the silvery membrane that covers it. It is a hard-working muscle, which makes it a tough piece of meat, best suited for slow cooking. Silverside makes a great pot-roast or can be cut into small pieces for stewing. The larger muscle is often cured in a brine and used to make corned beef, or it can be turned into bresaola. Topside is more tender than silverside and can be slow-roasted as a whole piece, cut into strips for frying or minced for burgers.

C: Knuckle

The knuckle or round, is cut from the group of muscles above the knee. It is a tasty piece of meat that can be sold as a cheaper cut for oven- and pot-roasting or braising. Sometimes it is sold ready-diced and is great for slow-cooked casseroles and curries. Sliced, pounded and crumbed, it can make terrifically tasty schnitzels.

D: Rump

The rump is a particularly tasty piece of meat from lower down the animal's back. It is made up of several muscles, separated by connective tissue and small sinews, and these are what account for its reputation as being a bit chewy. In fact rump meat itself is really quite tender. Rump can be sold as a large roast or sliced into steaks and medallions. Sometimes it is sold ready-diced for stewing and braising.

E: Tenderloin

This is also called the eye-fillet, and it is the prized and most tender muscle in the whole animal. There are two tenderloins that sit on the underside of the animal's spine, tucked in below the striploin. Because this muscle does very little work it is very tender. It can be roasted as a whole piece in a hot oven, or cut into thick steaks for grilling or frying.

F: Flank and Skirt

The flank is cut from the belly of the animal, beneath the striploin. It is very fatty, but also very tasty. Flank needs to be cooked very slowly in a casserole. The skirt is a group of lean muscles from inside the flank of the animal. These pieces of meat are lean and tasty, but tough, so they are best suited to long, slow cooking. It is perfect for casseroles, stews and pie fillings.

G: Striploin

This is sometimes known as the sirloin. There are two striploins, which are the long muscles that run along either side of the animal's spine. Striploin can be cut into a large piece for roasting, or sliced into steaks. Boneless steaks are also called New York cut; while bone-in steaks are called Porterhouse and T-bone, depending from where they are cut. This meat is tender, and perfectly suited to grilling, barbecuing and roasting.

H: Cube Roll

This is more commonly known as the scotch fillet (off the bone) or the rib-eye (on the bone). A bone-in rib-eye is the equivalent of a rack of lamb, and makes a magnificent standing rib roast. The rib-eye can also be sliced into rib-eye steaks. These cuts have a good covering of fat, which keeps them moist. They are full of flavour and are wonderful for roasting and grilling.

I: Blade, Chuck, Neck and Bolar

Blade and chuck are often sold in large pieces as braising steak, or cut into small pieces for stews and casseroles. They are cut from the area surrounding the animal's shoulder. The neck is sometimes called the clod and is usually sold as stewing steak. Bolar (sometimes called 'butcher's roast') is part of the blade, and is a big muscle, layered with fat and gelatine. It is wonderful for slow-braising, but funnily enough, when thinly sliced and quickly grilled, it can make a very tasty steak. Any chewiness is far outweighed by the flavour.

J: Brisket

Cut from the belly of the animal, but further forward from the flank and skirt muscles. Brisket can be fairly fatty and tough and needs long, low-temperature, slow cooking. It is often sold in a roll, and is a great cut for curing in a salt brine.

K: Shin

A bargain-basement cut from the top of the animal's foreleg. Beef shin can be cooked on the bone – in fact it can be cut into sections through the bone as for an osso buco (see page 72). Off the bone it is usually sold as gravy beef, and is ideally suited to slow-cooked stews and casseroles.

HOW DO YOU KNOW WHEN IT'S COOKED?

My preferred way of testing for doneness is to measure the internal core temperature of any cut of beef, using a digital instant-read thermometer inserted into the thickest part of the meat.

Remember that the reading will rise by about 5°C as the meat rests, so begin checking the temperature about 10 minutes before the end of the recommended cooking time.

rare	medium–rare	medium	medium–well	well done
35°C	45°C	55°C	65°C	75°C

If you don't have a digital thermometer, then use the thumb-to-finger test for doneness (see page 29).

The perfect steak

A good piece of grilled steak is one of the simplest meals you can make, yet many people worry endlessly about how to cook it properly. Here are my top 10 tips, some of which might seem obvious, but believe me, they will all help you understand how to cook the perfect steak.

1. Buy the best quality meat that you can afford. That way you get a head-start when it comes to flavour and texture.

2. Choose the right cut. For instance, if you like your steak butter-soft, choose a piece of eye-fillet; if you want super-tasty and don't mind a bit of a chew, choose rump, skirt or hangar.

3. Steaks come in all shapes and sizes, so there's no perfect formula for timing. For instance, a 250 g steak that is flat and thin will cook more quickly than a 250 g steak that is thick. See point 9 to learn about testing for doneness.

4. Don't cook your steak straight from the fridge. Let it come to room temperature about 30 minutes before you plan to eat.

5. Prepare for cooking by rubbing the steak all over with a little olive oil. Use your hands to smear it on evenly, then season the meat with salt and pepper just before you put it on the grill. Both the oil and seasoning will help stop the meat from sticking to the grill. They'll help seal the surface and ensure that it caramelises to a lovely deep brown, which will make it taste better, too.

6. You can cook steaks on the barbecue, on a ridged griddle pan, or in a frying pan (I don't really recommend cooking steak under an overhead grill). Each has its own merit, although each is slightly different. At the restaurant we cook our steaks on a massive flame-grill, so the steaks get a wonderful lightly charred flavour. You'll achieve a similar result at home using a barbecue. I also like cooking steaks in griddle pans because they can be heated to a high temperature and you get attractive stripe markings from the ridges. If you prefer to fry your steaks in a frying pan, then make sure you use only the barest minimum of oil or they run the risk of being a bit too greasy. And of course you won't get any attractive griddle markings from a flat surface either.

7. Ideally you want to be able to create a range of temperatures from very hot to medium–hot, which is dead easy on the barbecue, and less easy with a griddle or frying pan. Why is it important? Well, it's particularly important with a big thick piece of meat that is going to take longer to heat to the centre. With a thin piece of meat you can cook it over a fierce heat very quickly. With a big thick piece it is likely to burn on the outside before the heat penetrates to the centre. With big thick steaks you want to move the steak to a medium heat after the initial searing over a high heat. Alternatively, transfer it to the oven to finish cooking after the initial searing.

8. Which brings us to turning. Some people insist that you should only turn your steak once during the cooking process. I like to turn my steaks between three and five times depending on the thickness. I find that this way the meat cooks evenly and ends up tender and juicy inside. I actually turn the meat at right-angles, which means you get an attractive cross-hatching of griddle marks. Here's what actually happens when the steak is cooking: immediately the meat hits the heat, the moisture inside rushes away from the heat source up to the surface of the meat where it eventually cooks away. When you turn the steak over, the moisture rushes back in the other direction. If you turn the meat several times as it cooks, less moisture will escape and your steak will stay lovely and juicy in the centre.

9. Testing for doneness is another bugbear for people. This is something that you learn through practice and you will become more confident over time. Many experts warn against cutting into the steak to see how the steak looks, but if you're a novice cook, then this is a straightforward approach. You do run the

risk of losing some of the internal juices, so I suggest you move the steak off the heat and leave it to rest for 2–3 minutes before making a small incision into the thickest part of the meat.

A far better way to test for doneness is to press the steak with your finger. Essentially, the more yielding the steak is under pressure, the rarer the steak. Some people use the little trick of feeling the fleshy base of your thumb as you touch it to the fingers on your hand: thumb to index finger = rare; thumb to middle finger = medium–rare; thumb to ring finger = medium to medium–well; thumb to little finger = well done. To be honest, one sure-fire way of knowing how well cooked your steak is, is to use a meat thermometer and I strongly recommend using one of these until you gain confidence in your own judgement. At La Luna I have a big notice stuck above the grill to remind the chefs about internal core temperatures. 35ºC = rare; 45ºC = medium–rare; 55ºC = medium; 65ºC = medium-well; 75ºC = well-done. The beauty of this method is that it removes all the guess-work.

10. Finally, and perhaps most importantly of all, once the steak is cooked, you must rest it. As I've outlined above, while the meat is cooking, the moisture inside heats up and moves away from the heat source. There's a lot of activity going on inside that piece of meat! Letting it rest away from the heat source allows the juices to settle back to the centre of the meat and the fibres will all relax, becoming nice and tender. As a simple rule of thumb, allow an equal amount of resting time as the meat took to cook. So in other words, if the steak took 4 minutes to cook, allow it to rest in a warm spot for 4 minutes before serving. You can always put it back on the heat for a final warm-through. 30 seconds on each side should be enough.

This is one of my favourite steaks. It's not as pricey as eye-fillet, but is lovely and juicy and has a great flavour. Serve with mustard or relish, or top with your favourite flavoured butter (page 248–9).

Scotch fillet

---

2 x 350 g Scotch fillet steaks
extra-virgin olive oil

sea salt flakes
freshly ground black pepper

Remove the steak from the refrigerator at least 30 minutes before you want to eat. Preheat your grill or barbecue to medium–high.

Rub the steaks all over lightly with oil and season them generously with salt and pepper. Cook the steaks over a medium–high heat for 2 minutes, then turn and cook for a further 2 minutes. Turn again, this time at a 180-degree angle, and cook for another 2 minutes. Turn for a final time, and cook for 2 more minutes. The steaks should be cooked medium–rare, and be neatly cross-hatched with marks from the griddle. Use the thumb-to-finger test for doneness, or check the interior of the meat with a meat thermometer.

Transfer the steaks to a warm plate and cover them loosely with foil. Leave them to rest for 4 minutes before serving.

Serves 2

I think this on-the-bone steak is probably my all-time favourite. It's cut from the saddle, and is made up of sirloin on one side of the bone and eye-fillet on the other. It's incredibly tasty, and needs nothing more in the way of flavour additions than good salt, freshly ground pepper, and a drizzle of extra-virgin olive oil.

Ask your butcher for a big steak – at least 600 g, and about 5 cm thick. This will give you enough meat for two people to share. A steak this thick will take much longer to cook on a grill or barbecue, so I prefer to cook it in the oven after first sealing it in a griddle pan over a high heat. Serve with Thyme- and Garlic-Scented Mushrooms (page 313) or Sautéed Spinach and Chilli (page 312).

T-bone for two

1 x 850 g T-bone steak
extra-virgin olive oil
sea salt flakes

freshly ground black pepper
lemon wedges to serve (optional)

Remove the steak from the refrigerator 30 minutes before you want to eat. Preheat your grill or barbecue to high and your oven to 200°C.

Rub the steak all over lightly with oil and season it generously with salt and pepper. Cook the steak over a high heat for 2–3 minutes on each side, so that it is well coloured. Now transfer it to the oven for 10 minutes, turning once or twice. Alternatively, move the steak to a cooler part of the grill or barbecue and cook it for a further 12–15 minutes, depending on the heat of the grill and the thickness of the steak. Turn the steak every minute or so to prevent it burning.

Because of the bone, you'll find that the meat won't cook evenly: it will be rarer close to the bone and towards the edges it will be medium or even medium–well done. Use the thumb-to-finger test for doneness, or check the interior of the meat with a meat thermometer.

Transfer the steak to a warm plate and cover it loosely with foil. Leave it to rest for 5–6 minutes before carving.

To serve, cut the two sections of meat away from the bone and carve into thick slices. Serve with more salt and pepper, extra-virgin olive oil and the lemon wedges if using.

Serves 2

Spicy hangar steak with smoky flavours

Although the best known steak cuts come from thick muscles, such as the rump, loin and rib, there are several other steaks that come from flat muscles, cut from the shoulder blade, chest and side of the animal. Four in particular – bolar blade, skirt steak, flank steak and hangar steak – have become more popular in recent times because they are less expensive than prime fillet or sirloin. They are a bit chewier, it's true, but they have a great, deep, beefy flavour. I especially like hangar steak – so called because it is cut from the muscle that hangs down the side of the belly.

1 x 1 kg piece hangar steak
  or bolar blade
lemon wedges to serve
toasted garlic bread to serve

Spicy rub
1 tablespoon cumin seeds
1 tablespoon coriander seeds
2 tablespoons medium–hot
  dried chillies
1 tablespoon black peppercorns
1 tablespoon white peppercorns
2 tablespoons dried oregano
1 teaspoon sweet paprika
1 teaspoon salt

Carrot–herb salad
2 Lebanese cucumbers, finely sliced
3 spring onions, finely sliced
1 red pepper, seeded and finely sliced
1 large carrot, grated
2 cups coriander leaves
2 cups parsley leaves
1 tablespoon sesame seeds
juice of 1 lemon
½ garlic clove, crushed
3 tablespoons extra-virgin olive oil
salt
freshly ground black pepper

To make the spicy rub, first toast the cumin and coriander seeds separately in a hot dry pan until golden and aromatic. Now pound all the ingredients separately, using a mortar and pestle or a spice grinder, then mix all ingredients together. You're aiming for an aromatic rub that is still a little coarse, not a smooth powder. If not using immediately, store in an airtight jar and use within 4 weeks.

When ready to use, massage the rub into the meat so it is well covered. Cover and refrigerate overnight to allow the flavours to develop.

Preheat your grill or barbecue to medium–high. Cook the steak for 4 minutes, then turn and cook for a further 4 minutes. Turn again, this time at a 180 degree angle, and cook for another 4 minutes. Turn for a final time and cook for 4 minutes. The steaks should be cooked medium–rare and neatly cross-hatched with marks from the griddle. Remove the steak from the heat and leave to rest for 8 minutes in a warm place.

To make the salad, combine the cucumber, spring onion, pepper, carrot, herbs and sesame seeds in a large mixing bowl. In a small jug, whisk together the lemon juice, garlic, extra-virgin olive oil and seasonings to make a dressing. Pour onto the salad and toss gently.

To serve, tip the salad out onto a large serving platter. Slice the steak thinly on the diagonal and arrange over the salad. Serve with lemon wedges and toasted garlic bread.

Serves 4

Pepper- and thyme-crusted fillet of beef

Yes, it's a bit expensive, but a really top-quality piece of beef fillet makes a great dinner party meal. It's dead-easy to prepare and cook and it looks really impressive too. I like to serve beef fillet rare, with Creamed Spinach (page 312), Thyme- and Garlic-Scented Mushrooms (page 313) and Garlic- and Rosemary-Roasted Potatoes (page 296). You might also like to make a quick gravy in the roasting pan, and jazz it up with Red Wine Reduction (page 332).

1 x 1.3 kg eye-fillet of beef
1–2 tablespoons Dijon mustard
1 tablespoon salt
1 tablespoon freshly ground
  black pepper

1 tablespoon chopped thyme
2 tablespoons olive oil

Tuck the skinny tail-end of the fillet underneath so that the beef is an even thickness all along its length. Tie securely with butcher's string at 5 cm intervals. Smear liberally with mustard then season with salt and pepper and sprinkle with thyme. Refrigerate until needed, but bring to room temperature 30 minutes before you plan to eat.

Preheat the oven to 195°C. Heat the oil in a heavy-based roasting tin and brown the fillet all over. Transfer to the oven and roast for 15 minutes (for rare). If you're using a meat thermometer, the internal core temperature should be 40°C. Transfer the cooked beef to a hot dish, cover with foil and leave it to rest for 8–10 minutes in a warm spot. When ready to serve, snip off the string and carve into thick slices. Serve with your choice of gravy and accompaniments.

Serves 6

You can serve these shashliks with pita bread and salad if you like, but I prefer my grandad's choice of Buttery Rice Pilaf (page 304).

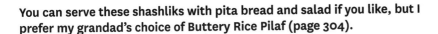
Grandad Peter's beef shashlik

1 kg beef rump, cut into 3 cm cubes
2 medium onions, cut into 3 cm dice
2 red peppers, cut into 3 cm dice
100 g button mushrooms
200 g thick-cut rashers smoky bacon, cut into 3 cm dice
salt
freshly ground pepper

Marinade
1 cup red wine
2 garlic cloves
2 bay leaves
3 sprigs thyme
½ medium onion, roughly chopped
2 tablespoons olive oil
1 teaspoon freshly ground black pepper

Place the cubed beef in a shallow container. Add the marinade ingredients and use your hands to toss well so the beef is evenly coated. Cover with plastic wrap and leave to marinate in the refrigerator overnight.

When ready to cook, preheat your barbecue to high. Drain the marinated beef and pat it dry on kitchen paper. Thread the beef, onion, pepper, mushrooms and bacon onto skewers, alternating to your liking.

Season the shashliks lightly then grill for 8 minutes, turning them frequently, so they colour and cook evenly.

Remove the shashliks from the heat and serve with pilaf.

Serves 4

Standing rib roast

Also known as a baron of beef, this is roasting at its best. A standing rib has everything: a thick layer of creamy fat on the surface of the meat that becomes crisp and golden in the oven, a lovely marbling of fat through the meat that adds flavour, and the rib bones, which keep the meat moist and juicy and are great to chew on!

This magnificent roast should be served with all the trimmings: Michael's Yorkshire Puddings (page 306), Garlic- and Rosemary-roasted Potatoes (page 296), Garlicky Green Beans (page 308), Horseradish Cream (page 342) and gravy made with the pan juices.

2 sprigs rosemary
2 tablespoons salt

2 tablespoons freshly ground
   black pepper
1 x 3 kg standing rib roast
   (about 5 ribs)

Preheat the oven to 220°C.

Strip the leaves from the rosemary and toss them with the salt and pepper. Rub this mixture all over the beef, working it into both the fat and the meat. Sit the beef on a rack inside a large roasting tin. Roast for 20 minutes, then lower the heat to 180°C and roast for a further 40 minutes. The beef will be cooked medium–rare when the internal core temperature reaches 45°C.

Remove the beef from the oven and transfer it to a warm plate. Leave it to rest for 30 minutes and take to the table to carve.

Serves 6–8

Roast stuffed brisket of beef

When it's cleaned and trimmed, brisket forms a large flat piece of meat, which is ideal for stuffing and rolling up. It's the perfect cut for feeding a lot of people cheaply! The brisket is a fairly fatty piece of meat that comes from the breast of the animal; in fact it often comes with the breastbone still attached. For this recipe ask your butcher to remove the breastbone and to cut the meat to a rough rectangle. He may also trim the meat for you, and score the surface layer of membrane so that the meat doesn't shrink as it cooks.

Because of its fattiness, this is a cut that works brilliantly with the strong, salty flavours of the stuffing. Serve it with Garlic- and Rosemary-roasted Potatoes (page 296) and your choice of gravy.

1 x 3.5 kg beef brisket
salt
freshly ground black pepper

Greek olive and caper stuffing
200 g kalamata olives, pitted
  and roughly chopped
1 cup homemade sourdough
  breadcrumbs
½ cup chopped parsley
6 garlic cloves, chopped
2 tablespoons capers, chopped
2 anchovies, chopped
3 tablespoons dried oregano
1 tablespoon salt
1 tablespoon freshly ground
  black pepper

Preheat the oven to 165°C.

To prepare the brisket, lay it out on your work surface, and trim away any excess chunks of fat and sinew. If the butcher hasn't already done so, use a sharp knife to score the membranes that cover the surface.

To make the stuffing, mix the ingredients together thoroughly. Season the brisket all over with salt and pepper and spread the stuffing evenly over the meat leaving a border. Roll the brisket up and tie securely with butcher's string at 5 cm intervals.

Place the rolled brisket on a rack inside a large roasting tin. Roast for 3 hours, turning every 30 minutes so that it browns evenly.

Remove from the oven and leave in a warm place to rest for at least 30 minutes before carving.

Serves 12

Beef shin is one of those bargain-basement cuts that are fantastic for long, slow cooking. It's often sold off the bone as gravy beef and makes great pies and soups. Here I cook it on the bone as a tasty pot-roast, and the meat's intrinsic chewiness softens down to a melting tenderness. Ask your butcher to trim the meat and to 'french' the bone for you for a neat presentation.

This pot-roast is definitely a better-the-next-day sort of dish, as the flavours develop and intensify with time. It's a meal in its own right, but I like to serve it with a big bowl of Creamy, Buttery Mash (page 296) and a bottle of full-bodied red wine.

Pot-roasted beef shin with smoky bacon and baby onions

1 x 1.8 kg beef shin
salt
freshly ground black pepper
2 tablespoons olive oil
150 g butter
250 g thick-cut rashers smoky
  bacon, cut into 4 cm dice
2 anchovy fillets
2 medium onions, chopped
2 medium carrots, chopped

2 sticks celery, chopped
6 garlic cloves, halved
400 g button mushrooms,
  halved
2 cups red wine
3 cups beef stock
3 sprigs thyme
2 bay leaves
2 cloves
200 g green olives
chopped parsley to serve

Preheat the oven to 150°C.

Season the beef with salt and pepper. Heat the oil in a heavy-based casserole then sear the beef until evenly browned all over. Lift the beef out onto a plate.

Add the butter to the casserole. Fry the bacon and anchovies until the bacon begins to brown and the anchovies start to melt. Add the onion, carrots, celery and garlic and stir together well. Lower the heat and sauté gently for 5–8 minutes, or until the vegetables soften.

Add the remaining ingredients to the casserole and bring to a gentle simmer. Season to taste then cover and transfer to the oven. Cook for 1 hour then remove the lid from the casserole and cook for a further 1½ hours. By the end of the cooking time the beef should be completely tender and falling away from the bone.

When ready to eat, sprinkle generously with parsley and serve with plenty of mashed potatoes.

Serves 6

Hot roast beef sandwich

One of the best things about roast beef dinners is making sandwiches from the leftovers. I usually fry up some onions and bacon and warm through the beef slices as I love the contrast these warm ingredients make with the cold butter on good crusty bread.

This is not so much a recipe, as a list of suggested ingredients; but obviously you should feel free to create your own sandwich masterpiece.

heaps of salted butter
1 onion, cut into rings
a few rashers of bacon (optional)
leftover roast beef, thinly sliced
1 loaf crusty sourdough bread
your favourite mustard (I use a mix
  of hot English and French grain
  mustards)

good-quality mayonnaise
iceberg or cos lettuce or rocket leaves
thick slices of ripe tomato
thick slices of your favourite
  tasty cheese

Melt a generous knob of butter in a heavy-based frying pan. Sauté the onion rings until soft and golden, then transfer to a warm plate. Fry the bacon until crisp, then transfer to a warm plate. Lower the heat and add the beef slices to the pan. Fry very gently until just warmed through.

Slice the bread and spread with lots of butter. Assemble with your choice of ingredients and eat with a good cold beer or a glass of milk.

When it comes to spare ribs, don't just think of pork. Beef short ribs are brilliant! They do need a fair amount of marinating and pre-cooking, but to my mind, nothing beats the smoky charred flavour they get from the barbecue, or the caveman satisfaction of chewing on a juicy bone.

Serve the ribs with American Slaw (page 316), Potato Salad (page 298) and lots of napkins to wipe those sticky fingers.

Barbecued beef short ribs

2.5 kg beef short ribs, cut into
10 cm lengths

Spicy marinade
3 onions, roughly chopped
6 garlic cloves, roughly chopped
4 small red chillies, seeded and
roughly chopped
½ cup brown sugar
2 tablespoons smoked paprika
2 tablespoons ground ginger
¼ cup soy sauce
¼ cup chopped coriander leaves
2 cups red wine
¼ cup extra-virgin olive oil
¼ cup sherry vinegar
1 tablespoon salt
1 tablespoon freshly ground
black pepper

To make the marinade, combine all the ingredients in a food processor and pulse to form a paste.

Arrange the ribs in a large shallow container. Pour on the marinade and use your hands to toss well so the ribs are evenly coated. Cover with plastic wrap and leave to marinate in the refrigerator for up to 48 hours, but at least overnight.

Preheat the oven to 160°C. Transfer the ribs to a large roasting tin and cover with aluminium foil. Bake for 40 minutes, basting with the marinade every 10 minutes or so. Remove from the oven and leave to cool. You can prepare the ribs to this stage up to 4 days ahead of time.

When ready to cook, preheat your barbecue to medium–high. Barbecue the ribs until warmed through and caramelised to a sticky dark brown, around 3 minutes on each side. Baste with the marinade frequently.

Serves 6

Hungarian goulash soup with sour cream and chives

On my first visit to Hungary in the early 1990s I had dinner in a well-known restaurant, famous for local specialties. I was eager to try the country's most famous dish … but it turned out to be a tourist rip-off and I couldn't have been more disappointed. When I got back to Melbourne I had a go at making goulash myself, and I'm pleased to say that it was delicious!

The flavours of caraway, smoked paprika and cumin make a brilliant soup, too – especially when topped with a good dollop of sour cream.

1 kg braising beef (blade or gravy),
   cut into 1 cm dice
1 tablespoon caraway seeds
2 tablespoons sweet smoked paprika
1 tablespoon ground cumin
1 tablespoon cayenne pepper
1 teaspoon salt
1 teaspoon freshly ground black pepper
¼ cup olive oil
4 red peppers
2 medium onions, finely diced
6 long red chillies, seeded and
   finely chopped

1 litre beef stock
1 cup white wine
¼ cup sherry vinegar
2 cups tomato passata
500 g tomatoes, skinned, seeded
   and chopped
2 bay leaves
4 sprigs thyme
2 large potatoes, peeled and
   finely diced
200 ml sour cream, to serve
smoked paprika, to serve
2 tablespoons snipped chives,
   to serve

Place the diced beef into a large mixing bowl with the spices, salt and pepper and toss well so it is evenly coated.

Heat half the olive oil in a heavy-based saucepan or casserole over a medium heat. When the oil is sizzling, brown the beef in batches, so that the heat stays high. Transfer the browned beef to a plate.

Halve the peppers lengthwise and rub them all over with a little more of the olive oil. Grill, skin-side up, until black and charred. Transfer to a bowl and cover with plastic wrap. When cool enough to handle, peel off the skin and slice away the seeds and pith. Chop roughly and place in a processor. Blitz on high to form a rough purée.

Add the remaining oil to the casserole with the onion, puréed peppers and chillies and lower the heat. Sauté gently for 5 minutes, or until the onion starts to soften. Return the beef to the casserole and sauté for 2–3 minutes. Add the stock, wine and sherry vinegar to the casserole and stir well. Add the tomato passata, tomatoes and the herbs and bring to the boil. Lower the heat and stir in the potatoes. Simmer gently for 1 hour, uncovered, stirring from time to time. Top up with extra stock or water if needed.

Taste just before serving, and adjust the seasoning to your liking. Ladle into bowls and top with a dollop of sour cream, a sprinkle of paprika and chopped chives. Serve with warm crusty bread.

Serves 6–8

Beef Bourguignon

This rustic French dish is so much more than just a beef stew. When it's made properly, with loads of mushrooms and shallots and tasty bits of smoky bacon, it's out of this world. If you have the time, you can marinate the beef overnight in the red wine. The marinade can then be added to the casserole, but make sure you skim it first to remove any impurities.

1 kg lean braising beef (chuck, blade or rump) cut into 2 cm dice
salt
freshly ground black pepper
2 tablespoons olive oil
100 g thick-cut rashers smoky bacon, cut into 2 cm dice
150 g butter
10 shallots, chopped
1 medium onion, finely diced
1 medium carrot, thinly sliced

200 g button mushrooms (halved if they're large)
1 tablespoon smoked paprika
1 cup good red wine
1½ litres good-quality beef stock
2 tablespoons cornflour mixed to a paste with a little water
½ cup sour cream
¼ cup snipped chives
¼ cup chopped parsley

Season the beef with salt and pepper. Heat the olive oil in a heavy-based casserole over a medium heat. When the oil is sizzling, brown the beef in batches, so that the heat stays high. Transfer the browned beef to a plate.

Add the bacon to the casserole and fry until golden brown. Transfer to a plate with the beef.

Add the butter to the casserole and when it sizzles, add the shallots. Fry over a medium heat until the shallots start to soften and begin to colour a lovely golden brown. Lower the heat and add the diced onion and carrot. Sauté for 5 minutes until they start to soften. Add the mushrooms and sauté for 4 minutes, stirring from time to time.

Stir in the paprika then add the wine and stock. Return the beef and bacon to the casserole, increase the heat until the liquid boils, then lower the heat and simmer gently, uncovered, for 1½ hours, or until the meat is tender. Top up with stock or water if drying out.

To thicken the sauce, stir in the cornflour paste. Simmer for a further 5 minutes, until the sauce thickens. Serve with the sour cream and fresh herbs and plenty of buttered new potatoes.

Serves 6

This is probably one of the first recipes that people learn how to cook – usually with fatty supermarket mince, tinned tomatoes and dusty dried herbs. But don't underestimate a good Bolognese. When it's made with a mixture of top-quality beef, pork, bacon and salami, it's a different thing altogether. And don't just serve Bolognese sauce with spaghetti; try different shapes of pasta and even Gnocchi (page 301). As with all minced meat dishes, I recommend that you choose the cut appropriate to the dish, and either mince it yourself or ask your butcher to mince it for you.

This recipe makes 2½ litres of sauce – enough to feed six hungry diners, with plenty left over to freeze.

Best-ever Bolognese sauce

150 g butter
2 onions, finely diced
6 garlic cloves
1 small carrots, finely grated
½ stick celery, finely grated
2 bay leaves
600 g lean minced beef
   (rump, topside or girello)

350 g minced pork (shoulder or leg)
200 g smoky bacon, minced
300 g salami, minced
1 cup red wine
2.5 litres tomato passata
salt
freshly ground black pepper
1 well-packed cup basil leaves

Melt the butter in a large heavy-based saucepan. Add the onion, garlic, carrot, celery and bay leaves and sauté gently for 5 minutes, or until the vegetables start to soften. Add the minced meats and fry until evenly browned. Use a spatula or wooden spoon to break up any lumps.

Add the wine and passata and stir well. Season to taste and bring to the boil. Lower the heat and simmer gently for 2½ hours, stirring from time to time. Stir in the basil just before serving the sauce with your choice of pasta or gnocchi and plenty of freshly grated parmesan.

Makes 2½ litres

Chilli beef ragù with cornbread topping

When I lived in Canada, Monday night was football night. My mates and I used to settle down to watch the game with a big bowl of chilli beef and plenty of cold beers. A word of warning: I like my chilli hot! Feel free to reduce the quantity of dried and fresh chillies to your degree of tolerance.

1 kg chuck, blade or rump steak, cut into 2 cm dice
2 tablespoons smoked paprika
1 tablespoon dried chillies
½ tablespoon cumin seeds, dry-roasted and ground
½ tablespoon coriander seeds, dry-roasted and ground
1 teaspoon salt
1 teaspoon freshly ground black pepper
¼ cup olive oil
4 red peppers
2 onions, finely diced
6 garlic cloves, crushed
2 long red chillies, thinly sliced

1 litre tomato passata
2 cups beef or chicken stock
½ cup red wine
1 cup basil leaves
1 cup coriander leaves

Cornbread topping
2 cups self-raising flour
1 cup fine polenta
1 tablespoon chopped rosemary
1 teaspoon salt
2 cups milk
4 eggs
300 g cooked corn kernels
2 tablespoons olive oil

Preheat the oven to 160°C. Place the diced beef into a large mixing bowl with the spices, salt and pepper and toss well so it is all evenly coated.

Heat half the oil in a large, heavy-based casserole over a medium heat. When the oil is hot, brown the beef in batches, so that the heat stays high. Transfer the browned beef to a plate.

Halve the peppers lengthwise and rub them all over with a little more of the olive oil. Grill, skin-side up, until black and charred. Transfer to a bowl and cover with plastic wrap. When cool enough to handle, peel off the skin and slice away the seeds and pith. Chop roughly and place in a processor. Blitz on high to form a rough purée.

Add the rest of the oil to the casserole and lower the heat. Add the onion, garlic and chillies and sauté gently for 5 minutes, or until the onion starts to soften. Return the beef to the casserole and sauté for 2–3 minutes. Add the tomato passata, puréed peppers, stock and wine and bring to the boil. Transfer the casserole to the oven, and cook, covered, for 2 hours. The ragù can be prepared to this stage ahead of time.

When ready to eat, preheat the oven to 200°C. Stir the fresh basil and coriander into the ragù and pour it into a large gratin dish.

To make the cornbread topping, combine the dry ingredients in a large mixing bowl. Whisk together the milk, eggs, oil and corn in a separate bowl, then stir into the dry ingredients to make a thick yellow batter.

Spread the batter over the chilli beef and bake for 30 minutes until the topping is risen and golden and the chilli beef underneath is bubbling.

Serves 4 hungry men

Big Aussie beef burger

When it comes to using minced beef, I strongly suggest that you don't buy it ready-minced from the supermarket. Go to your butcher and choose the appropriate cut for the dish – for burgers I'd suggest lean rump or topside – and ask him to mince it for you. That way you can be sure you're getting great quality, as well as correct balance of fat and lean meat. And of course you can always mince it yourself if you've got a mincer at home.

It's best not to make your burgers too far ahead of time. Fry or grill them, depending on how you feel. I like to sling them on the barbie, as I love the smoky, charred flavour, and the way they stay pink and juicy inside. Serve with all or some of the suggested accompaniments and good-quality oven-baked chips.

Burgers

1 kg lean minced beef
100 g thick-cut rashers smoky bacon, very finely diced
1 small onion, finely diced
2 garlic cloves, finely chopped
1 teaspoon fresh chilli, finely chopped
3 tablespoons Dijon mustard
2 tablespoons Worcestershire sauce
1 egg, lightly beaten
2 tablespoons chopped parsley
2 teaspoons salt
2 teaspoons freshly ground black pepper
olive oil for grilling

Burger accompaniments

6 good-quality burger buns or ciabatta rolls, split in half
1 small lettuce, leaves separated
Caramelised Onions (page 311)
12 slices beetroot
12 slices tomato
12 rashers grilled bacon
6 fried eggs
6 slices tasty cheese
tomato sauce or ketchup

Preheat your grill or barbecue to medium–high.

To make the burgers, combine all the ingredients, except for the oil, in a large mixing bowl. Use your hands to scrunch everything together so that the onion and flavourings are evenly distributed. Shape into 6 patties, making them as neat as you can, and about 2.5–3 cm thick.

Brush each burger lightly with oil and arrange them on your grill or barbecue. Cook for 4 minutes and then turn them over. Continue to cook until they're done the way you like them. This will depend on the heat of the grill, the thickness of the burger and, of course, personal preference.

Serve everything in the middle of the table so your guests can build their own burgers, the way they like them.

Serves 6

Oma's Dutch croquettes

These croquettes are one of my mother-in-law's specialties and a closely guarded family secret that she hasn't even really shared with her five daughters! I have spent years trying to wheedle out the recipe from all these women, and the version that follows is based on what my sisters-in-law were prepared to reveal of what they know.

Croquettes are a Dutch favourite and are fantastic served with Mayonnaise (page 340) and Adrian's One-Size-Fits-All Mustard (page 343). If you dip them into the egg and breadcrumbs twice you'll get an extra-crunchy coating.

50 g butter
50 g plain flour
1 cup hot milk
salt
300 g leftover cold roast beef, finely chopped, minced or whizzed in a food processor
½ onion, finely diced
1 tablespoon ketjap manis
1 tablespoon chopped thyme leaves
¼ cup chopped parsley
1 teaspoon freshly ground black pepper

Crumb coating
2 eggs, lightly beaten
⅓ cup milk
1 cup plain flour
2 cups homemade breadcrumbs
pinch of salt
vegetable oil for deep-frying

Melt the butter in a small, heavy-based saucepan. Stir in the flour to make a paste (roux), and cook, stirring all the time, for about 3 minutes. Gradually mix in the hot milk to make a béchamel sauce. Bring to the boil, then lower the heat and simmer for 5 minutes to get rid of the floury taste. Add a pinch of salt to season then tip the béchamel into a large mixing bowl and leave to cool.

Place the remaining ingredients into a food processor and whiz until smooth. Tip into the mixing bowl with the cooled béchamel sauce and stir in well to form a thick paste. Taste and adjust seasoning to your liking. Cover with plastic wrap and refrigerate for a few hours until chilled.

Form the croquette mixture into chunky little logs – you should get about 24 in total. Whisk the egg and milk together and set up a little production line of 3 dishes containing the flour, the egg mixture and the breadcrumbs. Roll the croquettes in the flour first, then dip them into the egg mixture and then the breadcrumbs so they are evenly coated. For an extra-crunchy coating dip the croquettes into the egg and breadcrumbs for a second time then refrigerate for 30 minutes.

Heat the oil in a deep-fryer or a heavy-based frying pan to 180°C. Preheat the oven to 100°C. Fry the croquettes in batches until golden brown all over, about 5 minutes. Drain briefly on a wire rack and transfer to the oven to keep warm while you fry the remaining croquettes. Serve with mayonnaise and mustard for dipping.

Makes 24

VEAL

TENDER
+
TASTY
=
SHANKS!

Veal

I grew up in a very Italian household, which means that we ate a lot of veal. My Nonna Yole was a brilliant cook and the whole family would descend upon her for our favourite Saturday night meals of veal cotelette, involtini or osso buco. I realise now that this was quite unusual. Veal has never been as popular or as widely available in Australia as it is in Europe – and it has always been expensive – so I was very lucky to have been introduced to it from such a young age.

Things are changing, though, and you'll find dishes like veal shanks popping up on more and more bistro and restaurant menus. Certain cuts of veal are brilliantly suited for this sort of slow-cooked dish because they have a very high collagen content that breaks down to a beautiful sticky richness. This gelatinous quality is why restaurant kitchens love to use veal bones when making stocks. They not only add a delicate flavour, but lots of body and sheen.

And who among us doesn't love the famous Austrian Wiener schnitzel, made from wafer-thin slices of veal, coated in crumbs and fried to juicy crispness? Veal offal is also much prized – think of delicately pink and tender slices of liver, or creamy, rich sweetbreads. These are always a sell-out when we feature them on the menu at La Luna Bistro.

On the downside, veal can be hard to find and does have a reputation for being pricey. There is also a lot of confusion about what veal exactly is, and what makes for good quality veal. And on top of these things, there is widespread resistance to eating veal because of the industry's reputation for questionable production practices and an apparent reluctance to eat such young animals. But if you are concerned about this latter aspect, then you'd better become vegetarian. The fact is that veal calves are slaughtered at a similar age to lambs and pigs.

There are, however, more understandable grounds for concern when it comes to animal welfare and veal. To understand the controversy, we first need to understand that veal is a by-product of the dairy industry. If we humans want to drink milk, then we have to accept that it goes hand in hand with thousands of baby calves being removed from their mothers. Without a veal industry, most of these calves would be slaughtered within hours of their birth.

Most ethical objections to veal actually centre on certain methods of its production: in particular, the traditional Dutch method of raising the baby calves in confinement in crates or small pens. These sorry animals are confined to such a degree that they are unable to turn around (the objective being to prevent them moving and developing muscle, which would make their meat less tender). And their diet is restricted entirely to milk formula, which causes them terrible digestive problems, to keep the meat pale and tender.

Let me say straight away that I find this an appalling and unnecessary level of cruelty. But thankfully, this crate system of production has been banned in most countries and there is a growing insistence on more humanely reared veal. The Australian veal industry is certainly kinder. Once weaned from their mothers, our veal calves are reared in large open barns with unrestricted access to milk and to a cereal-based diet. Although it is essentially an indoor environment, the barns are open at either end to natural light. Organic veal calves have greater access to the outside world, and are even encouraged to nibble on grass.

The veal meat from calves raised in both these ways is, of course, somewhat pinker than the 'true' milk-fed veal. But surely it is an acceptable trade-off? In fact most Italians – who after all eat more veal than anyone else in the world – have always preferred their veal to be pinker and fuller-flavoured than 'white' veal.

There is one other category of veal in Australia, known as 'bobby' veal. 'Bob' calves are male calves sold off by dairy farmers who have neither the expertise or interest in raising veal for meat. They range in age from four days to two weeks, and are sold straight away for meat. The fact that this meat is so young doesn't mean that it is better than veal raised especially for the premium meat market. In fact because it is so young bobby veal tends to be rather bland and tasteless and has a dry, chewy texture.

VEAL AND NUTRITION

Australians eat very little veal, especially when compared with our European cousins, such as the French and the Italians. It's a shame because, nutritionally speaking, veal is fantastic. It is a naturally lean meat because the animals are slaughtered before much fat or marbling has developed. But it is nutrient-dense, with a paltry 200 g supplying us a significant percentage of our daily requirements for protein, zinc, niacin, magnesium and vitamin B12.

HOW AND WHERE TO BUY VEAL

Although its availability is increasing, veal is still something of a seasonal item and the best times to find it are in winter or spring. It is definitely something of a gourmet item and you are almost certainly going to have to go to a specialist or Continental butcher to find it. Or ask your own butcher if he can source good-quality veal for you.

As I outlined above, age and diet both affect the appearance and quality of veal: the whiter the meat, the greater the proportion of milk it will have been fed. Sometimes veal with a pinkish hue is marketed as rosé veal or organic veal. Any veal that looks rather reddish is almost certainly not veal at all, but will be from yearling beef.

Veal is categorised according to the weight and age of the calf. In Australia, some of the best veal is considered to come from French breeds of cattle, such as the Charolais. This veal will be from animals that have been slaughtered between three and four months of age, and they will weigh between 75–90 kg.

As with all meat, you should choose veal that looks moist, but not slimy or sticky.

Chapter 4 / Veal

STORING VEAL

- Because it has virtually no fat, veal is more perishable than other red meats; treat it like chicken or pork.
- You won't find 'aged' or 'hung' veal, so it will be very fresh when you buy it.
- Unwrap and refrigerate all veal immediately.
- Store it in a Tupperware container, or sit it on a rack on a plate and cover it with a tea towel.
- Large cuts of veal will keep for up to four or five days.
- Smaller cuts should be used within three days.
- For most cuts, if you rub them with a bit of olive oil, or even cover them in a marinade they will keep a bit longer as it delays the oxidisation process.
- Cubed or minced veal should be used within two days.

WHICH CUT TO BUY

Veal are clearly much younger animals than their older brothers and sisters, which means that they break down to a more limited range of smaller cuts. In fact veal cuts are probably more similar to cuts of lamb than beef.

The tender prime cuts make up a small part of the animal and are expensive. So it makes sense to make good use of the secondary cuts, such as the breast, neck and shoulder. These cuts really shine when they are cooked long and slow in braises and casseroles.

A: Shanks and Shin

These are best cut from the hindquarter as they tend to be meatier and less stringy than the forequarter equivalent. Veal shanks are great for braising as they cook down to wonderfully sticky and tender meat. Cut across the bone into thick slices the shank and shin are used for the classic Italian dish, osso buco. Each piece contains a cross-section of the bone, with an interior of juicy marrow.

B: Silverside, Topside, Knuckle and Girello

Cut from the thigh of the calf these can be roasted on the bone or divided into the various muscles for slow-roasting and pot-roasting. The whole silverside is used for the classic dish vitello tonnato. The topside is often rolled up and tied for roasting. Knuckle is a smaller round muscle, great for a mini pot-roast or small schnitzels. The girello is tiny in very young veal, but in older animals it can be used for vitello tonnato or braised in butter and tomato passata for slicing and serving with pasta.

The thigh can be opened out and cut on the bias into thin slices – also called escalopes or scaloppine – for schnitzels and for saltimbocca. Try to avoid slices that are cut straight across the boned-out leg. You'll end up with several awkward-sized bits held together by connective tissue, which won't cook evenly in the pan. Ask your butcher to cut slices from a single large muscle.

C: Rump

This is also known as the round of veal, and it can be roasted whole on the bone, or sliced across the grain into slices, as with the leg muscles.

D: Loin

Many of the prime cuts come from the loin, although they are very small. The loin can be left whole on the bone or cut into chops (the equivalent of porterhouse or T-bone steaks). Some upmarket butchers will trim up the loin on the bone to create a frenched veal rack, which can also be cut into individual chops. Off the bone the loin is divided into the tenderloin and the backstrap – the eye or fillet of veal. These both make tender medallions and steaks, when cut into slices.

E: Flank and Breast

From the belly of the calf there is little meat to be had on the flank. The breast is also known as brisket and needs long, slow cooking, to melt it to juicy tenderness. It is traditionally boned out and stuffed, for roasting or poaching. Breast meat is sometimes ready-diced as 'pie veal', and it makes brilliant casseroles, pie fillings and terrines.

Veal cuts

A. shanks and shin / B. silverside, topside, knuckle and girello / C. rump / D. loin E. flank and breast / F. forequarter / G. feet

F: Forequarter

This yields the other prime roasting joint of veal, the shoulder. Shoulder chops are ideal for grilling, while the whole shoulder is often boned out, stuffed and rolled. Bone-in shoulder makes a wonderful pot-roast. Diced shoulder and diced brisket are the classic cuts for making blanquette de veau – a rich, creamy veal casserole.

G: Feet

Calves' feet yield copious amounts of gelatine, and are often added to a braise or a stew to give it body and sheen.

THINGS TO REMEMBER WHEN COOKING VEAL

Because veal is such a lean meat, you do need to take care to keep it moist – especially the tender-and-top-dollar cuts, such as scaloppine and chops. These will benefit immeasurable from being marinated in olive oil with lots of fresh herbs. And with these small cuts, always err on the side of undercooking, rather than run the risk of it drying out. They should be lovely and pink in the middle, and not cooked through to dry chalky whiteness.

Large lean cuts, such as the silverside, round or leg also need to be kept moist. You can either baste them with lots of butter and wine, wrap them in caul fat or even drape the surface of the meat with bacon rashers. Larger secondary cuts tend to be fattier and have more connective tissue, so are less likely to dry out. But as with all braised dishes, make sure that they cook very gently, for maximum juiciness.

HOW DO YOU KNOW WHEN IT'S COOKED?

Because veal are young animals, their muscle fibres and connective tissue are not as developed, as in older beef cattle. This means the meat can sometimes be a little chewy. For this reason I like to cook veal a little more than beef. Again, my preferred way of testing for doneness is to measure the internal core temperature using a digital instant-read thermometer.

Roasted leg, chops and racks of veal should be cooked to around 55°C. At this temperature the meat will still be pink and juicy, but the slightly longer cooking will help to break down the connective tissue, and the meat will be more tender.

rare	medium–rare	medium	medium–well	well done
35°C	45°C	55°C	65°C	75°C

THINGS THAT LOVE VEAL
Anchovies, breadcrumbs, butter, capers, cream, garlic, lemon, marjoram, mushrooms, olive oil, olives, oregano, parsley, rosemary, sage, salt, shallots, thyme, tomatoes, white pepper, white wine.

Classic veal schnitzel

Who can resist a schnitzel with its golden crunchy coating and tender interior? I remember the days when 'Wiener' – or Viennese – schnitzel seemed to feature on just about every restaurant menu in town. But strangely, it seems to have gone out of fashion. These days, if you want a decent schnitzel, you'll probably have to make it yourself – thank goodness they're really easy.

Don't worry that you'll have to spend a fortune on the most expensive scaloppine cut from the fillet. Schnitzels are usually made using a cheaper cut from the leg. Just make sure that your butcher cuts the scaloppine on the bias from a single leg muscle to create single slices. They should definitely not be sliced straight through the boned-out leg, as that will mean each slice is made up of several different muscles and won't cook evenly in the pan.

I like to serve these schnitzels with a Fresh Herb Salad (page 314) and Potato Salad (page 298).

1 kg veal leg meat, cut into 15–20 scaloppine
3 eggs
1 cup milk
1 cup plain flour
3 cups homemade breadcrumbs
2 tablespoons chopped thyme
2 tablespoons dried oregano
zest of 2 lemons, finely chopped
1 teaspoon salt
1 teaspoon freshly ground black pepper
olive oil for frying
butter for frying
1 lemon to serve

Place each scaloppine between two squares of plastic wrap and pound with a rolling pin or meat mallet to about 5 mm thick. If you're nice to your butcher, he might do this for you.

Whisk the eggs and milk together in a large shallow dish. Tip the flour into a separate dish. Mix the breadcrumbs with the herbs, lemon zest and seasoning and pour onto a large plate. Season each scaloppine lightly with a little salt and pepper then dip them into the flour, then into the egg mixture and then into the breadcrumbs so they are evenly coated.

Heat the oil and butter in a large heavy-based frying pan until it is sizzling. Fry the scaloppine, two at a time for 2–3 minutes, or until the undersides are golden brown. Turn and cook for a further 1–2 minutes. Remove from the pan and drain briefly on a wire rack. Serve straight away with a big squeeze of lemon juice and the herb and potato salads.

Serves 6

Saltimbocca alla Romana

Saltimbocca means 'jump in the mouth', which I can only assume refers to the vibrant flavours of the pancetta, sage and wine. Saltimbocca are very easy to prepare and are a great example of quick-cooking at its best. You can either buy a whole piece of veal and cut it into thin slices yourself, or buy scaloppine from the butcher. Personally, I don't like the scaloppine to be hammered so thin that there is nothing to chew on, and worse still, they dry out. Keeping them about 1 cm thick means they'll be moist and juicy.

12 veal scaloppine, about
  10 cm x 1 cm thick
salt
freshly ground black pepper
12 sage leaves
12 slices pancetta (or I sometimes
  use prosciutto)

3 tablespoons olive oil
1 garlic clove, crushed, but left whole
½ cup white wine
75 g butter
2 tablespoons chopped sage
¼ cup chopped parsley

Lay the veal scaloppine out on your work surface. Season lightly, then top each with a sage leaf and a slice of pancetta and flatten gently with a meat mallet or the back of a heavy knife. I find this is all you need to do to keep everything together, but feel free to secure them with a toothpick if you prefer.

Place the oil and garlic in a large, heavy-based frying pan and heat very gently. Once the garlic starts to colour, remove it from the pan. Increase the heat to medium and add 4 scaloppine to the pan, pancetta-side down. Fry for 2 minutes until golden brown, then turn and fry for 2 minutes on the other side. Transfer to a warm plate while you cook the remaining scaloppine.

Tip out any oil from the frying pan then add the wine and bubble vigorously until reduced by half. Add the butter and chopped sage to the pan and simmer for a minute or two until the butter has melted to form a thick, shiny sauce. Stir in the parsley and spoon over the saltimbocca.

Serves 4

Stuffed breast of veal with bacon and buttered shallots

The breast is a wide, thin piece of meat than can be opened out and stuffed, and then rolled up to create a plump, easy-to-slice log. It benefits from long, slow cooking in a little stock, which keeps it moist and tender. This is my kind of dish, with everything cooked in the one pot, creating its own sauce along the way. Once cooked, you can lift out the veal and reduce the braising liquid to form a thicker sauce. But I usually serve it as is, with Tomato-Braised Beans (page 309) and plenty of Creamy, Buttery Mash (page 296) or crusty bread to soak up the juices.

1 x 1. 5 kg veal breast
salt
freshly ground black pepper
3 tablespoons olive oil
50 g butter
20 shallots
3 cups good-quality veal or
   chicken stock

Stuffing
150 g butter
2 medium onions, finely diced
4 garlic cloves, crushed
250 g smoky bacon, finely diced
2 cups homemade breadcrumbs
¼ cup chopped parsley
1 tablespoon chopped thyme
salt
freshly ground black pepper

To make the stuffing, heat the butter in a heavy-based frying pan over a low–medium heat. Add the onion and garlic and sweat gently for 5 minutes until soft, but not coloured. Add the bacon to the pan and sauté for 3–4 minutes. Stir in the breadcrumbs and herbs and season to taste. Mix everything together well then remove from the heat and leave to cool.

Preheat the oven to 160°C.

Lay the veal breast out on your work surface and season lightly. Arrange the cooled stuffing down the centre of the meat then roll it up fairly tightly and secure at 5 cm intervals with butcher's string.

Select a casserole dish that will contain the veal snugly and place over a medium heat. Add the oil and brown the veal on all sides. Transfer the veal to a plate and add the butter to the casserole. Add the shallots and sauté for 5 minutes, turning continuously, until they begin to soften and colour. Add the stock and bubble for a minute or so, then return the veal to the pan. Cover and transfer to the oven for 1½ hours. Remove the lid and baste the veal, then cook for a further hour, covered, until the veal is very tender.

Serves 6

Braised shoulder of veal with sage and rosemary

This is a simple yet very elegant dish, with a tasty stuffing that flavours the meat from within. Serve with Creamy, Buttery Mash (page 296) to absorb the sauce and your choice of green vegies.

1.2 kg veal shoulder, boned
salt
freshly ground black pepper
¼ cup sage leaves
¼ cup rosemary
4 garlic cloves, sliced

150 g bacon, cut into strips
1 x 450 g pork fillet or Scotch fillet
150 g butter
2 cups white wine
½ cup chopped parsley

Preheat the oven to 175°C.

Lay the veal shoulder out on your work surface, skin-side down. Season with salt and pepper then scatter on the herbs and garlic slices. Lay the bacon strips over the surface of the veal then arrange the pork fillet lengthwise down the centre. Roll the veal up tightly and secure with butcher's string at 6 cm intervals.

Heat the butter in a heavy-based casserole. Sauté the veal until evenly browned all over. Add the wine to the casserole then cover with its lid and transfer to the oven. Cook for 1½ hours then remove from the oven. Lift the veal out of the casserole on to a warm plate.

Boil the remaining liquid in the casserole vigorously until reduced to a syrupy sauce.

To serve, slice the veal thinly and serve drizzled with a little sauce and sprinkled with parsley.

Serves 4–6

Veal involtini

This is one of those slightly retro dishes that I really love – probably because it takes me back to my childhood. My nonna used to make involtini for us as a treat, and one of the things I remember most clearly was the way she used to tie them up with cotton threads.

1 kg veal leg meat, cut into 20–30
  small scaloppine
salt
freshly ground black pepper
100 g butter
1 cup white wine
1 cup veal or chicken stock

Stuffing
50 g pitted green olives
2 anchovies
2 hard-boiled eggs, whites only
½ cup homemade breadcrumbs
½ cup chopped parsley
zest of 1 lemon

Put the stuffing ingredients into a food processor and pulse to form moist crumbs.

Lay the veal scaloppine out on your work surface. Season lightly, then place 1 spoonful of the crumb mixture at the end of each slice and shape it into a little log. Roll the veal up and around the filling and secure with toothpicks – or cotton, if you're feeling adventurous.

Melt the butter in a heavy-based casserole until just sizzling. Add the involtini and sauté for a few minutes until evenly browned. Add the wine and stock to the pan and bring to a gentle simmer. Cook, uncovered, for 1 hour, turning the involtini in the liquid every so often. By the end of the cooking time the liquid will have evaporated and the involtini will be golden brown and slightly sticky.

Serve the involtini with lots of crusty bread for mopping up the juices.

Serves 4 as a main course or 6 as a starter

Vitello tonnato

When Nonna made this dish for the family I used to think that she was just fobbing us off with leftovers. Shame on me! Now I understand just how much effort and love went into giving us all the very best and tastiest meals.

Vitello tonnato is best made a day or two ahead of time, which allows the flavours to develop and intensify. It's a great party dish as it feeds many people and most of the work is done in advance.

1 kg veal topside or silverside, trimmed, but left whole
2 carrots, cut into large slices
2 onions, quartered
2 sticks celery, cut into large dice
2 garlic cloves, halved
1 bay leaf
6 peppercorns
1 teaspoon salt

Sauce
1 x 150 g best-quality tuna in olive oil, drained
2 tablespoons extra-virgin olive oil
juice of 1 lemon
2 tablespoons capers
6 anchovy fillets
salt
freshly ground white pepper
2 tablespoons Mayonnaise (page 340)
chopped parsley to serve

Place the veal in a heavy-based saucepan or casserole dish that contains it snugly. Add the vegetables, garlic, bay leaf, peppercorns and salt and enough cold water to just cover the meat. Bring to the boil, then lower the heat and simmer gently for 1½–2 hours, covered, until the veal is very tender. Leave the veal to cool in the poaching stock overnight. Strain the stock and discard the vegetables, then return the veal to the stock and refrigerate.

To make the sauce, combine all the ingredients, except for the chopped parsley, in a food processor and blitz to a smooth paste. Dilute with a few spoonfuls of the cool poaching stock to form the consistency of thin cream.

Lift the veal out of the stock and pat it dry. Slice it thinly and arrange in overlapping layers on a large serving platter. Cover with the sauce then chill before serving. Ideally, I like to leave the vitello tonnato overnight for the flavours to develop, but you'll need to cover it with plastic wrap to prevent the sauce discolouring too much.

Bring the vitello tonnato to room temperature before garnishing with chopped parsley and serving with a simple green salad.

Serves 8

These meatballs – or polpetti as they're called in Italian – are a great favourite with my family. In fact my nonna has been making them as far back as I can remember. And she nearly always serves them with Peperonata (page 307). Nonna would never use truffled pecorino, of course. Yes, it's a bit of a luxury, but it adds a lovely earthy depth to the finished dish. Both the truffled pecorino and porcini powder are available from specialist food stores or delicatessens.

If you omit the cheese from this dish, it becomes virtually fat-free. Serve it with a salad of green leaves and mixed garden herbs, and a drizzle of the peperonata dressing, and you can almost think of it as health food! For a heartier meal, serve with spaghetti and loads of grated parmesan – or truffled pecorino if you can afford it.

Italian meatballs with peperonata and shaved pecorino

300 g lean veal leg meat
300 g pork leg meat
2 garlic cloves, finely chopped
2 teaspoons porcini powder
2 tablespoons chopped sage leaves
¼ cup chopped parsley
2 tablespoons chopped basil
¼ teaspoon ground allspice
2 teaspoons salt

2 teaspoons freshly ground black pepper
1 tablespoon grated parmesan
2 cups chicken stock
olive oil
Peperonata (page 307), to serve
100 g truffled pecorino (or parmesan or provolone)

To make the meatballs, cut the veal and pork into cubes and place in a large mixing bowl with the garlic, porcini powder, herbs, seasonings and parmesan. Toss to combine, then mince or process to a not-too-smooth paste.

Wet your hands to stop the mixture sticking and roll into 24 even-sized balls. Heat the chicken stock in a medium saucepan until just simmering. Poach the meatballs in batches for 8 minutes, then remove with a slotted spoon and drain on kitchen paper. Transfer to a container and leave to cool. You can make the meatballs to this stage up to 3 days in advance.

When ready to eat, heat the oil in a large, heavy-based frying pan. Fry the polpetti for 6–8 minutes, until warmed through and golden brown all over. Serve with peperonata and shavings of truffled pecorino.

Serves 6 as a starter or light meal

Veal shanks with Italian flavours

It's hard to believe these days, but shanks used to be one of the cheapest cuts going. Several of my butcher friends tell me stories about the days when they'd throw a few shanks to regular customers as a bit of a thank you. But these days, butchers get top dollar for each shank, and they've become a favourite dish on restaurant menus. In this recipe, the eggplant helps thicken the sauce to a wonderful lusciousness that brilliantly complements the soft, melting texture of the veal. I like to serve these shanks with Soft, Herby, Cheesy Polenta (page 300) and a big dollop of Basil Pesto (page 344) added just before serving.

2 medium eggplants
6 veal shanks
salt
freshly ground pepper
1 tablespoon smoked paprika
¼ cup extra-virgin olive oil
150 g butter
1 medium onion, finely diced
2 medium leeks, cut into 2 cm rounds
10 garlic cloves, roughly chopped
1 carrot, sliced into rounds
200 g green olives, pitted

2 cups white wine
1 litre veal or chicken stock
1 kg roma tomatoes, skinned,
  quartered and seeded
1 cup basil leaves
½ cup chopped coriander
½ cup chopped parsley
1 cup cooked chickpeas
2 medium zucchini, sliced
juice of 2 lemons
Basil Pesto (page 344), to serve

Preheat the oven to 180°C and lightly oil a baking tray.

Prick the eggplants all over with a fork, then roast for 20 minutes until very soft. Remove them from the oven and transfer to a wire rack. When cool, peel away the skin and chop the flesh roughly.

Season the veal shanks with salt, pepper and the paprika. Heat half the oil with half the butter in a heavy-based casserole. Sauté the shanks over a high heat until evenly browned all over then transfer to a plate and keep warm.

Add the remaining oil and butter to the casserole over a medium heat. Add the onion, leeks, garlic and carrot and sauté for 5 minutes, or until they begin to soften. Add the eggplant and olives and sauté for 2 minutes.

Return the veal shanks to the casserole. Pour on the wine and stock then add the tomatoes and half the fresh herbs. Transfer to the oven and cook for 1 hour, covered. Add the chickpeas and zucchini to the casserole and cook for a further 30 minutes. By the end of the cooking time the veal should be very tender and begin to fall away from the bones.

Stir in the lemon juice and scatter on the remaining herbs just before serving with a big dollop of pesto.

Serves 6

Nonna Yole's osso buco

Most people have a dusty bottle of port lurking around in the back of a cupboard, and here's a great way to use it up. Osso buco is a classic Italian recipe that uses the veal shin, cut through the bone into thick chunks. It's a brilliant slow-cooked dish that really makes the best of what seems to be a bony and rather mean cut. You end up with meltingly soft meat and a juicy knob of marrow to suck from the bones. It may not be elegant, but it's delicious.

Ask your butcher to cut your osso buco pieces from the hind shin, as they have more meat on them than those from the foreleg.

This osso buco recipe comes from my Nonna Yole. It is traditionally served with risotto alla Milanese, but I like to serve it with Red Wine Risotto (page 305), or Soft, Herby, Cheesy Polenta (page 300).

¼ cup olive oil
2 kg veal shin, cut crosswise into
  5 cm slices
100 g butter
4 anchovies
10 garlic cloves, crushed
2 onions, diced
1 carrot, sliced
2 sticks celery, sliced
200 g olives, pitted
50 g capers
2 bay leaves

1 cup red wine
1 cup port
1 litre tomato passata
salt
freshly ground black pepper
1 cup basil leaves

Gremolata
zest of 1 lemon
2 tablespoons chopped parsley
½ garlic clove, finely chopped
  (optional)

Preheat the oven to 175°C.

Heat the oil in a heavy-based casserole and brown the veal pieces all over. Transfer the browned veal to a plate and keep warm.

Add the butter to the casserole and when it starts to sizzle add the anchovies, garlic and onion. Sauté over a medium heat until the anchovies begin to melt. Add the carrot and celery and sweat for about 5 minutes until they begin to soften. Add the olives, capers and bay leaves to the casserole then pour in the wine, port and tomato passata. Season with salt and pepper and stir in half the basil leaves.

Bring to the boil then lower the temperature to a simmer. Cover the casserole and transfer to the oven for 1½ hours, or until the meat is meltingly tender. Check the casserole from time to make sure that the meat is always covered with sauce.

Once the veal is cooked, remove the casserole from the oven. If the sauce is too thin, remove the lid from the casserole and boil vigorously on the stovetop for 5–10 minutes until reduced.

Mix together the gremolata ingredients and scatter onto the osso buco just before serving.

Serves 6

This dish gets its name from the French word 'blanc', which means white. The paleness of the creamy sauce complements the veal's light colour and flavour. It is essentially a delicate stew, and I like to serve it with Buttery Rice Pilaf (page 304) and a green salad.

Blanquette de veau

1 kg veal shoulder, boned
1 large onion, quartered
2 sticks celery, cut into 5 cm lengths
2 medium carrots split lengthways
2 garlic cloves
2 bay leaves
3 sprigs thyme
5 peppercorns
1 teaspoon salt

Sauce
20 shallots
250 g button mushrooms
4 garlic cloves, crushed
2 sprigs thyme
1.2 litres reserved veal poaching
   stock (see veal method)
100 g butter
100 g plain flour
½ cup chopped parsley

Place the veal in a heavy-based saucepan or casserole dish that contains it snugly. Add the vegetables, garlic, bay leaves, thyme, peppercorns and salt and enough cold water to cover the meat. Bring to the boil, then lower the heat and simmer gently for 2 hours, skimming frequently, until the veal is very tender. Leave the veal to cool in the poaching stock. Strain and discard the vegetables. Cut the veal into 2 cm pieces and return to the stock. Refrigerate until ready to proceed.

To make the sauce, combine the shallots, mushrooms, garlic, thyme and a splash of the reserved stock in a small saucepan. Simmer, covered, for 10–15 minutes, or until the shallots are tender.

Melt the butter in a heavy-based saucepan and stir in the flour over a low heat to make a smooth paste (roux). Gradually add the rest of the reserved stock, stirring continuously, to make a smooth sauce. Simmer for 20 minutes, stirring from time to time, until the sauce thickens to a rich, velvety cream.

Add the diced veal and the reserved shallot-mushroom mixture and simmer for 5 minutes. Season to taste and scatter on the chopped parsley before serving.

Serves 6

LAMB

5

WHO DOESN'T
LOVE A LAMB
ROAST?

Lamb

We Australians have a special fondness for lamb. According to the well-worn cliché, the country rode its way to wealth on the sheep's back, and a lamb roast seems to be everyone's favourite dinner. In fact, if we have such a thing as a national dish, a barbecued lamb chop would have to be a good contender for the title. As for me, I love the fact that lamb has such a distinctive flavour that responds brilliantly to bold seasonings and a variety of cooking techniques.

Sheep were one of the very first animals to be domesticated, about 9000 years ago, by nomads in Mesopotamia – a region that corresponds roughly with modern Iraq. This was probably no great feat, given that sheep are very easy animals to handle and have a naturally gregarious temperament and a strong herding instinct. Better still, they will happily graze on the most barren terrain, which makes them much easier to farm than cattle or pigs. Early communities prized sheep as much for their thick woolly coats, milk and tallow fat as for their meat.

In Middle Eastern countries today, when people talk about meat, they pretty much mean lamb. And because this region is so strongly linked with many of the world's major religions, it is not surprising that lamb has become the meat of choice at feast days around the world. For Christians, a paschal lamb has particular significance at Easter as the symbol of Christ. Jewish New Year and Passover celebrations would be unthinkable without lamb, while Muslim communities ritually slaughter and feast upon whole roasted lambs on religious holidays and family celebrations.

AUSTRALIAN LAMB

For us Aussies, both sheep and lamb are strongly linked with our history and our sense of identity. They were introduced to the country in 1788, with the First Fleet, and early pioneers, such as John Macarthur, Samuel Marsden and Governor King, realised straight away how suited they were to the Australian rural landscape. Within 50 years of settlement, wool had become the country's main export, with an annual wool clip in excess of two million kilograms.

The Australian sheepmeat industry – in other words lamb, and to a lesser extent, mutton – has generally been a by-product of the wool industry, but in the last few decades it has evolved into a significant industry in its own right. While Australian lamb doesn't contribute as much to our economy as wool, we do spend around $2 billion on our lamb every year, and eat around 24 million servings of it every week.

Australia also plays a big part in the world demand for lamb. We produce around 7 per cent of all the lamb and mutton, and we're the second largest exporter of lamb in the world – after New Zealand – and the largest mutton exporter. While our lamb industry is generally considered to be well managed and untainted by many of the welfare issues that are commonplace in other intensively farmed animals, it is in our export market for live sheep, as opposed to lamb meat, that we have been widely – and rightly – criticised.

In terms of breed, the Merino sheep has always been the hero of the Australian wool industry and even today around two-thirds of all our sheep are Merino or Merino-cross. Although they are best known for the excellent quality of their wool, Merino lambs also make pretty good eating. It is more common, though, to cross Merinos with other stocky, early-fattening breeds for prime lamb. Many of these are British breeds and the main choices are the Leicester, Poll Dorset, Cheviot and Suffolk. However, most Australian lamb comes from crossing Merinos with Dutch Texel sheep.

A lot of studies suggest that the breed of the animal doesn't actually make a huge difference to its flavour. The animal's diet and environment have much more of an impact, and in this respect we are lucky in Australia. Our lamb is widely considered to be consistently mellow and sweet-flavoured, largely because it is predominantly grass-fed on pasture. As with the beef cattle industry, though, there has been a growing tendency in recent years for our lambs to be put to feedlots for fattening prior to slaughter. The idyllic vision of woolly lambs nibbling on tender green grass is only true up to a point. Many lamb farmers have uniformity and consistency of texture and flavour as their priority, and animals that are dependent upon pasture land are clearly vulnerable to the effects of drought. Generally speaking, though, Australian lamb has escaped the less appealing aspects of intensive farming, such as unnatural feeds, growth promoters and confined living space, that beset other animals and the meat is considered to be top-notch.

Uniquely Australian

One of my very favourite meats is Australian saltbush lamb, which gets its distinctive flavour from munching on this extraordinary plant. Saltbush is native to Australia and is one of the only plants in the world that thrives in saline terrain. The plant can take salty water into its system, absorb the salt and offload it into a few sacrificial leaves and use the remaining pure water to grow on. Not only does saltbush act to improve the land it grows on, but sheep seem to thrive on the stuff.

To my mind this is a brilliant and sustainable way of raising lamb, making them less susceptible to the fickleness of our climate and less reliant on grain. Lamb that has been fed on saltbush tends to be a bit leaner and the meat is darker than that of pasture-fed or grain-finished lamb. It also tends to be very moist as the animals drink a lot. The meat tastes quite intense, although not at all salty.

LAMB AND NUTRITION

Lamb has somewhat fallen out of favour in recent years because of worries about its levels of saturated fats. In Australia we eat around 11 kilograms of lamb and 3 kilograms of mutton every year, substantially less than beef, the other red meat. As often seems to be the case with nutritional issues, things are not as cut and dried as, 'it's good for you' or 'it's bad for you'. Lamb these days is bred to be much leaner than it was several decades ago, and the industry built a very successful 'Trim Lamb' marketing campaign around this very issue in the 1990s. Nutritional studies actually show that half the fat in today's lean lamb is of the unsaturated kind, similar to that in olive oil. Furthermore, palmitoleic acid, a 16-carbon monounsaturated fatty acid found in lamb, is known to possess strong antimicrobial properties.

STORING LAMB AND MUTTON

- Because it comes from a young animal, lamb is not usually aged. It is a fresh meat that is best eaten quickly, and typically it arrives on the dining table within a week of slaughter.
- Mutton comes from an older animal, and benefits from dry-aging for two to three weeks.
- Unwrap and refrigerate lamb and mutton immediately.
- Store it in a Tupperware container, or sit it on a rack on a plate and cover it with a tea towel.
- Large joints of lamb or mutton will keep up to five days.
- Smaller cuts, such as chops and medallions, should be used within three days.
- For most cuts, if you rub them with a bit of olive oil, or even cover them in a marinade they will keep a bit longer as it delays the oxidisation process.
- Cubed or minced lamb should be used within two days.

As with all meats, lamb is high in protein. It is also a good source of iron, zinc and the B vitamins, and contains trace elements, such as copper, manganese and selenium. Lamb is high in CLA (conjugated linoleic acid), which is linked with boosting immunity and inhibiting certain cancers and diabetes. Interestingly, saltbush lamb has been found to have higher levels of vitamin E.

HOW AND WHERE TO BUY LAMB

The meat from Australian sheep is eaten at every age, from a few weeks to several years old, and it is easy to recognise because it is branded accordingly. True lamb – the lamb we eat most of the year round – is usually around 3–12 months of age, and is defined as being lamb by the absence of adult teeth. You can recognise it by the red ribbon stripe, branded on its carcass.

Spring lamb is really a bit of a marketing term. It refers to the time of year that the lambs are born and sold – winter and spring, respectively. Spring lamb is often thought to be particularly delicious because the animals eat plenty of young green shoots. By the end of a hot Australian summer, lambs that are actually born in springtime may have had to make do with a sparser diet and less rainfall – particularly in drought years.

By the time it has grown two adult teeth the animal is known as 'two-tooth' or 'hogget', which is indicated by six round stamps branded on the carcass. Some less scrupulous butchers may try to sell you hogget instead of lamb, but you should be able to identify it by the darker colour of the meat. Having said that, some people actually prefer hogget to lamb because of its more developed flavour. If you want to try it for yourself, you are more likely to be able to find it at farmers' markets or in country areas.

If lamb has more than two teeth (18–24 months of age), then it becomes the stronger-flavoured mutton, which you'll either love or loathe. Mutton is identified by four circular brand marks on the carcass.

I definitely fall into the 'love it' camp with mutton. I think there is nothing quite like the intense flavour of these beasts – it's a fullness and richness that is often lacking in the immature youngsters. You may find mutton more appealing if you think of it in the same way as beef; that is, as a mature animal that has had time to develop a bit of character. But like beef, mutton does need a bit of hanging (dry-aging), to tenderise it. Surprisingly, mutton doesn't necessarily need to be braised. If it's been properly aged, then it makes for a delicious roast.

At the other end of the spectrum is baby milk-fed lamb, which you will find in specialist butchers. True milk-fed lamb is aged between two weeks and a month or so old. Milk-fed lamb is the dish par excellence for feast days in the Arab world and the Mediterranean, where it is often roasted whole on a spit.

Lamb is widely available, although you'll probably have to go to a specialist butcher to buy mutton. As is always the case when you're buying meat, you need to take care to buy the appropriate cut for the recipe you plan to make. You are more likely to find a larger selection of cuts at a good butcher than you will in a supermarket. Supermarkets tend to limit their stock to a smaller range of the more popular cuts, such as chops and lamb roasts. Of course the only way they're going to expand their range is if we customers ask. But in the meantime I'm going to encourage you – as I do throughout this book – to find yourself a good butcher and make him your friend.

And what should it look like? Well, lamb meat should be a light, rosy pink colour. As it gets older, the meat darkens, so mutton is more of a deep burgundy red. Don't buy any lamb that has a bit of a dry, brownish tinge to it. The texture of lamb should be fairly fine-grained and it should be firm, not flabby. The fat should be creamy-white and dry, not yellow and sticky.

WHICH CUT TO BUY

Most lamb is fairly tender because it comes from a young animal, but you still need to give some thought to choosing the right cut for each method of cooking. Don't make the mistake of choosing the less expensive cuts, which are layered with plenty of connective tissue and fat, and thinking you can get away with quick-cook methods like grilling or barbecueing. As outlined in Chapter 1, the various muscles are put to varying degrees of work, and need to be treated accordingly.

A: Shank

There was a time when lamb shanks were virtually given away as cheap off-cuts. These days they are recognised for what there are: a nice meaty cut (from the bottom-end of the leg) that cooks down to delectably tasty tenderness. Lamb shanks are not as generous as veal shanks, but they are similarly rich in gelatinous connective tissue that is released by long, slow cooking.

B: Leg

Everyone recognises a leg of lamb and I think most of us would have a go at roasting one. They are brilliant when studded with garlic and sprigs of rosemary and oven-roasted until pink and juicy. The leg can also be boned and butterflied (the meat opened out flat) for grilling on the barbecue. Or it can be cut into steaks, which are great for grilling, barbecuing or quickly frying in a hot pan.

C: Chump (Rump)

The chump is sometimes sold attached to the leg, which makes for a monster-roast indeed. When removed, it is the equivalent of beef rump, and makes a very neat and tasty roast. Sometimes the chump is cut into chops, which are good and meaty.

D: Loin

Equivalent to beef sirloin, the loin gives us some of the most tender lamb, and comes in a variety of ways, both on and off the bone. There are actually two loins, attached in the middle (at the backbone); when sold together, these form the very grand roasting cut known as the saddle. You are probably more likely to find a single loin, which is called the shortloin when left on the bone. When cut off the bone, the loin is also called a strap or backstrap. It is sometimes sold with a flap of fat still on, and the whole thing is rolled up and tied for roasting. Loin and middle loin chops are lovely and tender, and are ideal for grilling or barbecuing as quickly as possible.

E: Best End

Also known as the rack (of the first eight ribs), and one of the best-loved and luxurious cuts of lamb. As with the saddle, each lamb has two racks, one on either side of the backbone. They are wonderful for roasting – rubbed with a marinade or even with a crunchy coating of crumbs. For a real celebration your butcher can form the two racks into a circle to create a crown roast. The rack can also be cut into its individual ribs, when they are called cutlets. I especially love them when they are dipped into egg and breadcrumbs and deep-fried to make very tasty little morsels.

GOAT

It's hard to find goat meat in the average high street butcher, so you'll probably be surprised to learn that Australia is the world's leading goat-meat exporter. Our industry is evolving from a small, cottage industry to a genuine economic and environmentally sustainable one, valued at around $20 million per annum.

This makes perfect sense when you realise how well-suited goats are to the Australian climate and terrain. They graze happily on unproductive land, doing less damage than sheep and cattle. They breed prolifically – even in drought conditions – and are exceptionally hardy.

Goat meat meets many of our modern-day requirements for leanness, and it is tender and juicy. It has a similar flavour to lamb and is ideally suited to long, wet cooking techniques, which makes it popular for curries and braises. Whole baby goats (kid) are brilliant for spit-roasting. You'll be most likely to find goat at butchers in neighbourhoods where there is a diverse ethnic population – especially of Greeks, Africans, Indians or Middle Easterners.

Lamb cuts

A. shank / B. leg / C. chump
D. loin / E. best end / F. breast
G. shoulder / H. forequarter
and neck / I. foreshank (shin)

F: Breast
This is often dismissed as being overly fatty, but I think it can be cooked very successfully. It's best when filled with a tasty stuffing, then rolled up and slowly pot-roasted. It will produce a lot of fat, which you'll need to drain off, and will benefit from a final blast in a hot oven to brown the outside. You may prefer to use the breast for mincing (it makes great sausages).

G: Shoulder
This is one of my favourite cuts of lamb. I think the shoulder makes a much tastier roast than the leg, largely because it has more fat. Otherwise the shoulder can be braised, when I think it marries well with strong flavours. Either method will bring out its intrinsic stickiness. With the bone removed, the shoulder can be stuffed and rolled – its fat content will keep it good and juicy inside.

H: Forequarter and Neck
Chops cut from the forequarter and neck are brilliant for slow-cooked casseroles and braises as they are marbled with plenty of tasty fat. But whatever you do, don't think you can sling them on the barbie; they need long, slow cooking to make them tender and succulent. Try them for a Lancashire hotpot or even a Moroccan tagine.

I: Foreshank (Shin)
Equivalent to the hindquarter shank, but a much less meaty part of the beast. They need to be cooked very slowly to release their goodness.

HOW DO YOU KNOW WHEN IT'S COOKED?
My preferred way of testing for doneness is to measure the internal core temperature of any cut of lamb, using a digital instant-read thermometer inserted into the thickest part of the meat.

Remember that the reading will rise by about 5°C as the meat rests, so begin checking the temperature about 10 minutes before the end of the recommended cooking time.

rare	medium–rare	medium	medium–well	well done
35°C	45°C	55°C	65°C	75°C

If you don't have a digital thermometer, then use the thumb-to-finger test for doneness (see page 29).

THINGS THAT LOVE LAMB
Allspice, black pepper, cinnamon, coriander, cumin, eggplant, garlic, lemon, marjoram, mint sauce, olive oil, oregano, peppers, red wine, redcurrant jelly, root vegetables, rosemary, salt, shallots, spinach, thyme, tomatoes, yoghurt.

Barbecued butterflied lamb with honey and rosemary

There are lots of muscles in the leg that all work together as the animal walks and skips around, so it is a really tasty bit of meat with all sorts of different textures to chew on. There is often quite a lot of external fat on the leg that melts in the heat of the barbecue to keep the meat lovely and moist. Be careful not to let it drip onto the charcoal too much, or you'll get flames, which can burn the meat.

When you butterfly a leg of lamb – which is a fancy way of saying you remove the bone and open it out flat – it greatly cuts down the cooking time. It also helps the meat absorb all the lovely flavours of the marinade and the barbecue. Sometimes I like to cut the butterflied lamb into pieces and grill them as free-form chunks. Either way, slice the lamb thinly and serve it with Big Greek Salad (page 315), Tzatziki (page 342) and warm pita bread, so everyone can make their own pita sandwiches.

If you're not confident about doing the boning and butterflying yourself, ask your butcher to do it for you.

1 x 2.5 kg leg of lamb, bone removed and butterflied
3 stalks fresh rosemary
½ cup white wine
8 garlic cloves, chopped
¼ cup olive oil
¼ cup honey
¼ cup chopped parsley
1 tablespoon salt
1 tablespoon freshly ground black pepper
zest and juice of 2 lemons

Open the leg of lamb out flat and trim away any excess fat. Use the tip of a sharp knife to stab grooves into the meat all over. Cut into 6 even pieces, or leave whole, depending on your mood.

Strip the leaves from the rosemary stalks and bruise them with a pestle or the flat blade of your knife. Chop roughly and rub all over the lamb. Transfer to a shallow dish or plastic container that it will fit into snugly.

Mix all the remaining ingredients together, except for the lemon zest and juice, and pour over the lamb. Use your hands to rub in well. Cover, refrigerate and leave to marinate overnight or for a few hours.

When ready to cook, light your barbecue or heat your oven to medium–high. Remove the lamb from the fridge and bring it to room temperature. Cook the lamb for around 20–30 minutes for medium-rare, turning continuously. Leave it to rest for 15 minutes in a warm spot before serving. Individual portions will take 10–15 minutes for medium.

Just before carving, pour the lemon juice and zest over the lamb. Slice thinly and serve with lots of warm pita bread, salad and tzatziki.

Serves 6–8

Double-thick lamb chops on rosemary skewers

Double-thick loin chops are perfect for the grill or barbecue, as their juicy plumpness means they're harder to overcook or worse, burn. Coming from the loin, they are lovely and tender with great flavour. Ask your butcher to cut you nice fat chops, about 5 cm thick, and to leave the flank flap attached.

Rosemary is the perfect partner to lamb and I like to use long, strong stalks to make 'skewers'. You'll need to strip away most of the leaves from the stalk, leaving a sprig at one end. Slide a metal skewer through the chop first, then ease the rosemary skewer in alongside it and remove the metal one.

Serve with Potato Salad (page 298) and Eggplant Salsa (page 345).

12 double loin chops
12 long, strong rosemary stalks
salt
freshly ground black pepper

Marinade
1 garlic clove, crushed
1 tablespoon balsamic vinegar
1 tablespoon dried oregano
1 tablespoon coarsely ground
 black pepper
1 tablespoon fresh thyme leaves
3 tablespoons extra-virgin olive oil

Put the marinade ingredients into a mortar and pound to a fairly smooth paste. Rub over the chops, cover with plastic wrap and refrigerate overnight.

When ready to cook, preheat your grill or barbecue to medium–high. Wrap the flank flap around the chop to cover the small piece of fillet and skewer with a stalk of rosemary to hold it in place. Season all over with salt and pepper. Cook the chops for 12 minutes for medium–rare, turning frequently. Serve hot from the grill.

Serves 6

Lamb kofte kebabs

These spicy minced meat kebabs are popular all around the Middle East and Eastern Mediterranean. Think of them as a sort of skinless sausage, moulded around a skewer. If you can, try to find long, flat metal skewers for this dish as they hold the kofte better.

You can serve these kebabs the traditional way, stuffed into warm pita bread with salad and tzatziki, but for a change, I sometimes partner them with Buttery Rice Pilaf (page 304) and zucchini slices, sautéed with garlic in a little olive oil.

1 kg lamb leg or shoulder, minced
½ onion, finely diced
2 garlic cloves, crushed
1 tablespoon ground sumac
1 tablespoon cumin seeds,
  dry-roasted and ground
2 teaspoons chilli powder

1 teaspoon coriander seeds,
  dry-roasted and ground
¼ cup chopped coriander leaves
¼ cup chopped parsley leaves
1 tablespoon salt
1 tablespoon freshly ground
  black pepper

Combine all the ingredients in a large mixing bowl. Use your hands to squish everything together thoroughly, so that the onion, garlic, spices and herbs are evenly distributed. Cover and refrigerate for 20 minutes to allow the flavours to develop.

When ready to cook, preheat a barbecue or griddle to its highest temperature. Use wet hands to divide the kofte mix into 12 portions and mould each one around a flat metal skewer into a long sausage shape.

Cook the kofte for 5–8 minutes, turning frequently, until golden brown and cooked through. Serve with your choice of accompaniments.

Serves 4–6

Roast lamb with lots of garlic

Most Aussie families find it hard to go past a succulent roast lamb dinner. This is my favourite way of cooking it – studded with garlic and served up with the classic trimmings: Creamy Pommes Dauphinoise (page 297), Minted Peas (page 308) and not forgetting Mint Sauce (page 344)!

As well as looking pretty cool, the studding procedure is really easy and helps the flavours to permeate the meat. I always cut the garlic into little slivers and roll them in salt and pepper. That way, when you stick them into the meat, they add plenty of flavour to the inside.

1 x 2 kg leg of lamb
8 garlic cloves, peeled and cut
  into slivers
2 tablespoons salt
2 tablespoons freshly ground
  black pepper

rosemary sprigs
olive oil
2 carrots
2 onions
2 sticks celery

Preheat the oven to 175°C.

With a small sharp knife, pierce the lamb all over, making incisions about 3 cm deep. If you're feeling artistic, you can do this in neat lines. Roll the garlic slivers in salt and pepper and push them into the holes. You can either do this randomly, or create a neat pattern, alternating the garlic slivers with little sprigs of rosemary.

Season the lamb once more and rub it all over with oil. Sit it on a rack inside a large roasting tin and place in the oven. After 40 minutes scatter the vegetables around the lamb and roast for a further 40 minutes. I like my lamb to be nice and pink, so I cook it until the internal core temperature reaches 55°C.

Remove the lamb from the oven and transfer it to a warm plate. Leave it to rest for 30 minutes in a warm place before serving.

Serves 6

Roast saddle of lamb with spinach–herb stuffing

This is definitely a dinner party dish to impress and you'll need to ask your butcher for help. The saddle is made up of the two loins from each side of the lamb's back (see the diagram on page 80) that are held together by the surface layer of fat which finishes in long flaps, also known as 'aprons'. Ask your butcher to bone out the saddle for you, leaving the flaps long enough to roll under the joint. Ask him to remove the two little fillets and to keep them separately. And then ask him to remove most of the outer layer of fat so that you end up with a lovely neat piece of meat, perfect for stuffing, rolling up and roasting. When you carve it, you get lovely elegant slices.

I like to develop the spinach theme by serving the lamb with Creamed Spinach (page 312), as well as Creamy Pommes Dauphinoise (page 297) and Red Wine Reduction (page 332).

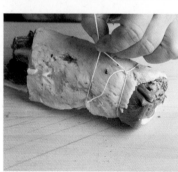

1 x 2.2 kg lamb saddle (bone-in weight)
salt
freshly ground black pepper
3 tablespoons olive oil

Spinach–herb stuffing
100 g butter
1 small onion, finely diced
2 garlic cloves, finely chopped
1 bunch spinach, stalks removed
   and rinsed well
1 tablespoon fresh thyme leaves
1 tablespoon parsley, chopped
1 tablespoon chervil, chopped
1 teaspoon salt
1 teaspoon freshly ground
   black pepper

To prepare the stuffing, first melt the butter in a heavy-based frying pan over a medium heat. Sweat the onion and garlic for 5–10 minutes until soft, but not coloured. Remove from the heat and leave to cool.

Bring a large saucepan of water to the boil and blanch the spinach leaves for 30 seconds. Drain well, squeezing to extract as much moisture as you can. Cool then chop roughly. Put the spinach into a food processor or liquidiser with the fresh herbs, salt and pepper and blend to a smooth paste.

When ready to cook, preheat your oven to 200°C.

Lay the saddle of lamb, skin-side down, on your work surface. Season lightly then spread on the spinach-herb stuffing as evenly as you can, leaving a border around the edge. Arrange the skinny fillets down the centre of the saddle then roll up to form a neat, fat log. Tie securely with butcher's string at 5 cm intervals.

Heat the oil in a heavy-based roasting tin and brown the lamb all over. Transfer to the oven and roast for 14 minutes for rare, 18 minutes for medium–rare, or 25 minutes if you like it well done. Remove from the oven and leave to rest for 10 minutes in a warm spot.

Remove the string, carve into thick slices, and serve with your choice of accompaniments.

Serves 8

There's no doubt that this is a bit of a show-off dish. The 'crown' is actually two racks of lamb that have been cut through the backbone and chine so that they can be formed into a circular crown. It looks pretty fancy and should be brought to the table and served in a suitably grand style. This is the time to bring out all your best silverware and crockery. And get Dad to brush up on his carving skills – although to be honest, it's dead-easy to carve: you just cut between the ribs with a sharp knife. Allow about four ribs per person. For a full-on presentation, fill the middle of the crown with Garlic- and Rosemary-roasted Potatoes (page 296), and serve with Minted Peas (page 308).

You'll need to ask your butcher to prepare the crown for you. But he'll love it, as it's a classic preparation, and will give him a chance to show off his skills. As well as forming the crown, he'll 'french' the racks for you, which means he'll scrape the meat and sinews away from the bones so they look nice and neat and clean. Just do him a favour and give him a few days notice, to organise things. And if your butcher is anything like mine, he'll invite himself along to eat it with you and drink all your beer!

Crown roast with minted peas

1 x 16-point lamb crown roast
olive oil
1 tablespoon salt

1 tablespoon freshly ground
  black pepper
1 tablespoon fresh rosemary,
  roughly chopped

Preheat the oven to 200ºC.

Rub the lamb all over with a little oil then season with the salt, pepper and rosemary. Transfer to a rack inside a large roasting tin and wrap the bones with foil, which will stop them burning and discolouring. To cook medium–rare, roast for 20 minutes.

When the lamb is cooked, remove from the oven, cover loosely with foil and leave to rest for 15 minutes in a warm place. To serve, transfer the lamb onto a serving platter and pile the potatoes into the middle. Serve with minted peas and your favourite gravy.

Serves 4

Lemony lamb shank soup with lentils, spinach and smoky eggplant

When my brother and I were children, my nonna used to make this soup for us in the winter. She learned to make it in Eygpt, which is where she grew up, and tells me that the original version uses a leafy green Middle Eastern vegetable called melokheya. Melokheya has a distinctive slippery texture and a sharp lemony flavour and this is a characteristic of the soup. It's hard to find melokheya in Australia, (although you should be able to find it in the freezer section of Middle Eastern stores), so I often substitute spinach and lemon juice instead. This is a great soup for breakfast on a cold winter's morning as it gives you a real energy boost for the day ahead.

Lamb stock
2 kg lamb shanks
2 medium onions, roughly chopped
2 carrots, roughly chopped
2 sticks celery, roughly chopped
1 head garlic, cut in half crosswise
1 medium bulb fennel, roughly chopped
2 bay leaves
1 tablespoon fennel seeds
1 teaspoon salt
1 teaspoon freshly ground black pepper

Soup
3 eggplants
¼ cup extra-virgin olive oil
½ tablespoon ground cumin, roasted
½ tablespoon ground coriander, roasted
6 garlic cloves, crushed
2 medium onions, cut into 1 cm dice
2 medium carrots, cut into 1 cm dice
2 sticks celery, cut into 1 cm dice
1 medium fennel bulb, cut into 1 cm dice
1 cup brown lentils, well rinsed
2 big handfuls baby spinach leaves, well rinsed
¼ cup chopped parsley leaves
¼ cup chopped coriander leaves
2 tablespoons chopped dill
squeeze of lemon juice

To make the stock, combine all the ingredients in a stockpot or large heavy-based saucepan. Cover with cold water and bring to the boil slowly. Skim away any scum or impurities as they rise to the surface. When the stock boils, lower the heat and simmer gently, uncovered, for 2 hours, skimming frequently. By the end of the cooking time the meat should be very tender and falling away from the bones. Leave to cool slightly, then strain the stock into a jug or bowl. Chop the meat roughly and set aside.

Prick the eggplants all over with a fork then sit them directly on the flame of your stove burners. Set the flame to low–medium heat and cook for 10 minutes, turning frequently until the eggplants are blackened and blistered and have collapsed. Remove from the flame and sit them on a small cake rack in a sealed plastic bag. Leave to cool for 10 minutes then peel away the skin from the flesh with a small sharp knife. Chop the flesh roughly and set aside.

In a large heavy-based saucepan, heat the oil. Add the spices and sauté over a gentle heat. Add the garlic and sauté for 2 minutes. Add the vegetables and toss to coat in the oil. Sauté for 2 minutes then add the chopped eggplant and the lamb stock. Bring to the boil, then lower the heat and simmer for 30 minutes.

Add the chopped lamb to the pan with the lentils. Simmer for 15 minutes, until the lentils are soft. Just before serving, throw in the spinach and allow it to wilt. Scatter on the fresh herbs and finish with a squeeze of lemon juice.

Serves 6–8

I love shanks because they are flavoursome, juicy and gelatinous, and when braised in a tasty sauce they become the food of kings, especially when served with Soft, Herby, Cheesy Polenta (page 300) or Creamy, Buttery Mash (page 296). Another great thing you can do is remove the cold meat from the bones, wrap it in caul fat and roast it in the oven. You can reduce the braising liquid to make a sauce and serve it alongside the roasted meat.

Incidentally, I never brown shanks before braising them, but instead just seal the outside of the meat gently in oil. I find it allows the flavours of the sauce to penetrate the meat better.

Braised lamb shanks with tomatoes and red peppers

¼ cup olive oil, plus 1 extra tablespoon
6 lamb shanks (ask your butcher to 'french' them for you)
4 red peppers
150 g butter
8 garlic cloves, crushed
2 large onions, cut into 2 cm dice
4 carrots, cut into 1.5 cm slices
4 sticks celery, cut into 1.5 cm slices
2 tablespoons paprika
2 bay leaves
3 cups tomato passata
2 cups red wine
½ cup basil leaves
½ cup roughly chopped parsley
1 tablespoon salt
1 tablespoon freshly ground black pepper

Preheat the oven to 160°C.

Heat the oil in a heavy-based casserole over a low heat. Add the lamb shanks and seal without colouring, still over a low heat. Transfer the shanks to a large plate.

Halve the red peppers lengthwise and rub them all over with the extra tablespoon of olive oil. Grill, skin-side up, until black and charred. Transfer to a bowl and cover with plastic wrap. When cool enough to handle, peel off the skin and slice away the seeds and pith. Chop roughly and place in a blender. Blitz on high to form a rough purée.

Add the butter to the casserole and increase the heat. Add the garlic, onion, carrot, celery, paprika and bay leaves and sauté gently for 5 minutes, or until the vegetables start to soften. Return the lamb shanks to the casserole and add the pepper purée, passata and wine. Stir well then add the half the fresh herbs and season with salt and pepper. Bring to a simmer, then cover and transfer to the oven. Cook for 2–2½ hours, by which time the lamb should be very tender and falling from the bone.

Scatter on the remaining herbs and serve with soft polenta or creamy mashed potatoes.

Serves 6

Shoulder of lamb braised with garlic, olive oil and eggplant

This is a really popular dish at La Luna Bistro. I find diners love the way the long, slow cooking makes the lamb all sticky and garlicky. Don't be tempted to skimp on the oil; it really is a key component of the dish. When extra-virgin olive oil is called for in a recipe such as this, I always use the best quality I can find. If you're just using it for frying, when most of the oil will be tipped out, then you can use a slightly cheaper one.

I often make this dish using whole baby lamb, or sometimes capretto, which are two-week-old baby goats. As is the case here, the meat is chopped into chunks on the bone before cooking.

Serve with Nonno's Cake (page 299) or couscous.

2 x 1 kg forequarter lamb legs, chopped through the bone at 4 cm intervals to give 12 pieces
1 tablespoon salt
1 tablespoon freshly ground black pepper
1 cup extra-virgin olive oil
12 garlic cloves
¼ cup fresh rosemary leaves (discard the stalks)

2 medium onions, cut into 1 cm dice
2 carrots, cut into 1 cm dice
2 sticks celery, cut into 1 cm dice
1 cup basil leaves
2 large eggplants (around 700 g total weight), cut into 2 cm dice
2 cups white wine
1 litre lamb or chicken stock
½ cup chopped parsley to serve

Preheat the oven to 160°C. Season the meat with salt and pepper.

Heat the oil in a large casserole dish. Add the lamb pieces and sauté over a medium heat until they colour a light golden brown. Transfer the sealed lamb pieces to a plate and keep warm.

Lower the heat and add the garlic cloves and rosemary to the pan. Leave to sweat gently for a few minutes, until soft but not coloured. Add the diced onion, carrot, celery and basil and sweat gently for 2–3 minutes. Add the diced eggplant and sweat for a further 4–5 minutes, stirring from time to time. Return the lamb pieces to the casserole and pour on the wine and enough of the stock to cover. Increase the heat and bring to a gentle simmer. Cover the casserole and cook in the oven for 2–2½ hours, or until the meat is very tender and comes away from the bone.

Stir in the parsley and serve with wedges of Nonno's Cake or couscous.

Serves 6

The forequarter is a secondary cut made up of many different muscles, with lots of connective tissue and fat. It is ideally suited to long, slow cooking. This is a great recipe to cook ahead of time as all the flavours intensify. As it cools, the fat rises to the surface and forms a protective seal, so you can happily make it up to four days in advance. It makes a hearty meal in itself, but I usually offer some warm crusty bread too, to mop up the sauce.

Rolled forequarter of lamb braised in a rich mushroom sauce

225 g butter
9 garlic cloves, crushed
500 g mixed mushrooms (halved if they're large)
¼ cup water
1 teaspoon salt
1 teaspoon freshly ground black pepper
1 x 2 kg forequarter of lamb, boned
¼ cup olive oil
2 onions, finely diced
2 carrots, cut into 2 cm dice
2 sticks celery, cut into 2 cm dice

1 cup red wine
¼ cup Madeira or port
1.5 litres meat stock or water
5 sprigs thyme
½ cup chopped parsley to serve

Mushroom stuffing
125 g sautéed mixed mushrooms (see above)
6 garlic cloves, thinly sliced
2 tablespoons fresh thyme leaves
1 tablespoon fresh rosemary leaves

Preheat the oven to 160°C.

Melt 75 g butter in a heavy-based saucepan. Add 3 garlic cloves, mushrooms, water and a pinch of salt and pepper and bring to a simmer. Cook over a low–medium heat for 5–10 minutes, or until the mushrooms release their liquid. Use a slotted spoon to lift out around a quarter of the mushrooms for the stuffing. Reserve the remaining mushrooms in their liquid for the braise.

To make the stuffing, slice the mushrooms thinly and mix them with 6 garlic cloves and herbs.

Lay the lamb forequarter, skin-side down, on your work surface. Season with salt and pepper then spread on the mushroom stuffing. Roll the forequarter up to form a fat log and tie securely with butcher's string at 5 cm intervals.

Heat the oil in a heavy-based casserole dish and brown the lamb all over. Remove it from the dish and transfer to a large plate. Add 150 g butter to the dish and melt over a medium heat. Add the onions and sauté gently for 5 minutes until soft, but not coloured. Add the remainder of the garlic cloves, carrot and celery and sauté for a further 5 minutes. Add the reserved mushrooms and their liquid, together with the wine, Madeira, stock and thyme, and bring to the boil. Return the lamb to the dish and cover with a lid or aluminium foil. Bake in the oven for 2–2½ hours.

At the end of the cooking time, remove the dish from the oven. Lift out the lamb and transfer it to a large plate. Place the casserole over a high heat and bring to the boil. Cook until reduced by half, to form a lovely thick sauce. You can prepare the dish to this stage up to 3 days ahead of time. Return the lamb to the casserole and leave to cool. When completely cold, cover and refrigerate.

When ready to eat, reheat the casserole in a medium oven for 20 minutes. Lift the lamb out of the casserole and remove the string. Cut into thick slices and serve with plenty of sauce and a generous sprinkling of chopped parsley.

Serves 6

Lancashire hotpot

One of my favourite winter warmers, this old-fashioned English dish combines full-flavoured lamb with layers of potato and onion. I like to throw in lots of garlic and rosemary, and sometimes I add a couple of anchovies when I'm sweating the onions. They melt down and add a great savoury undertone. Lancashire hotpot makes a great filling meal just on its own, but I really like to serve it with Minted Peas (page 308) crushed with the back of a fork to make them mushy.

3 tablespoons olive oil
12 lamb chump chops (about 1 kg)
100 g butter
8 onions, sliced (about 1.5 kg)
8 garlic cloves, crushed
2 bay leaves
1 tablespoon fresh rosemary leaves

6 potatoes, peeled and cut into
  1 cm slices (about 1 kg)
salt
freshly ground black pepper
4 sprigs thyme
1 litre hot lamb or chicken stock
  (or even just water)

Preheat the oven to 180°C.

Heat the oil in a heavy-based casserole over a medium heat. Add the lamb chops and sauté until evenly browned then transfer to a large plate and keep warm.

Add half the butter to the casserole and sweat the onions, garlic, bay leaves and rosemary for 10–15 minutes until soft, but not coloured. Remove half the onion mixture from the casserole to a large plate.

Arrange half the potato slices on top of the onion in the casserole and season generously. Arrange the lamb chops on top of the potatoes then spread the remaining onions on top. Scatter on the sprigs of thyme, then top with the remaining potato slices. Season again, then dot the surface of the potatoes with the remaining butter. Pour in enough hot stock to just reach the top layer of potatoes.

Cover the casseorole and bake in the oven for 45 minutes. Remove the lid and return to the oven for a further 30 minutes. You want the potatoes to be nice and golden brown and a bit crunchy on top. Make sure everyone gets a bit of the crisp potatoes when you serve up.

Serves 4–6

Lamb salad with spinach, goat's cheese and chickpeas

This tasty salad is a great way to use up lamb leftovers. I often make it after we have slow-cooked lamb for dinner. You can make a really quick-and-easy meal by using a selection of items from the deli counter and canned chickpeas – just make sure you rinse them very well to get rid of that 'tinny' flavour.

Serve with lots of warm crusty bread as a lazy lunch or quick weeknight dinner.

600 g leftover lamb, roughly torn by hand into bite-sized pieces
100 g baby spinach leaves, washed and dried
2 cups cooked chickpeas (or 1 x 400 g can, drained and well rinsed)
200 g goat's feta
200 g marinated red peppers
100 g sun-dried tomatoes
1 small bunch frisée (curly endive), inner pale leaves only
½ cup pine nuts
½ cup currants
½ cup coriander leaves

Dressing
juice of 1 lemon
3 tablespoons extra-virgin olive oil
1 teaspoon smoked paprika
½ teaspoon salt
½ teaspoon freshly ground black pepper

Combine all the salad ingredients in a large mixing bowl.

To make the dressing, whisk all the ingredients together. Pour over the salad and toss everything together gently.

Serves 6

Orecchiette pasta with slow-cooked lamb sugo

Lamb neck is one of those inexpensive-but-tasty cuts. It's often overlooked as being tough, as it is full of connective tissue. But this makes it lovely and gelatinous when cooked. And being on the bone, it's full of flavour.

Cooked long and slowly in a rich tomatoey braise, lamb neck makes the perfect pasta sauce. Serve it with lots of parmesan, some crusty bread and a bottle of good Italian wine.

Lamb sugo
2 x 800 g lamb necks (ask your butcher to chop each neck in half, so they'll fit in your casserole dish easily)
salt
freshly ground black pepper
¼ cup olive oil
2 medium onions, roughly chopped
2 medium carrots, roughly chopped
2 sticks celery, roughly chopped
6 garlic cloves, crushed
2 bay leaves
½ cup fresh basil leaves
1 cup red wine
1. 5 litres tomato passata

500 g orecchiette pasta
100 g butter
½ cup roughly chopped parsley
extra-virgin olive oil to serve
grated parmesan or pecorino to serve

Season the lamb necks with salt and pepper. Heat half the oil in a heavy-based saucepan or casserole dish and brown the lamb all over. Transfer the browned neck pieces to a plate and keep warm.

Add the rest of the oil to the casserole. Add the onion, carrot, celery, garlic, bay leaves and basil and sauté gently for 5 minutes, or until the vegetables start to soften. Stir in the red wine and tomato passata then return the lamb necks to the pan. Season again and bring to a simmer. Cover the casserole and cook for 2–2 ½ hours, stirring regularly to ensure the sauce doesn't stick to the bottom and burn. By the end of the cooking time the meat should be very tender and fall away from the bones. Leave to cool slightly, then discard the bones. Chop the meat roughly and return it to the sauce. The sugo can be made to this stage ahead of time and kept in a sealed container in the fridge for up to 4 days.

When ready to eat, heat the lamb sugo in a large saucepan. Bring another large saucepan of salted water to the boil. Add the orecchiette pasta and cook according to the packet instructions. Drain the pasta and stir in the butter until it melts. Tip into the sugo and toss well to coat the pasta evenly. Scatter on the parsley and serve with a drizzle of extra-virgin olive oil and a handful of parmesan.

Serves 6

Goat is ideally suited to making curries as it has a strong, rich flavour. This recipe brings back memories of my childhood days in Malaysia, when my dad was in the air force. Don't be put off by the number of ingredients. They're all easy to find, and the method is simple: you just whiz the curry paste up in a processor.

This curry is quite spicy, but it also uses lovely creamy coconut milk, which tempers the heat. Serve with roti bread or Coconut Rice (page 306).

Malaysian goat curry

Curry paste
1 large onion, finely chopped
6 garlic cloves, crushed
2 tablespoons grated ginger
1 small red chilli, seeded and finely chopped (or more to taste)
¼ cup desiccated coconut
1 teaspoon ground cumin
2 teaspoons ground coriander
½ cup chopped coriander leaves
2 x 400 g cans coconut milk
3 tablespoons vegetable oil
juice of 1 lime

1 x 1 kg goat leg, cut into 2 cm dice
2 cups water
1 stalk lemongrass, bruised
2 kaffir lime leaves
1 teaspoon salt
1 teaspoon freshly ground black pepper
¼ cup chopped coriander leaves
juice of 1 lime
¼ cup toasted grated coconut to serve

To make the curry paste, combine all the ingredients in a food processor and pulse to form a paste.

In a large mixing bowl, toss the diced goat meat with the curry paste, making sure it is well coated. Transfer to a large heavy-based saucepan or casserole dish and add the water, lemongrass and lime leaves. Add the salt and pepper and bring to the boil. Lower the heat to a simmer, cover and cook for 1½ hours until the goat is very tender.

At the end of the cooking time, stir in the coriander and lime juice. Serve with a sprinkling of toasted coconut and some roti bread or coconut rice.

Serves 6, or 4 hungry blokes

PORK

"IT'S NOT JUST ABOUT THE CRACKLING"

Pork

Although I don't like to play favourites, I think I could be happy eating nothing but pork and pork products for the rest of my life. It's not just about the crackling – although who doesn't love its salty, tasty crunch? – it's more that pork appeals directly to the butcher and chef in me.

There's no doubting the pig's versatility. It provides us with everything from a fantastic roast dinner to tasty chops and spare ribs for the barbecue. And with a bit of processing and preserving magic, we can transform it into all sorts of fresh and cured sausages, pâtés, terrines, hams and bacon. You really can eat every part of the animal – except for the squeal, of course.

Despite the fact that in some cultures, such as Judaism and Islam, there is a prohibition against eating pork, it is still the world's most popular meat by a long way. It is the meat of choice in many European and Asian countries; in China, where it was first domesticated, they eat around a third of the world's pork. Here in Australia we've been steadily eating more of it over the last few years; in fact we've nearly doubled our consumption since the turn of the current century and now eat around 23 kilograms of pork every year.

Unfortunately, it is this ever-increasing world demand for pork that has led to it being one of the most intensively farmed – and abused – of all domesticated animals. I've been to a pig factory-farm – and believe me, they are factories – and it was not pretty. More than any other industry, pig farming is a numbers game – it's about getting as many big pigs to the marketplace as quickly and as cost-effectively as possible. As a result, the average pig endures a tormented life in overcrowded pens with virtually no freedom of movement. They are pumped full of antibiotics and growth hormones and fed a rigidly controlled diet. In these conditions pigs change from being naturally sociable and intelligent animals, to aggressive, miserable creatures.

Even worse, the meat from these massive porkers is so bland and flabby as to be barely worth bothering with. Our obsession with low-fat meat products means that pork in many First World countries has been bred to ultra-leanness, entirely at the expense of texture and flavour.

AUSTRALIAN PORK

Compared with other countries, the Australian pork industry has invested considerable time, money and research into minimising the negative effects of intensive farming practices. In very recent years the industry has introduced more rigorous animal welfare requirements and I have to say that in my experience most modern pig farmers do seem to care about their animals, if only because it makes better commercial sense.

There's no getting away from the fact, however, that most pig farming in Australia is big business, geared towards maximum cost efficiency. Some massive piggeries carry as many as 10,000 breeding sows, and nearly 5.5 million pigs are slaughtered every year. Sixty-five per cent of Australian pork production is sold as fresh meat, while the remainder is processed into bacon, hams and smallgoods.

The main breeds in large-scale Australian piggeries are the Large White and the Landrace, whose long loins are particularly prized in the bacon industry. They have been bred over the years to gain weight fast and to be more tolerant of intensive farming conditions.

Numbers of old-fashioned, 'rare-breeds', such as the Berkshire, Wessex Saddleback, Tamworth and Large Black are declining, and these days they are really only found in small free-range piggeries that cater to a growing niche market. And to be honest, this is probably a good thing, because this type of pig wouldn't survive five minutes in a modern piggery. These old-fashioned breeds are only suited to natural living conditions, so it takes a dedicated farmer to make the commitment to raising them.

These small, free-range and rare-breed farmers are the true heroes of the Australian pork industry. This type of small-scale farming is inevitably more personal, with a far greater emphasis placed on the animal's environment and diet. These happier animals live outdoors and are free to move around and explore their environment and (of course) roll around in the mud. They are fed a varied diet of grass, grains and vegetables and given time to develop marbled flesh and generous subcutaneous layers of flavoursome fat. As far as I'm concerned, this is the way pigs should live, and I do everything in my power to support these dedicated farmers.

Having said that, these small-scale farmers are definitely battling against the odds. It is a far costlier way of farming and the animals are more susceptible to the vagaries of our difficult climate. As a result, the supply of this specialist pork can be inconsistent and, for the home cook, much harder to source. Thankfully there are a few larger piggeries that are moving towards producing free-range pork on a larger scale, and this is becoming far more widely available.

PORK AND NUTRITION

The first thing to bear in mind is that pork is actually a red meat, despite the marketing campaign that promoted it as 'the other white meat'. Much is made of the fact that modern pork is lean, and indeed, when pork is trimmed of any visible fat it is lower in kilojoules and cholesterol than beef, lamb or even chicken. It is also a good source of protein, B vitamins, zinc, potassium and iron.

HOW AND WHERE TO BUY PORK

Around 60 per cent of Australian pork is sold through the major supermarkets, Woolworths/Safeway and Coles, and only 25 per cent is sold through independent butchers. The most popular cuts are roasts, chops, spare ribs, sausages and mince and, sure enough, these are the cuts that you'll see in the supermarket chill cabinets.

More pleasingly, though, a few of the more upmarket supermarkets are beginning to stock 'free-range' and 'organic' pork, and this delights me no end. If you are presented with such a choice in your own supermarket, then please try it. I promise you won't be disappointed. But it is more likely that you will have to go to a butcher to find quality pork and pork products. But believe me, you will find it tastes so much better.

Because here's a funny thing: I am told time and time again by my customers at La Luna Bistro, that the main reason they don't cook more pork at home is because it is a bit dry and tasteless. They tell me that pork somehow doesn't taste as 'piggy' as it used to, and that it is bland and boring. It astounds me that they don't understand that this is the inevitable consequence of having all the fat bred out to meet the apparent consumer demand for leanness. Yes folks, in the world of meat, fat equals flavour and there's no escaping it.

Another thing to bear in mind is that most decent pork butchers – and those customers in the know – prefer to buy meat that comes from female pigs (sows). This is generally considered to be sweeter, while meat from male pigs (boars) is stronger flavoured. Indeed meat from a true, mature boar often has a hard texture and an unpleasant urine 'taint'. Castration is one way of avoiding this problem, although most farmers insist that pigs these days are slaughtered at such a young age, that there is no need for them to be castrated. Not everyone is convinced by this argument (which may well be largely to do with cost). Certainly most good pork butchers, especially Continental and Asian butchers, still insist on sow meat only, even if they have to pay more for it.

Pigs are slaughtered at a relatively young age: around three to five months for 'porkers' and four to five months for 'baconers', when they weigh 50–60 kg and 70–100 kg, respectively. Whether you're buying your pork from a butcher or from a supermarket, fresh pork should look exactly that – fresh (it is never aged, like beef). So always choose meat that looks moist and has a bit of a shine to it. It should not look dry and shrivelled, and certainly not sticky or slimy. The fat on pork should be creamy and smooth, rather than yellow and the meat itself should be a rosy pink. Organic and free-range pork may even be a darker reddish-pink.

For very special occasions you might want to try cooking a suckling pig. These are the definitive cut for banquets and celebrations and are usually roasted whole. We have special suckling pig dinners at La Luna Bistro, and they are always sold-out within days. I buy my suckling pigs from a specialist pig farmer in the western part of Victoria. They usually weigh around four kilograms, which is tiny, but I know that they have been reared and slaughtered in impeccable conditions.

STORING PORK

- Because it is lean, with minimal fat and connective tissues, pork is more perishable than other red meats; treat it like chicken or veal.
- You won't find 'aged' or 'hung' pork, so it will be very fresh when you buy it.
- Unwrap and refrigerate all pork immediately.
- Store it in a Tupperware container, or sit it on a rack on a plate and cover it with a tea towel.
- Large cuts of pork will keep for up to four days.
- Smaller cuts should be used within three days.
- Cubed or minced pork should be used within one to two days.

WHICH CUT TO BUY

When choosing your pork cut, the same general rules apply as with other meat. Harder working muscles, or meat which is more substantially layered with fat, needs longer, slower cooking. Tender prime meat, such as the loin, medallions or cutlets, are ideal for quick cooking.

A: Trotter

Although pig's trotters are the darling of trendy restaurant menus these days, (especially when boned out and stuffed), they are quite challenging for the home cook, as they contain very little meat. Trotters are generally considered as being offal, and I talk about them more on page 205.

B: Leg/Ham

Most pork legs are cured to make hams, and there are few things as impressive as a baked glazed Christmas ham, prettily studded with cloves. Fresh pork legs also make brilliant roasts. Broken down, the leg gives us the knuckle, silverside, topside, girello and rump. The rump can be sold bone in or out for roasting. With a wonderful layer of crackling and a jug of apple sauce, this is one of our most familiar cuts.

C: Loin

On pigs the loin is very long, extending from the shoulder all the way back to the leg. It is the source of many wonderful cuts, and they are all fairly lean (especially when the fat is removed), tender and tasty. Meat from the loin is especially good at taking on flavour from marinades and herb or spice rubs.

Cuts from the loin include a rack of pork, chops, cutlets, fillet (tenderloin), medallions and butterfly steaks. The whole loin may be sold rolled up and tied for roasting. And then there are the spare ribs, often sold as American-style ribs. Finally, when cured, the loin gives us back bacon.

Pork / Choice cuts

A. trotter / **B.** leg/ham
C. loin / **D.** belly / **E.** shoulder
F. head / **G.** hock

THINGS THAT LOVE PORK

Apple sauce, bay leaves, cabbage, calvados, cider, curry powder, fennel, garlic, ginger, mustard, onions, paprika, pepper, pickled cherries, prunes, rosemary, sage, salt, sauerkraut, sour cream, star anise, tarragon, thyme, white wine.

D: Belly

Belly is primarily used for making streaky bacon and pancetta, the Italian equivalent. It is thickly layered with fat and brilliantly versatile. It can be braised or roasted or cut into strips and grilled. Although it is fatty, it is a wonderfully tasty and succulent part of the animal, which is all too often overlooked.

Spare ribs are cut from inside the thick end of the belly. They are wonderful when slow-roasted in a tasty marinade, then finished on the barbecue.

E: Shoulder

The whole shoulder is huge, and it is generally broken down into the neck end spare ribs, the blade and down at the top of the leg, the hand. The neck end can also be cut off the bones to give a Scotch roast (also called the collar butt). When cured, it makes collar bacon. The boned-out blade gives a picnic shoulder roast. The hand is brilliant when pickled, or slow-cooked. Cured, it becomes picnic ham.

Cubed meat from the shoulder is fantastic for making pork casseroles or curries, which need long, slow cooking.

F: Head

An incredibly productive part of the pig, which again, is generally sold as offal (see page 201).

G: Hock

The hock is the first joint of the leg after the hand. It is not very meaty, being made up mainly of connective tissue, skin and bone. But it yields wonderful gelatinous juices when slowly cooked, which are brilliant in stews. Smoked hocks are wonderful when braised with lentils or boiled up with split peas to make pea and ham soup.

HOW DO YOU KNOW WHEN IT'S COOKED?

One of the reasons that people so often find pork a disappointment is because it is so often overcooked. The main reason for overcooking is because of lingering concerns about the trichonosis parasite, which was prevalent in the days that pigs were fed largely on table scraps and all sorts of other raw foods. The parasite is actually killed (and the meat safe to eat) at 59°C, but to allow a margin of error for uneven cooking within a piece of pork, in those days, pork was always cooked to a minimum of 80–85°C. In reality, the trichonosis has been eradicated from Australian pork, and these days you don't have to cook the hell out of it to be safe.

My preference is to cook tender cuts of pork to medium, so that they are moist and juicy (there really is nothing worse than overcooked, dry, stringy pork). For really successful pork cookery I strongly believe that a digital meat thermometer is absolutely essential. It takes all the guesswork out of doneness, and you can be absolutely sure that the pork is cooked through, without it being overcooked. Most food authorities today recommend cooking pork to an internal temperature of 75°C – and remember that the reading will rise by about 5°C as the meat rests, so you can happily take it out of the oven at about 70°C. Pork cooked to these temperatures may still have a rosy pink tinge about it – but that shouldn't be cause for panic. It will be perfectly safe, but succulent and juicy.

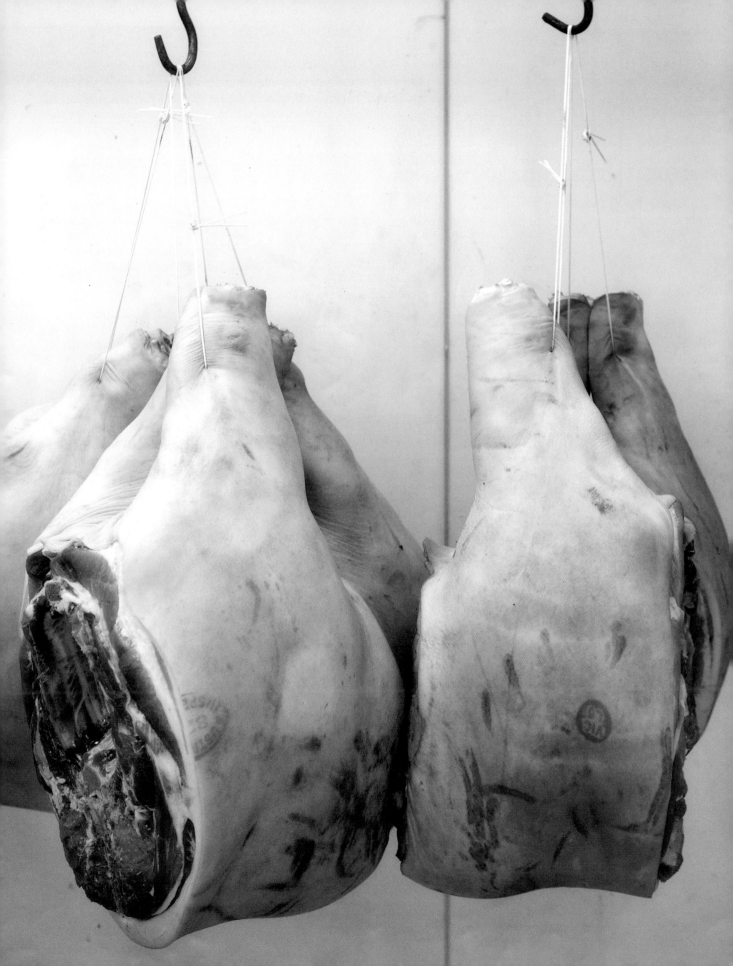

Pork fillet medallions with prosciutto and porcini butter

Pork fillets, cut from the tender and fairly lean loin area, are great for a quick and very stylish meal. The prosciutto adds extra flavour and helps the medallions hold their shape. The porcini butter adds a lovely earthiness.

You can use metal or wooden skewers for this dish, but if you use wooden ones, remember to soak them in water for at least 30 minutes before threading on the pork medallions.

I like to serve these medallions with Eggplant Salsa (page 345) and Green Bean Salad with Feta Dressing (page 314).

6 pork fillets (about 1.5 kg total weight)	**Marinade**
18 slices prosciutto	1 tablespoon chopped thyme
salt	1 tablespoon chopped sage
freshly ground black pepper	2 tablespoons olive oil
olive oil	zest of 1 lemon
120 g Porcini Butter (page 348)	1 teaspoon freshly ground black pepper

Lay the pork fillets out on your work surface. From the thick end, cut 2 even-sized medallions, about 5 cm thick. This will leave a longer, thinner tail-end piece. Make an incision half-way along this remaining piece, nearly all the way through. Fold the skinny tail-end underneath to form a third medallion that is roughly the same size as the other two. Repeat with all 6 pork fillets, so that you end up with 18 medallions in total.

Mix the marinade ingredients together in a large mixing bowl. Rub into the medallions so they are evenly coated. Cover and transfer to the fridge to marinate for 1 hour or overnight.

When ready to cook, preheat your barbecue or grill to medium–high. Wrap a slice of prosciutto around each pork medallion and skewer them in batches of three. Season with pepper and a little salt – but remember that the prosciutto is quite salty. Brush lightly with oil and grill for 8 minutes. Turn the skewers every couple of minutes, to ensure that they cook evenly.

Serve the pork medallions on their skewers, topping each with a slice of porcini butter that will melt and create a delicious sauce.

Serves 6

Vanilla-grilled T-bone chops

This might seem like an unlikely combination, but pork has its own underlying sweetness that actually goes really well with vanilla. These chops smell amazing while they're cooking, and they taste pretty amazing too.

I like to serve them with a tangy salad. White Bean, Blood Orange and Watercress Salad (page 318), Cabbage, Apple and Tarragon Salad (page 318) and Beetroot, Lemon and Coriander Salad with Extra-virgin Olive Oil (page 317) are all good choices.

1 tablespoon brown sugar
1 vanilla bean, split and seeds scraped
zest of ½ orange
1 tablespoon chopped fresh thyme
2 tablespoons olive oil

1 tablespoon sherry vinegar
6 x 350 g pork T-bone chops
salt
freshly ground black pepper

Combine the sugar, vanilla, orange zest and thyme in a mortar and grind together. Stir in the oil and vinegar to form a paste.

Arrange the pork chops in a large shallow container. Pour on the marinade and use your hands to rub it in evenly. Cover with plastic wrap and leave to marinate in the refrigerator overnight, or for a minimum of 2 hours.

When ready to cook, preheat the grill to medium–high. Season the chops with salt and pepper and cook for 8–10 minutes, until the chops are just cooked to juicy pinkness. Serve with your choice of salad.

Serves 6

Fancy crumbed pork cutlets

I love just about anything that's crumbed and fried. For me, it's perfect comfort food. This dish was inspired by one of the best meals I've had on my travels. I had arrived in Vienna late at night and very hungry. The only place serving food was a tiny bar and even though I didn't speak a word of Austrian I was able to make it clear that I was hungry. The bartender brought me a beer and shortly afterwards a plate of crumbed pork chops with red cabbage and mustard arrived. The pork chops were moist and succulent, the crumb coating crisp and crunchy. It was the ideal feed for a late-night traveller and I happily stayed for a few more beers.

People are often scared about deep-frying because they think it's bad for you. And I have to admit that one of the reasons the Viennese pork chops were so delicious was because they were fried in lard. I'm suggesting the slightly healthier option of vegetable oil. Now I'm not pretending that this sort of dish is ever going to be health food, but equally, I don't think you should be too militant about what you eat. Think of this type of meal as an occasional treat, rather than an everyday dinner. Don't forget to drain the cutlets briefly on a wire rack after they're cooked to remove any excess oil.

6 x 300 g pork cutlets (cut from
  the rib end)
2 tablespoons sherry vinegar
1 garlic clove, crushed
1 teaspoon freshly ground black pepper
1 tablespoon fresh thyme
3 tablespoons Dijon mustard
4 eggs, lightly beaten

½ cup milk
½ cup plain flour
2 cups homemade breadcrumbs
vegetable oil, for deep-frying
lemon wedges to serve
Red Cabbage with Apple and Caraway
  (page 310), to serve

Trim away the skin and excess fat from the pork chops. In a large mixing bowl, combine the vinegar, garlic, pepper and thyme. Rub into the chops and leave to marinate for at least 1 hour, or preferably overnight.

Remove the cutlets from the marinade and pat them dry with paper towels. Brush each cutlet all over with mustard.

Whisk the eggs and milk together and set up a little production line of 3 dishes containing the flour, the egg mixture and the breadcrumbs. Dunk the cutlets in the flour first and shake off any excess. Dip them into the egg mixture and then the breadcrumbs so they are evenly coated. For an extra-crunchy coating dip the cutlets into the egg and breadcrumbs for a second time then refrigerate for 30 minutes.

Meanwhile, heat the oil in a deep-fryer or a large, heavy-based frying pan to 180°C. Preheat the oven to 160°C.

Fry the chops, 3 at a time, for 8–10 minutes until golden brown all over. Drain briefly on a wire rack and transfer to the oven to keep warm while you cook the rest. Serve with lemon wedges and red cabbage.

Serves 6

Smoky barbecued spare ribs

Pork belly is one of my all-time favourite cuts of meat – and you'll see I've got a few recipes for it in this book! (See page 116 and 126). These belly spare ribs are perfect for long, slow cooking on the barbecue (a kettle barbecue is ideal), and you'll want to get yourself some hickory woodchips (they're readily available) for that authentic smoky flavour. You'll need about one to two cups of woodchips.

The secret to great ribs is a great marinade. The recipe here is pretty spicy as I love a big chilli hit, but do reduce the amount to your liking. You can use beef ribs instead of pork ribs, if you prefer, but remember not too trim away to much of the fat. It will render down as it cooks to the consistency of crispy bacon.

Serve your ribs American barbecue-style, with American Slaw (page 316), Potato Salad and your favourite barbecue sauce. I also like to serve cornbread, which you can make following the recipe on page 46.

Marinade
1 cup soft brown sugar
1 cup beer (choose your favourite brand)
2 cups Homemade Tomato Sauce (page 343)
½ cup runny honey
3 tablespoons Worcestershire sauce
1 onion, finely diced
4 garlic cloves, crushed
3 spring onions, finely chopped
¼ cup chopped coriander (leaves, stalks and roots)

2 tablespoons ground ginger
1 tablespoon ground cumin, dry-roasted
1 tablespoon chilli flakes (or to taste)
1 tablespoon cayenne pepper (instead of, or as well as, the chilli flakes, depending on how strong you feel)
1 tablespoon smoked paprika

2 kg pork belly spare ribs

To make the marinade, combine all the ingredients in a mixing bowl to form a paste.

Arrange the pork belly spare ribs in a large shallow container. Pour on the marinade and use your hands to rub it in evenly. Cover with plastic wrap and leave to marinate in the refrigerator overnight or for up to 2 days. Turn the meat around in the marinade every 6 hours or so.

When ready to cook, light your kettle barbecue. When the coals die down to 180°C (most kettle barbecues have a temperature gauge to help with this) add a small handful of the woodchips to each side of the coals and place the pork belly on the grill. Pull down the hood of the barbecue and cook the pork for 3 hours. Every 45 minutes or so add a few more woodchips to keep the smoke going.

After about 3 hours, the ribs will be beautifully soft and tender and will fall apart in your hands as you rip into them. Eat with the suggested accompaniments and lots of cold beers to wash down the chilli!

Serves 4

Asian-style sticky spare ribs

This dish is the real thing. It uses a whole rack of proper spare ribs – the ones that come from the belly of the pig – which are not the same as the baby back ribs that many people buy for barbecuing. Real spare ribs are a bit chewy, but they have an amazing flavour. For this dish I like to slow-cook the ribs first as one big rack – which means they're great for entertaining as you can do most of the work ahead of time. After they've cooled, I cut them into individual ribs that are cooked on the barbecue. Serve with Asian Slaw (page 316) and Coconut Rice (page 306).

Marinade
¼ cup sherry vinegar
¼ cup brown sugar
2 tablespoons ground ginger
¼ cup ketjap mannis
3 garlic cloves
¼ cup tomato sauce
2 tablespoons hoisin sauce

½ cup chopped coriander
¼ cup olive oil
1 tablespoon freshly ground black pepper
1 tablespoon chopped chilli

6 pork belly spare ribs (about 2 kg)

To make the marinade, combine all the ingredients in a mixing bowl to form a paste.

Arrange the pork belly spare ribs in a large shallow container. Pour on the marinade and use your hands to rub it in evenly. Cover with plastic wrap and leave to marinate in the refrigerator overnight.

Preheat the oven to 150°C. Lift the spare ribs into a large roasting tin and pour in the marinade and 2 cups of water. Cover with aluminium foil and bake for 1½ hours, basting with the marinade every 15 minutes. Remove from the oven and leave to cool. Tip the liquid from the roasting tin into a small saucepan. Bring to the boil over a high heat, then lower the heat and cook until reduced to a sticky glaze. You can prepare the ribs and glaze to this stage up to 4 days in advance.

When ready to cook, preheat your barbecue or grill to medium–high. Cut the ribs apart between the bones and cook for 3–4 minutes on each side, basting with the glaze from time to time. Serve the ribs with any leftover glaze and your choice of accompaniments.

Serves 6–8

Rack of pork with fennel–garlic rub

Meat roasted on the bone has a sweeter, more intense flavour, and of course a roast rack always looks very impressive. I prefer to use a rack from a smaller animal, as it's more elegant, so ask for a rack that weighs no more than 2 kg, with the chine bone removed.

One of the main points of this dish is the crunchy crackling. Rubbing the skin with a salty herb mixture helps, by drawing moisture out, but even more important is the scoring. Your butcher will probably oblige with this too, so ask him nicely to score through the skin and surface layer of fat at 1 cm intervals. Not only does this help with the crunch-factor, but scoring into the layer of fat encourages it to melt away during the cooking, and as it does, it bastes the meat, keeping it moist and tender.

Serve with Char-grilled Asparagus with Pesto and Parmesan (page 311) and Soft, Herby, Cheesy Polenta (page 300).

---

1 x 6-rib rack of pork (about 2 kg), scored
2 tablespoons salt
1 tablespoon freshly ground black pepper

1 tablespoon fennel seed
1 tablespoon fresh thyme
1 garlic clove
1 tablespoon fresh rosemary
3 tablespoons olive oil

Preheat the oven to 220°C.

Use a sharp knife to 'french' the bones, by neatly scraping away any skin, fat and meat from them – or ask your butcher to do this for you. You might also like to wrap the bones in aluminium foil, which will stop them burning. Place the pork on a rack inside a large roasting tin.

Pound the remaining ingredients in a mortar or liquidiser to make a paste. Rub the pork all over with the paste, taking extra care to work it into the scored skin.

Roast the pork at 220°C for 20 minutes, then lower the temperature to 175°C and roast for a further 1 hour. If you are using a meat thermometer, the pork is cooked when the internal core temperature reaches 72°C.

Transfer the cooked pork to a hot dish and leave it to rest for 20 minutes in a warm spot. Remove the foil from the bones and use a sharp knife to cut the rack into 6 thick chops, each with its own crisp layer of crackling. Serve with your choice of accompaniments.

Serves 6

Shoulder of pork roasted with fragrant spices

Pork shoulder is often overlooked in favour of the leg or loin, because it is interlarded with fatty connective tissue. Of course this makes it very tasty, as well as perfect for long, slow roasting or braising. You'll usually find pork shoulder already boned, and sometimes rolled. I like to open the meat out and rub it inside with a fragrant paste of herbs, spices, garlic and salt. You can stick it in the oven to roast straight away, however I prefer to leave it to marinate overnight, so the flavours really permeate the meat. I use the blade part of the shoulder and ask my butcher to make sure the flap of skin is left attached, so I can use it to wrap around the meat.

Serve with Garlicky Green Beans (page 308), Sautéed Spinach and Chilli (page 312) and Creamy, Buttery Mash (page 296).

Fragrant spice paste
3 tablespoons extra-virgin olive oil
1 tablespoon fennel seed
1 tablespoon caraway seed
1 tablespoon cumin seed
1 tablespoon salt
1 teaspoon freshly ground black pepper
4 garlic cloves, roughly chopped
juice 1 lemon
¼ cup chopped coriander leaves

2 kg rolled pork shoulder
olive oil
salt

To make the fragrant herb paste, combine all the ingredients in a mixing bowl and stir well.

Unroll the pork shoulder and lay it out flat on your work surface with the skin-side facing up. Use a very sharp knife to score the surface in parallel lines, about 1 cm apart. Turn the meat over and make incisions all over the surface of the meat. Rub the paste into the meat, working it into the incisions thoroughly. Roll the shoulder up again and tie securely with string at 5 cm intervals. Transfer to the refrigerator and leave to marinate overnight, uncovered.

When ready to cook, preheat the oven to 220ºC.

Rub the pork skin with oil then season with salt. Place the pork on a rack inside a large roasting tin. Roast for 20 minutes then lower the oven temperature to 175ºC. Roast for a further 1 hour and 20 minutes, or until cooked. If you are using a meat thermometer, the pork is cooked when the internal core temperature reaches 72ºC.

Transfer the cooked pork to a hot dish and leave it to rest for 20 minutes in a warm spot before removing the string and carving.

Serves 8–10

Roast suckling pig

In countries all around the world, a suckling pig is considered an incredible treat for seriously special occasions. The meat is delicately flavoured and as soft as butter; the crackling is thin and crisp, like shards of toffee.

Traditionally, baby piglets were sold by farmers while still very young, so as to avoid the cost of raising them to maturity; after all, sows generally produce very large litters. In these days of mass production, though, baby piglets are less readily available. In fact you will definitely need to order your piglet from a specialist pork butcher. I buy mine from a free-range pig farmer in western Victoria, where I know the animals are reared in the very best conditions. True suckling pigs range in weight from around 4–8 kg and may have been slaughtered from several days old up to four weeks or so of age.

Another thing to bear in mind if you want to cook this dish at home is that you need to have an oven large enough to contain the whole piglet. Either that, or you'll need to have facilities for roasting your piglet on a spit over an oven fire.

1 suckling piglet (approx. 4 kg)
2 tablespoons salt
1 tablespoon freshly ground black
    pepper

1 bunch sage
1 bunch thyme
1 bunch rosemary
¼ cup olive oil

Preheat the oven to 220°C.

Wrap the ears and the tail of the piglet with aluminium foil to stop them burning. Sprinkle 1 tablesppon of the salt and all the pepper in the cavity of the piglet and stuff in the bunches of herbs. Rub the oil all over the piglet and sprinkle with the remaining salt. Place the piglet on a rack inside a large roasting tin, with the belly facing down.

Roast for 20 minutes. The skin will puff up and become crisp. Remove the piglet from the oven and lower the oven temperature to 175°C. After 5 minutes, once the oven has cooled a little, return the piglet to the oven and cook for a further hour. If you are using a meat thermometer, insert it into the shoulder or near the pelvis bone (the thickest parts). The meat is cooked when the internal core temperature reaches 72°C.

Transfer the cooked piglet to a hot dish and leave it to rest for 30 minutes in a warm spot. It is traditional to present and carve the roast piglet at the table, surrounded by its garnishes.

Serves 8–10

Preparing

Carving

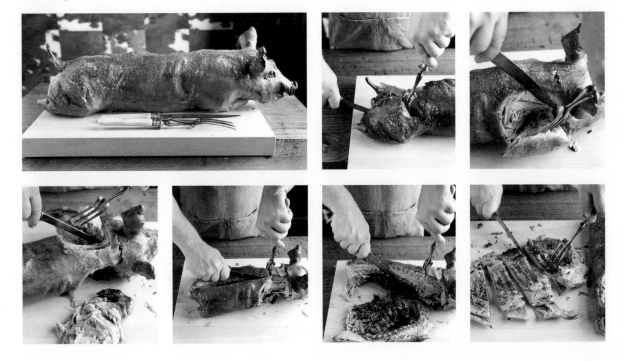

Crackling-wrapped rolled loin of pork

This is a great dish for serving lots of people. Because the bone is removed and the loin rolled, it slices easily and economically. The pork stays moist, and everyone gets the same amount of crackling. It is also a really easy dish to reheat, and will taste just as good.

Ask your butcher to bone the loin and keep enough of the belly flap to wrap around the meat to make a roll. Just show him the accompanying photograph in this book and he will know what you need!

Serve with Cabbage, Apple and Tarragon Salad (page 318).

2.5 kg pork loin
2 tablespoons salt
1 tablespoon freshly ground black pepper
6 garlic cloves, thinly sliced

¼ cup fresh thyme leaves
¼ cup fresh sage leaves
½ cup parsley leaves
¼ cup olive oil

Open out the pork loin and lay it, skin-side down, on your work surface. Rub in 1 tablespoon of the salt and all the pepper then scatter on the garlic and fresh herbs. Roll the loin up into a long log shape and tie securely with butcher's string at 5 cm intervals. You can prepare the pork to this stage up to two days in advance. The herbs and seasonings will permeate the flesh and add extra flavour.

When ready to cook, preheat the oven to 220ºC and place the pork on a rack inside a large roasting tin. Rub all over with oil and season with the rest of the salt. Roast for 20 minutes then lower the oven temperature to 175ºC and roast for 1 hour. The pork is cooked when the internal core temperature reaches 72ºC.

Transfer the cooked pork to a hot dish and leave it to rest for 30 minutes in a warm spot. Remove the string and carve into slices, each with a crisp layer of crackling. Serve with your choice of accompaniments.

Serves 8–12

Twice-cooked pork belly with toffee-crisp crackling

You can often buy salted pork belly from the butcher, but it is easy to do this yourself. Salting the meat draws out some of the moisture and really intensifies the flavour and colour of the meat. It also helps the skin to crisp up.

This dish requires a little planning, as you need to allow time for the initial curing and then slow-cooking. But it can be prepared to this stage ahead of time, and can then be very quickly cooked at the last minute. I think this dish looks amazing. I like to serve it with Braised Savoy Cabbage with Smoky Bacon (page 310) and a Caramelised Cherry and Brandy Glaze (page 333), both of which act as a foil to the richness of the pork.

Aromatic salt rub
500 g rock salt
1 bunch thyme, chopped
1 bunch sage, chopped
1 bunch rosemary, chopped
zest of 2 oranges
4 garlic cloves, chopped
2 tablespoons freshly ground black
  pepper
2 tablespoons ground allspice

1 x 2 kg piece pork belly, skin on
50 g butter
2 medium carrots, roughly chopped
2 onions, roughly chopped
2 leeks, sliced
2 sticks celery, sliced
2 bay leaves
1 tablespoon freshly ground black
  pepper
1 cup white wine
2 litres good-quality chicken stock
  or water
olive oil, for frying

To make the aromatic salt rub, combine all the ingredients in a bowl and mix together. Place the pork on a rack set inside a container and rub the salt rub all over the meat, packing it on thickly. Set a small chopping board on top of the pork and weight it down (cans from the pantry will do the job). Transfer to the refrigerator and leave for 4 hours to cure. After curing, rinse the pork well under running water then pat it dry.

Preheat the oven to 120°C.

Heat the butter gently in a large heavy-based saucepan. Add the carrots, onion, leeks and celery and sweat gently for 5 minutes until the vegetables start to soften. Add the bay leaves, pepper, wine and stock and bring to the boil.

Sandwich the pork between two sheets of baking paper, and place it, skin-side down in a deep roasting tin. Pour on enough of the boiling stock to immerse the pork. Cover the roasting tin, or weight the pork down with a wire rack. Transfer to the oven and cook for 3 hours, by which time the meat will be very tender. Remove from the oven and leave the pork in the liquid until cool enough to handle.

Transfer the pork to a tray lined with a clean sheet of baking paper. Weight it down again using the board and cans. When completely cold, transfer the pork to the refrigerator and leave it overnight.

When ready to cook, cut the pork into 8 cm x 8 cm portions. Heat the oil in a heavy-based frying pan. When the oil is hot, fry the pork pieces, skin-side down, for 4–5 minutes. The skin will quickly colour and crisp up. Turn and cook for 3–4 minutes on the other side, until golden brown. Serve hot from the pan with your choice of accompaniments.

Serves 6–8

Pork bones and puha soup

Over the years I've had lots of Kiwis working in my kitchens and they always ask me to save the pork neck so they can make pork and puha soup. I learned this particular recipe from my Kiwi mate Kurt on a visit to New Zealand. It's a traditional Maori dish, which uses all sorts of pork bones, the pork neck and any other random bits you have to hand. Puha is a leafy vegetable, like a cross between dandelion and watercress. It's not grown commercially, but is still widely available in some areas of New Zealand. I loved this soup so much that I tried to figure out how to make something similar back in Oz, using watercress. It's not an elegant dish, but it is very tasty and satisfying and is a great way of using up any scruffy old bits of pork you've got hanging around.

2 kg pork neck, pork hock, or whatever you've got, cut through the bone into smaller pieces
2 medium onions, roughly diced
4 garlic cloves
2 bay leaves
4 cloves

2 carrots, sliced
1 tablespoon salt
1 teaspoon freshly ground black pepper
2 bunches watercress, roughly chopped
lime juice to serve
chopped parsley to serve

Throw all the ingredients, except for the watercress, lime juice and parsley, into a large saucepan or casserole dish. Cover with cold water and bring to the boil, skimming away any foam or scum that rises to the surface. Lower the heat and simmer, uncovered, for 2½ hours, topping up with water if needed. You'll see that quite a lot of fat rises to the surface: skim off as much or as little as you like. Personally, I like to keep quite a lot of fat in the soup as this is what makes it so tasty. By the end of the cooking time the meat should be very tender and falling from the bones.

Just before serving, add the watercress and simmer for 5 minutes.

Ladle the soup into bowls and serve with a squeeze of lime and a sprinkling of parsley.

Serves 6–8

I'm pretty sure that my fondness for curries dates back to my early childhood in Malaysia. We had an Indian nanny who often did the cooking, and my brother and I grew to love spicy food from a young age. Pork neck is really well suited to this sort of slow-cooked dish, as it is threaded with lots of connective tissue that melts to make the meat succulent and juicy. This is a mild curry that will suit people who don't like chilli. I find that the sweetness of the raisins, brown sugar and apple cider works brilliantly with curry flavours. Serve with boiled rice and cool minted yoghurt.

Curried pork casserole with sweet spices

2 medium onions, diced
4 garlic cloves, sliced
2 tablespoons grated ginger
1 small bunch coriander, roots and stems chopped (reserve the leaves for garnish)
1 kg pork neck, diced
salt
freshly ground black pepper
3 tablespoons olive oil
2 tablespoons curry powder
2 sticks cinnamon

2 cloves
pinch saffron
2 tablespoons sherry vinegar
2 cups apple cider
2 cups good quality chicken stock or water
¼ cup brown sugar
¼ cup raisins
500 g potatoes, peeled and cut into 3 cm dice
juice of 1 lime
3 spring onions, finely sliced

Place the onion, garlic, ginger and coriander roots and stems into a liquidizer and blend to a purée.

Season the pork with salt and pepper. Heat the oil in a large, heavy-based casserole over a medium heat. When the oil is hot, brown the pork in batches, so that the heat stays high. Transfer the browned pork to a plate.

Add the onion purée to the casserole with the curry powder, cinnamon, cloves and saffron. Lower the heat and sauté for 5 minutes until the paste is fragrant. Return the pork to the casserole and add the vinegar, cider and stock. Stir in the sugar, then add the raisins and potatoes to the casserole and stir well. Bring to the boil, then lower the heat to a simmer and cover the pan. Cook gently for 1½ hours, after which the pork should be lovely and tender.

When ready to serve, squeeze on the lime juice and garnish with the reserved coriander leaves and spring onions.

Serves 4–6

Cabbage rolls

These are another of my Nonna Yole's specialties and they're equally delicious made with vine leaves. You can serve them warm or cold with a big dollop of yoghurt. Nonna always used to make her own yoghurt, strain it overnight to thicken, and flavour it with sweet new-season garlic from her garden.

l Savoy cabbage
2 tablespoons oil
1 onion medium, finely diced
6 garlic cloves, finely chopped
500 g finely minced pork
2 cups long grain rice
2½ cups chicken stock or water
½ cup chopped parsley

2 tablespoons chopped fresh mint
2 tablespoons dried mint
1 tablespoon dried oregano
1 teaspoon salt
½ teaspoon freshly ground black
  pepper
juice of 2 lemons

With a small sharp knife, slice out the core of the cabbage. Carefully separate the leaves, being careful not to tear them. Bring a large pan of salted water to the boil and blanch the cabbage leaves in batches for 1 minute. Lift them into a colander and rinse briefly in cold water. Leave to drain, then lay them out on a tea towel and pat dry all over.

Heat the oil in a heavy-based saucepan. Add the onion and garlic and sweat over a low heat for 5 minutes, or until soft and translucent. Add the minced pork and sauté over a medium heat until the pork starts to colour. Add the rice to the pan and stir well. Add 1 cup of stock to the pan and bring to the boil. Lower the heat to a simmer, then cover the pan and cook for 10 minutes, or until the liquid is absorbed. Stir in the herbs and season with salt and pepper, then tip the mixture out onto a shallow tray to cool.

Arrange the larger, tougher outer cabbage leaves in the bottom of a casserole dish or a heavy-based saucepan. Lay the remaining leaves out on your work surface. With a small sharp knife make a v-shaped cut in each leaf and slice out the tough stalky bit. Take 2 generous tablespoons of the cooled stuffing mixture and place on one of the prepared leaves, just above the incision. Roll up and over once, then fold in the sides and continue to roll up to form a neat package. Repeat until all the cabbage leaves and stuffing mixture are used up.

Place the cabbage rolls in the casserole dish, packing them tightly together. Season generously then pour on the remaining stock. Cover the casserole and cook over a low heat for around 20 minutes. Alternatively, cook the cabbage rolls in a 175°C oven for 20 minutes. When the cabbage rolls are cooked, pour on the lemon juice. Serve the cabbage rolls straight away, or leave them to cool. Serve with garlicky strained yoghurt.

Serves 4

GAME

FURRY,
FEATHERED
& WILD

Game

In ancient times all animals were wild things and we humans only got to eat them by using our wits to hunt them down. In those hungrier days we ate anything we could get our hands on, from badgers to bears and wild boar. But gradually we discovered that some animals were easier to herd together, and we were able to domesticate them to provide a more reliable source of food. These animals – cattle, sheep, pigs and poultry – still make up the bulk of meat that we eat today.

Those ancient instincts run deep, though, and for some of us, the thrill of the chase remains to this day – but now we only hunt animals and birds as a leisure sport, and rarely out of necessity. This is the category that we call 'game'. The reality though, is that very few of these animals are truly wild. In fact most of them are specifically bred and farmed on a commercial scale. In England and Scotland, for instance, grouse, pheasants, partridges and venison are all carefully managed on estates to provide sport for hunters.

In Australia, some hunting (of rabbits, kangaroo, goats) is done in the name of pest control, often by farmers, but there is also a growing leisure market for the hunting, shooting and fishing set. Most prefer the challenge of large wild game animals, such as Asiatic buffalo, Sambar deer and wild boar, as well as the 'sport' of the annual duck hunting season. But when it comes to buying and eating game in Australia, most of it is bred and farmed specifically for the table, and bypasses entirely the hunting part of the process.

Unless you live in the country or have farmer friends, you will find that the range of game available to most of us – and that includes chefs – is fairly limited. The Australian consumer is most likely to encounter deer (venison), rabbit, quail, pigeon (squab) and pheasant, but most of these will have been farmed, with only a very small percentage being truly wild. There is also a small, but growing market for our own native kangaroo, which of all the animals on our table is the only one that will have certainly lived a truly 'wild' life.

There are some game specialists who will be able to offer you wild rabbit, hare, venison or quail, as well as a few market stalls, especially in rural areas. If you are lucky enough to try these wild creatures, you'll find they are quite different from farmed game. Wild game is distinguishable from farmed game in two simple ways: by its flavour and by the leanness of its meat. When it comes to diet, wild game – be it furry or feathered – has a much more varied foraged diet, of wild grasses, berries, grubs and grains, than its farmed cousins. The flavour of the meat reflects this variety and is the reason why wild game has a deep, more intensely 'gamey' flavour.

Wild game animals and birds also have a much more free-ranging lifestyle than farmed animals. They cover more terrain – or migrate over long distances – so their harder working flesh is leaner, denser and tougher.

Hanging game

I was first introduced to the idea of hanging wild animals when I worked on a big country estate in Scotland many years ago. The game keeper explained how hanging the locally caught pheasants completely changed their texture and flavour. In the cool, airy cellar he pointed out a series of birds, hanging from the ceiling at various stages of aging. Some were almost turning green before our eyes, and I could hardly believe that people would actually want to eat them. After a few weeks cooking wild pheasants, though, I was converted, and these days I much prefer the more intense flavour of well-hung game, to the blander, less interesting flavour of quickly hung and farmed game.

I've talked about the benefits of hanging meat – dry-aging it – before (page 9), and there is no doubt that hanging wild game makes a big difference to its eating quality. As is the case with beef, hanging game animals and birds in a cool, well-ventilated place allows the enzymes in the flesh to work their tenderising magic.

Hanging also changes the flavour, developing those distinctive 'gamey' characteristics. This effect is especially strong in game birds and some small animals that are hung with their guts (entrails) still inside. The 'ripe' flavour begins in the guts, with the onset of decomposition, and then gradually spreads through the rest of the meat. The longer the animal hangs, and the warmer the conditions, the stronger the flavours will be. Some serious game gourmands like their game to be so well-hung that it actually smells and tastes quite rank.

There are no hard-and-fast rules about how long to hang each creature – it does depend on the individual species of bird or animal, so I believe it's best left to those who know what they're doing.

FURRY GAME

RABBIT

Although they make cute and furry pets, we Australians have mixed emotions when it comes to bunnies. They were introduced to the country in the mid-1800s to provide a quick-and-easy food source, but without natural predators, quickly grew to plague proportions, damaging the environment and competing with Australian livestock for feed. In the 1950s, the rabbit problem was famously decimated by the deliberate introduction of the myxomatosis virus – although they eventually developed immunity and their numbers returned to plague proportions once more.

Although recent efforts to control their numbers with the rabbit calcivirus have been more successful, to anyone who lives in rural Australia, the rabbit remains a rampant pest. The main problem with rabbits, of course, is that they breed like, well, rabbits! Each doe can produce a litter of between four and six kittens every month – generating a potential 10-fold increase in population over just six months. All of which seems a very good reason to eat as many of them as we can!

Ironically, it is actually fairly hard to find wild rabbit in most parts of Australia, although theoretically they are available all year round. Wild rabbits have darker, leaner meat than farmed rabbits, and are likely to be tougher. Farmed rabbit operations are strictly controlled (not surprisingly) mainly to supply the restaurant and export industries. They are paler, larger, meatier, and generally more tender than wild rabbits.

How to choose, store and cook rabbit

Good butchers and fresh food markets sell whole rabbits, ready for cooking (skinned, gutted, head removed). They are usually killed young, at around 10–12 weeks and generally weigh between 1 and 1.5 kilograms. You can also ask for older rabbits that have finished their breeding life. These are bigger and meatier and have more fat and flavour than the young rabbits.

You will probably also be able to buy various cuts of rabbit – the hindlegs and forelegs, the saddle and fillets. When choosing rabbit, always choose meat that looks smooth and a bit shiny. The liver and kidneys should be glossy and there should be no odour.

♥

THINGS THAT LOVE RABBIT
Bacon, brandy, fennel seeds, garlic, juniper berries, lemon, mushrooms, olive oil, olives, onions, pancetta, pepper, prunes, red wine, rosemary, sage, salt, shallots, thyme

Storing rabbit
- Because it is lean, with minimal fat and connective tissues, rabbit is more perishable than other meats; treat it like chicken or veal.
- Unwrap and refrigerate all rabbit immediately. Rub it with olive oil or cover in an oil-based marinade to protect it.
- Store it in a Tupperware container, or sit it on a rack on a plate and cover it with a tea towel.
- Rabbit should be eaten within two to three days.

A whole rabbit can be delicious when wrapped in bacon and roasted with garlic and onions and a splash of wine. But because the legs and saddle cook at very different rates I usually prefer to break them down into joints. Rabbit legs are wonderful for braising, while the tender saddle (which comes from the centre of the back and is made up of the two loins and tiny fillets) are great for quick cooking.

Because rabbit has virtually no body fat, you need to add it. I often marinate rabbit in a generous amount of olive oil before cooking it, or the meat can be wrapped in bacon, prosciutto or caul fat, to provide lubrication as it cooks.

KANGAROO
Kangaroo is the only meat in this book that is actually indigenous to Australia. With today's growing interest in eating 'locally', it seems to make perfect sense that we eat animals that grow on our own doorstep – especially when they breed prolifically, and are considered a pest in many parts of the country. Even Greenpeace has suggested that we should be eating more kangaroo to help reduce our output of greenhouse gases.

And yet the idea of eating our national symbol is something that many people find repellent. Kangaroo culls are always greeted with highly publicised emotional opposition. Yet government-approved management plans are aimed at a balanced approach to sustaining acceptable population levels of kangaroo and of the 48 species in Australia, only four are harvested commercially within strictly controlled quotas.

There seem to be many good reasons for eating kangaroo: it's widely available, relatively free of diseases, and entirely free of antibiotics or chemicals that are common in meat from other domestic animals. Simply put, it is one of the healthiest red meats there is. It is higher in protein and iron than any other meats and with a fat content of under 2 per cent, meat just doesn't come any leaner. Kangaroo has also been identified as the highest known source of CLA (conjugated linoleic acid), which is linked with boosting immunity and inhibiting certain cancers and diabetes. Funnily enough, even though we ourselves don't eat all that much of it, Australia now exports kangaroo meat to more than 55 countries around the world, in the European Union, the USA and Asia.

How to choose, store and cook kangaroo
Kangaroo is now fairly widely available in fresh produce markets, butcher's shops and even in supermarkets.

Kangaroo meat is a deep, rich red colour, with negligible surface fat. It is fairly densely textured and is usually sold trimmed and denuded of sinew. Primary cuts of kangaroo include the striploin (loin), fillet, rump, topside and minced or chopped meat. Kangaroo tails are also available, and apparently make delicious soup, but I have to confess that I usually give them to my dog as a big treat.

Kangaroo meat sold in supermarkets often comes pre-packed and portioned in MAP (Modified Atmosphere Packaging) trays. If unopened, MAP trays will keep for up to four weeks in the coldest part of your fridgerator.

Storing kangaroo

- Unless packed in MAP trays, all other kangaroo should be eaten as soon as possible after purchase.
- Unwrap and pat it dry all over. Rub it with olive oil or cover in an oil-based marinade to protect it.

Kangaroo has a distinctive rich and slightly gamey flavour. Meat from younger animals, or meat that is consumed within 1–2 weeks of killing will have a much milder flavour than older or aged kangaroo.

The wide range of cuts available lend themselves to a wide range of recipes, but as is always the case, you need to match the cut to the cooking method. Kangaroo needs to be handled and cooked like any other lean, low-fat game meat. The most popular techniques for the prime cuts are frying, grilling, barbecuing or briefly roasting at a high heat. You need to take particular care not to overcook kangaroo – pink is best. The only cuts that should be slow-cooked are the tail or shanks.

As you might expect, native Australian ingredients pair especially well with kangaroo, something indigenous cooks have known for thousands of years.

VENISON AND ELK

Venison is the culinary name for deer meat, of which elk is a variety. Deer were introduced into Australia and neighbouring New Zealand in the 19th century, but were not farmed seriously until the 1970s. Today New Zealand leads the world in deer farming, and both countries export venison meat around the world.

In fact, venison is one of the most widely consumed of all game meats, and continues to become more and more popular. Its main virtues are that it is an extremely lean and naturally tender red meat – perfect for today's health-conscious consumers. The only real downside is that it is relatively expensive to farm and process, making it something of a luxury product. Nearly all Australian venison is exported to Europe and South-East Asia, where they particularly value its 'purifying' health benefits.

How to choose, store and cook venison

Although there are wild deer populations in parts of Australia, nearly all venison sold is farmed, and comes from the red deer or fallow deer. It can be tricky to find, but most good butchers should be able to source it for you if you give them plenty of notice.

There is not a huge difference between wild venison and the farmed species, as both live relatively free-range lives. Deer are ruminants, and even farmed deer are allowed to graze naturally on pasture and grow at their own rate and in their own time. Farmed venison do lead less active lives than wild deer, which makes them slightly less lean and less intensely flavoured. The trade-off is that their flesh is more tender and they are usually slaughtered at a consistently younger age. Whether wild or farmed, venison needs to be hung to tenderise the meat and to develop the flavour.

THINGS THAT LOVE KANGAROO

Anchovies, beetroot, bush tomatoes, garlic, juniper berries, mustard, native peppercorns, olive oil, onions, paprika, pepper, port, red wine, salt, spinach, sun-dried tomatoes

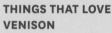

THINGS THAT LOVE VENISON

Allspice berries, anchovies, bacon, bay leaves, beetroot, chestnuts, garlic, juniper berries, lentils, mustard, olive oil, onions, pancetta, paprika, pepper, port, red wine, redcurrant jelly, rosemary, salt, sour cherries, thyme

Venison is often sold vacuum-packed, which in my view is a bit of a mixed blessing as I'm not a huge fan of the way vacuum-packed meat sits in a bath of its own blood. However, it's a good way of tenderising freshly slaughtered meat and is common in the venison industry.

Storing venison

- Vacuum-packed venison should be left in its wrapping until you are ready to cook it. It will keep for up to two weeks in the coldest part of your fridgerator. When you open the package, you will need to mop up any blood sitting on the surface of the meat. Any odour should disappear after a few minutes.
- Because it is lean, with minimal fat and connective tissues, venison is more perishable than other red meats; treat it like chicken or veal.
- Unwrap and refrigerate all venison immediately.
- Store it in a Tupperware container, or sit it on a rack on a plate and cover it with a tea towel.
- Large cuts of venison will keep for up to three days.
- Smaller cuts should be used within three days.
- Cubed or minced venison should be used within one or two days.

The primary cuts of venison are the haunch (leg) and saddle (which includes the eye-fillet), the breast (or flank) and shoulder.

The best cuts for roasting are the haunch and saddle, and on a larger deer the saddle is usually divided into chops and a loin that can be roasted on the bone or boned, stuffed and rolled. The loin is brilliant for roasting whole, or it can be cut into thick steaks for grilling, sautéing or barbecuing.

The breast and shoulder are rather tough cuts and are more suitable for braising. They also make a great filling for a hearty pie, or can be minced to make venison burgers or sausages.

The biggest challenge when cooking venison is to keep it moist. It is naturally very lean, so you need to be careful it doesn't dry out and become tough. Marinating before cooking in lots of olive oil helps, and large roasting cuts can be kept moist by draping them with bacon, pancetta or pork back fat, or wrapping it in caul fat.

FEATHERED GAME

QUAIL

These plump little game birds are surprisingly meaty, and are perfect for hand-held eating. They are very popular here in Australia, whether spiced and deep-fried the Chinese way, grilled Mediterranean-style with herbs and garlic, or stuffed and roasted whole.

Quail are funny little ground-dwelling birds, and different species can be found in Europe, Asia, North America and Africa. In the wild, quail are pretty easy to catch, as they prefer running to flying. Nevertheless, most commercially available quail in Australia is farmed on specialist poultry operations.

Although they do have a slight gamey taste, farmed quail are more delicately flavoured than wild quail, and are altogether meatier and more tender.

How to choose, store and cook quail

Quail are fairly widely available all year round, both fresh and frozen. Some upmarket supermarkets will stock them, but otherwise you will probably have to go to a specialist poultry seller or butcher.

Quail are usually sold on trays of 4–6 birds, depending on how big they are. Jumbo quail seem to be increasingly popular, and these weigh 200g or more, compared with 160–200g for medium-sized quail. Quail are sometimes sold spatchcocked, ready for barbecuing, which is to say they are split down the backbone and opened out flat. It's also a good method to employ with pigeon and poussin (baby chicken). Once spatchcocked, you can marinate the bird in olive oil and your favourite herbs.

For a fancy presentation, the flattened birds can be speared onto skewers, which help keep them flat on the grill.

I would allow one whole quail per person as a starter, and two each for a main course.

Storing quail
- Unwrap and refrigerate quail immediately. Rub with olive oil or an oil-based marinade to protect it.
- Store them in a Tupperware container, or sit them on a rack on a plate and cover it with a tea towel.
- Quail should be eaten within two to three days.
- Frozen quail should be thawed overnight in the refrigerator. Once thawed, rinse them and pat thoroughly dry.

Quail are very versatile birds, and can be roasted, grilled, barbecued, fried or braised. The main thing to remember is that it is a sin to overcook quail – to be really good and juicy the breast meat should be pale pink in the centre, and some even like it positively red. Whole quail will take around 8–10 minutes to cook in a 180–200°C oven. When flattened out (see page 156) they will cook on a hot griddle or barbecue in as little as three to four minutes. However you cook them, make sure you leave them to rest before eating.

PIGEON

The first thing to understand is that I'm not talking about those annoying noisy birds that leave their droppings all over public buildings and our cars! The pigeons that I love to eat are wood pigeons, and they are especially popular in Europe. Here in Australia they are virtually impossible to find, but we do have a fairly lively squab pigeon industry.

So what's the difference? Well wood pigeons are wild birds. They cover vast distances in the air hunting for food, which means that their meat is rather stringy and tough, even if dense and very tasty. Squab pigeon are farmed pigeons that are killed as fledglings, before they have even left the nest, so they are much more tender. The meat from squab pigeon is much less dark and gamey than wild pigeon, but it is still quite delicious.

THINGS THAT LOVE QUAIL
Bacon, chilli, coriander, cumin, garlic, ginger, honey, lemon, olive oil, pepper, pomegranate molasses, quince paste, raisins, red currant jelly, salt, star anise, thyme, vinegar

♥

**THINGS THAT LOVE
PIGEON**
Bacon, chilli, coriander,
cumin, garlic, ginger,
honey, pepper, raisins,
redcurrant jelly, rosemary,
salt, Sichuan pepper, soy
sauce, star anise, thyme,
vinegar.

How to choose, store and cook pigeon

Squab pigeon are not widely available – in fact you will probably have to go to a specialist poultry seller, or ask your own butcher to order them in for you. They are something of a luxury item in Australia, and you may find they cost as much – if not more – than a much larger chicken. On the upside, their meat is rich and meaty, and a little goes a long way, especially if you are happy to suck away at all the little bones, to extract every last little bit of tasty flesh.

Squab are usually sold as whole birds, ready plucked and drawn (gutted). Occasionally they come with their head and sometimes even their claws still attached, and you will need to trim them off. When buying squab, check to see that the skin is not torn or blemished. The meat should be darkish pink under a layer of creamy skin.

Squab are generally sold in two sizes: medium (300 g) and large (400–450 g). I would allow one small pigeon per person as a starter, and one large one for a main course.

Storing pigeon

- Unwrap and refrigerate pigeon immediately.
- Store them in a Tupperware container, or sit them on a rack on a plate and cover with a tea towel.
- Pigeon should be eaten within two to three days.
- Frozen pigeon should be thawed overnight in the refrigerator. Once thawed, rinse them and pat thoroughly dry.

Some fancy restaurants offer elaborate salads scattered with plump little seared pigeon breasts, but I think it is much more sensible to cook and eat the whole bird. They are perfect for filling with a hearty stuffing and roasting to a dark burnished bronze, or they can be spatchcocked like quail (see page 156) and grilled or barbecued. The Chinese are especially good at cooking pigeon: the birds are first poached in a master stock before being deep-fried to crisp perfection and served with spicy salt and a dipping sauce. As with other game, never cook these tender game birds beyond medium–rare.

PHEASANT

Anyone who has been to England or Scotland in the late autumn will know the thrill of seeing one of these gorgeous birds emerging from the misty undergrowth, and then taking off in a whirring flurry of feathers. When I was working on a large Scottish estate I became used to the regular crack of the rifles – a signal to expect delivery of a brace or two of birds.

Things are not nearly as romantic here in Australia. In fact, there is only one wild pheasant hunt (on King Island) in the country, and only farmed birds are commercially available. The drivers of the pheasant industry in Australia are undoubtedly Maggie and Colin Beer, who were pioneer farmers of the birds on their Barossa Valley property in the early 1970s. As a result, many of us are familiar with these tasty birds – if only through the famous and delicious Pheasant Farm Pâté.

Pheasants are believed to have originated in Asia, and were brought to Europe by Jason (of the Argonauts) while he was out searching for the Golden Fleece. From Greece they were then spread to Italy, from where the Romans spread them to all corners of their empire. Although there are nearly 50 species of pheasant around the world today, the most wildly consumed is the Chinese ring-necked bird.

How to choose, store and cook pheasant

Nowadays there are a number of top-notch pheasant farms in Australia – some even boast of being truly free-range – and pheasant and pheasant products are increasingly available.

Unless you purchase directly from the farmer, you will almost certainly have to order pheasant from a game specialist. They are available fresh between March and August, but you can find frozen pheasant all year around. As is the case with squab pigeon, pheasants are expensive, so you do need to think of them as a bit of a special occasion dish. However, you know you're going to get a quality bird. Dismiss any memory you may have of biting down on a piece of 'shot' in an English pheasant!

All pheasants are hung for a period of time before sale to tenderise the flesh. They are always sold plucked and drawn (gutted), often with the head and claws still attached. Always check to see that the skin is not torn or blemished. The meat is surprisingly pale and should have a thin creamy cover of flat.

Most farmed pheasant are processed between 16 and 20 weeks of age and weigh between 800g–1 kg. One pheasant makes a good meal for two people.

Storing pheasant

- Unwrap and refrigerate pheasant immediately.
- Store them in a Tupperware container, or sit them on a rack on a plate and cover with a tea towel.
- Pheasant should be eaten within two to three days.
- Frozen pheasants should be thawed overnight in the refrigerator. Once thawed, rinse them and pat thoroughly dry.

There are many people who think you can't go past the traditional English roast pheasant with all the trimmings (fried breadcrumbs or a fried crouton, bacon, and creamy bread sauce). But pheasant can also be pot-roasted or braised. The leg meat is brilliant when turned into a pie or even sausages. As with all game birds, pheasant is very lean, so you do need to be careful not to let the flesh dry out. Rub them with olive oil or marinate them before cooking, and drape the delicate breast meat with bacon, pancetta or pork back fat.

HOW DO YOU KNOW WHEN IT'S COOKED

Different game animals require cooking to varying degrees of doneness. Please refer to recipes for specific cooking times for each cut.

THINGS THAT LOVE PHEASANT
Bacon, butter, cabbage, fried breadcrumbs, garlic, ginger, grapes, honey, Madeira, orange, pears, pepper, port, raisins, red wine, salt, thyme, verjuice.

Roasted rabbit legs wrapped in prosciutto

For this dish you need to remove the thigh bones from the rabbit legs which creates a nice little pouch, perfect for stuffing. You'll need a small, sharp knife and a bit of patience, but otherwise it's not terribly difficult. And if you're not sure you're up to the task, then ask your butcher nicely if he'll do it for you.

Serve with Creamy, Buttery Mash (page 296) or Soft, Herby, Cheesy Polenta (page 300) and Fresh Herb Salad (page 314).

200 g butter, softened
2 tablespoons porcini powder
  (available from specialist food stores)
1 tablespoon chopped thyme
2 tablespoons chopped parsley

1 teaspoon salt
1 teaspoon freshly ground black pepper
6 meaty rabbit hind legs (thigh bones
  removed)
6 thick slices prosciutto

Preheat the oven to 200°C.

Place the softened butter in a mixing bowl with the porcini powder, chopped herbs and seasonings and beat everything together well. Divide the butter into 6 portions.

Lay out the rabbit legs on your work surface and season. Stuff a portion of butter into each thigh cavity then wrap each leg with a slice of prosciutto and arrange on a roasting tray.

Roast the rabbit legs for 8–10 minutes, until golden brown. Remove from the oven and leave to rest for 5 minutes. Serve each leg on top of a spoonful of mash, or slice each rabbit leg crosswise into 1 cm slices and fan them out, with the drumstick at a jaunty angle at one end.

Serves 6

Barbecued rabbit with roasted onion marinade

Farmed rabbit – which is ideal for this recipe – is tender and lean with a mild flavour that's enhanced by the roasted onion marinade.

Marinade
3 large brown onions, skin on
3 garlic cloves, finely chopped
¼ cup extra-virgin olive oil
1 tablespoon finely chopped coriander
1 tablespoon finely chopped parsley
1 teaspoon freshly ground black pepper

1 large rabbit, jointed
salt
freshly ground black pepper
olive oil
lemon wedges to serve

Preheat the oven to 180°C.

Roast the onions for about 20 minutes, until very soft and golden. When cool enough to handle, peel away the skins and chop the onions finely or purée in a food processor.

When cool, place the onion purée in a large mixing bowl and add the remaining marinade ingredients.

Make deep incisions into the rabbit pieces to open up the flesh. Rub in the marinade, working it well into the incisions. Cover the bowl and refrigerate overnight to marinate.

When ready to cook, preheat your barbecue or grill to medium. Season the rabbit pieces, then grill, turning frequently and brushing liberally with olive oil every few minutes. They will take around 5–10 minutes to cook, with the legs taking a little longer than the fillets. Serve piping hot, with wedges of lemon.

Serves 4

This is one of my favourite ways of cooking rabbit. I serve it with Soft, Herby, Cheesy Polenta (page 300) to soak up the wine-rich juices and a green salad tossed with a mustardy dressing.

Ask your butcher to show you how he joints the rabbit, and the next time you'll be able to do it yourself.

Rabbit braised with grapes and riesling

1 rabbit, jointed
salt
freshly ground black pepper
100 ml olive oil
10 shallots, peeled and halved
1 garlic clove, roughly chopped
1 stick celery, sliced

1 small carrot, sliced
2 tablespoons fresh tarragon
2 allspice berries
1 clove
2 cups seedless white grapes
750 ml riesling
2 cups good-quality chicken stock

Preheat the oven to 180ºC.

Season the rabbit pieces generously with salt and pepper. Heat 3 tablespoons of the oil in a heavy-based casserole and seal the rabbit in batches, until browned all over. Transfer to a warm plate.

Add the rest of the oil to the casserole dish and heat gently. Add the shallots, garlic, celery and carrot with 1 tablespoon of the tarragon and sweat over a low heat until they soften. Stir in the spices and 1 cup of the grapes and cook over a medium heat for 3 minutes, until the grapes soften. Add the wine and bubble vigorously for 5 minutes so that it reduces slightly. Return the rabbit pieces to the pan and add the chicken stock. Bring to the boil, then lower the heat to a simmer. Transfer to the oven and cook, uncovered for 45 minutes.

Towards the end of the cooking time add the rest of the tarragon and grapes to the casserole and simmer for 5 minutes. Serve with wet polenta or warm crusty bread and a simple green salad.

Serves 4

Rabbit galantine with date, pork and pistachio stuffing

This is one of the most popular dishes on the menu at La Luna Bistro. I really love the combination of salty prosciutto with the sweetness of the dates in the stuffing.

Don't be daunted by the idea of boning rabbits. Although it's a bit fiddly, it's actually much easier than you might think. And if you don't feel confident about doing this yourself, ask your butcher to help.

100 g dates, pitted and roughly chopped
3 tablespoons brandy
300 g lean pork, minced
50 g smoky bacon, diced
¼ cup shelled pistachio nuts, roughly chopped

2 tablespoons chopped parsley
1 tablespoon chopped thyme
½ teaspoon salt
1 teaspoon freshly ground white pepper
10 slices proscuitto
2 rabbits, boned

Soak the dates in the brandy for 5–10 minutes. Meanwhile, combine the minced pork, bacon, pistachios and herbs in a mixing bowl. Mix thoroughly and season well, then fold in the soaked dates and brandy. Cover and refrigerate until chilled.

On your work surface, spread out 2 large rectangular sheets of aluminium foil, one on top of the other (they need to be about 10 cm longer than the rabbit). Cover the foil with a layer of plastic wrap. Arrange the prosciutto slices crosswise, in an overlapping row along the centre. Place one rabbit directly on top of the prosciutto and spread the stuffing on top. Place the other rabbit directly on top, but facing in the opposite direction, and wrap the prosciutto slices up and around the rabbits until they meet. Wrap the rabbit up firmly in the plastic wrap and foil, folding the ends tightly underneath to form a round sausage.

Place the foil parcel in a saucepan that holds it snugly and cover with cold water. Bring to the boil slowly, then lower the heat to a gentle simmer. Poach gently for 55 minutes then carefully lift the rabbit out and place in a sink of iced water.

When the rabbit is cool, carefully unwrap and remove the foil and plastic wrap. The rabbit can be prepared to this stage up to 4 days ahead of time.

When ready to serve, preheat the oven to 180°C. Place the rabbit on a rack set into a roasting tin and cook for 20 minutes until golden brown. Leave to rest for 15 minutes before carving into thick slices.

Serves 6–8

Warm salad of barbecued kangaroo with spinach, pine nuts and beetroot jam

Kangaroo is best when cooked rare or medium-rare. This is ideal for the fillet, loin and rump, which are the most widely available cuts. Serve this salad with a dollop of Beetroot Jam (page 343) to bring out the underlying sweetness of the meat.

3 x 400 g kangaroo fillets
olive oil
300 g baby spinach leaves
200 g cherry tomatoes, halved
200 g soft goat's cheese, crumbled
100 g toasted pine nuts
3 tablespoons extra-virgin olive oil

2 tablespoons balsamic vinegar
salt
freshly ground black pepper
chopped parsley to serve
chopped thyme to serve
Beetroot Jam (page 343)

Dry the kangaroo meat thoroughly and trim away the silvery membranes. As soon as you can, rub the meat all over with oil, to prevent it discolouring.

Preheat a barbecue or griddle to high. Drizzle the kangaroo with a little more oil and cook it for 3–4 minutes, turning several times, until it is browned all over. Transfer to a warm plate, cover loosely with foil, and leave to rest for 5 minutes.

To make the salad, combine the spinach, tomatoes, goat's cheese and pine nuts in a large mixing bowl. Whisk the oil and vinegar together and pour onto the salad. Season with salt and pepper, toss together gently then divide between 6 plates.

Slice the kangaroo fillets on the diagonal and arrange on top of the salad. Scatter with the fresh herbs and serve with hot crusty bread and beetroot jam on the side.

Serves 6

Kangaroo meat is extremely lean, so to get the desired juicy consistency for burgers, you need to add minced pork belly to the mix. Even so, these burgers are best cooked rare or medium-rare or they run the risk of being dry and crumbly.

Serve with Homemade Tomato Sauce (page 343) and Oven-baked Organic Potato Chips (page 297) or with burger buns and your favourite accompaniments.

'Roo burger

800 g kangaroo fillet, finely minced
200 g pork belly, finely chopped
½ onion, finely diced
1 garlic clove, crushed
1 teaspoon Worcestershire sauce
1 teaspoon English mustard

1 egg, lightly beaten
2 tablespoons finely chopped parsley
1 teaspoon salt
1 teaspoon freshly ground black pepper
olive oil for grilling

Preheat your grill or barbecue to medium-high.

Combine all the ingredients, except the olive oil, in a large mixing bowl. Use your hands to scrunch everything together so that the pork belly, onion and flavourings are evenly distributed. Shape into 6 patties, making them as neat as you can, about 2.5-3 cm thick.

Brush each burger lightly with oil and arrange them on your grill or barbecue. Cook for 6 minutes for medium-rare, turning several times. Serve hot from the grill with your choice of accompaniments.

Serves 6

Venison meat is deep red, lean and has a wonderful rich gamey flavour. The prime cuts are tender and dense, which makes them perfect for eating raw in small amounts as a carpaccio. It's best to prepare this dish just before eating, as it does have a tendency to discolour over time.

Venison carpaccio

400 g venison (fillet, loin or topside)
1 tablespoon capers
1 anchovy fillet, chopped
1 tablespoon chopped parsley
2 tablespoons olive oil
salt flakes

freshly ground black pepper
4 tablespoons good-quality
  mayonnaise
75 g green olives, pitted and
  roughly chopped
¼ cup mustard cress or baby
  herb leaves

Use a very sharp knife to cut the venison into 18 slices. Sandwich each slice between two pieces of plastic wrap and flatten with a rolling pin or meat mallet to 3 mm thick.

Place the capers, anchovy and parsley in a mortar with 1 tablespoon of the olive oil. Pound to a smooth paste.

Brush the venison slices lightly with the remaining olive oil and arrange on a serving platter. Season lightly with salt and pepper and drizzle with mayonnaise. Dot with the anchovy paste, dividing it evenly between the venison slices. Garnish with the chopped olives and mustard cress and serve straight away with a glass of pinot noir.

Serves 6

Elk minute steak – for a special mate

Elk are native to North America, and a bit of a rarity in Australia. They're a large species of deer, second in size only to the moose, and their meat is extremely tasty. I have a special mate who raises elk just over the South Australian border, and at some point during the hunting season, I'll get a late night phone call, alerting me to the fact that there's been a shoot, and that I can expect an elk delivery. Two weeks later, after the elk has been hung, my mate will turn up in his ute with the elk on board. At La Luna Bistro we use every part of the animal for making sausages, pies and braises, and I always keep back a small part of the rib-eye to slice thinly and cook as a minute steak for my mate.

The fat on venison has an unpleasant flavour – make sure you trim it off.

4 x 150 g slices elk Scotch fillet
olive oil for frying
salt
freshly ground black pepper

extra-virgin olive oil
2 tablespoons chopped parsley
Oven-baked Organic Potato Chips
 (page 97), to serve

Preheat a grill, griddle or frying pan to high. Brush the meat with a little olive oil and season with salt and pepper. Cook for 30 seconds then turn and cook for another 30 seconds. Transfer the meat to a warm plate and leave to rest for 2 minutes.

Drizzle with extra-virgin olive oil and garnish with chopped parsley. Serve straight away with chips and salad.

Serves 4

Grilled venison rib-eye steaks

Venison rib-eye steaks weigh around 150 g each, which is a decent serve, given that the meat is so dense and richly flavoured. I like to use an aromatic spice rub and to grill them no more than medium–rare.

Serve with Beetroot, Lemon and Coriander Salad with Extra-virgin olive oil (page 317), to really bring out the underlying sweetness of the meat.

Aromatic rub
3 tablespoons olive oil
6 juniper berries, crushed
2 tablespoons fresh thyme
2 teaspoons freshly ground black
 pepper

2 allspice berries, crushed
 (or ¼ teaspoon ground allspice)

4 x 150 g rib-eye venison steaks
salt
freshly ground black pepper

Combine all the rub ingredients in a mixing bowl. Rub into the venison steaks, making sure they are evenly coated. Refrigerate for 4 hours, or overnight if possible. Bring the steaks to room temperature at least 30 minutes before cooking.

When ready to cook the steaks, preheat your grill or barbecue to medium–high. Season the steaks generously, then cook for 1 minute. Turn and cook for 1 further minute. Turn again, this time at a 180° angle, and cook for 1 more minute. Turn for a final time, and cook for a minute. The steaks should be cooked medium–rare and be neatly cross-hatched with marks from the griddle. Remove the steaks from the grill and let them rest on a warm plate for 2 minutes before serving.

Serves 4

Boned saddle of venison with mushroom stuffing

Venison saddle is one of those special-occasion cuts, from the tender back of the beast. Ask your butcher to bone out a small saddle and you'll end up with a manageably sized piece of meat that is beautifully tender. To add essential moisture, I like to wrap the saddle around a tasty stuffing, and then encase the whole thing in caul fat. That way the meat is lubricated from within and without.

If it all sounds a bit too ambitious, then by all means use a venison loin (off the bone), instead of the saddle. Pack the stuffing along the top of the meat and wrap it in caul fat before roasting.

Serve with Tomato-Braised Beans (page 309) and Creamy, Buttery Mash (page 296).

1 x 1.2 kg venison saddle (boned weight)
salt and pepper for seasoning
200 g caul fat, rinsed
olive oil

Mushroom stuffing
3 tablespoons butter
400 g mushrooms, sliced
salt
freshly ground black pepper
1 onion, finely diced
2 garlic cloves, finely chopped
2 tablespoons finely chopped parsley
1 tablespoons finely chopped thyme
3 juniper berries, crushed and finely chopped
¼ cup fresh breadcrumbs (optional)

To make the stuffing, heat 2 tablespoons of the butter in a heavy-based frying pan. When it sizzles, add the mushrooms. Season lightly and sauté over a medium heat until they are tender. Increase the heat and continue cooking until all the liquid has evaporated. Tip into a food processor or blender and blitz to a fairly smooth purée.

Wipe out the frying pan and heat the remaining butter. Sweat the onion and garlic over a low heat for 5 minutes, or until soft but not coloured. Stir in the fresh herbs and the juniper berries and season with a little more salt and pepper. Remove from the heat and leave to cool.

Combine the mushroom purée, onion mixture and the breadcrumbs in a bowl and mix together well.

When ready to cook, preheat your oven to 200°C.

Lay the venison saddle out on your work surface. Season lightly then spread on the mushroom stuffing as evenly as you can, leaving a border around the edge. Roll up to form a fat log and tie securely with butcher's string at 5 cm intervals. Wrap the caul around the stuffed saddle so that it is completely encased.

Heat the oil in a heavy-based roasting tin and sear the venison all over until golden brown. Transfer to the oven and roast for 12–15 minutes for medium–rare. Remove from the oven and leave to rest for 20 minutes in a warm spot.

Carve into thick slices and serve with your choice of accompaniments.

Serves 4–6

Pot-roasted venison with juniper, shallots and bacon

Game meats, whether furry or feathered, are naturally very lean and nearly always need some sort of extra fat added to stop them drying out. Barding is a simple and effective method where you drape or wrap the meat in fat. Lardo (salted, cured pork back fat) is perfect for this dish, but smoky bacon or pancetta will also do the job.

This is a deceptively simple dish that results in lovely moist meat. And I find the rather herbal and aromatic flavour of juniper goes brilliantly with venison's intense flavour. Try to use a casserole dish that will contain the meat snugly. I sit the shallots and garlic cloves underneath the meat so they caramelise and melt during the long, slow cooking. If you like, they can then be blended into some of the reduced cooking liquid, or a cup of jus, to make a beautifully tasty sauce.

Serve with Creamed Spinach (page 312) and Garlic- and Rosemary-roasted Potatoes (page 296).

1.2 kg venison topside or silverside	10 shallots
salt	3 garlic cloves
freshly ground black pepper	2 juniper berries
200 g thick-cut rashers smoky bacon or lardo	1 tablespoon chopped sage
	1 tablespoon chopped thyme
75 g butter	2 cups good-quality chicken stock

Preheat the oven to 200°C. Season the venison all over with salt and pepper then drape the surface neatly with slices of bacon or lardo.

Heat the butter in a heavy-based casserole dish. When it sizzles, add the shallots, garlic, juniper berries and herbs and sauté for 5 minutes until they begin to colour and soften. Add the stock to the casserole and bring it to the boil. Place the venison in the casserole, barded-side up – the stock should come no more than half-way up the meat. Place in the oven and roast for around 1 hour. Check from time to time to ensure the bacon is not browning too quickly. If it does, cover the casserole with foil.

Remove from the oven and allow the venison to rest for 15 minutes before serving with the pan juices.

Serves 6

Barbecued quail, Greek-style

This is a meal that transports me to the Mediterranean. The smoky char-grilled flavour of quail from the barbecue is lovely with a chunky, crunchy Greek salad.

Spatchcocking a bird – which means opening it out and flattening it – helps it to grill evenly. It is easy enough to do yourself. Use kitchen scissors to along both sides of the backbone. Remove the backbone completely and discard it. Open out the bird and turn it flesh-side up. Use the heel of your hands to squash the bird flat. I think it is also helpful to remove some of the fiddly bones – it just makes for easier eating! Once you've learned this technique, you can easily apply it to other birds, like chicken, poussin and pigeon.

6 quail
salt
freshly ground black pepper
olive oil, for grilling
lemon wedges, to serve
extra-virgin olive oil, for drizzling
Big Greek Salad (page 315) to serve

Marinade
2 garlic cloves, chopped
2 tablespoons extra-virgin olive oil
zest and juice of 1 lemon
1 teaspoon dried oregano
1 tablespoon chopped dill
1 tablespoon chopped parsley
1 teaspoon salt
1 teaspoon freshly ground black pepper

Trim the birds of their feet, wingtips and heads, as necessary. Spatchcock them as described above.

Combine all the marinade ingredients in a large mixing bowl. Add the quail to the marinade and use your hands to toss well so the birds are evenly coated. Cover with plastic wrap and leave to marinate in the refrigerator overnight.

When ready to cook, preheat your barbecue or grill to medium–high and season the quail lightly. Brush the grill with a little oil and place the birds, skin-side down, over the heat. Grill for around 2 minutes, then turn and grill for 1 further minute or so, or until cooked. Be careful not to overcook them – the breast meat should still be a little pink. Serve the quail hot from the grill with lemon wedges, a drizzle of extra-virgin olive oil and salad.

Serves 6 as a starter, or 2 hungry blokes as a meal

These are a favourite late-night snack of mine from Chinatown. Pigeon meat is rich and dark, and has a strong gamey flavour that works brilliantly with chilli-heat and prickly Sichuan pepper. It should be salty and spicy all at once, and leave a lingering buzz in your mouth and on your lips. You'll definitely need a few ice-cold beers to wash it down. But just a note about 'responsible cooking': deep-frying and alcohol consumption don't mix, especially when you're tired. So don't start your drinking until the cooking is all over!

Chilli-fried pigeon

4 x 450 g pigeons
2 tablespoons ground Sichuan pepper
1 tablespoon dried chilli flakes, or finely chopped fresh chilli
1 teaspoon salt
1 tablespoon freshly ground black pepper
4 tablespoons cornflour
vegetable oil for frying
lemon or lime wedges to serve

Spicy salt
1 teaspoon salt
1 teaspoon ground Sichuan pepper
1 teaspoon dried chilli flakes, or finely chopped fresh chilli
1 tablespoon chopped coriander

Dipping sauce
1 tablespoon finely chopped fresh chilli
¼ cup chopped coriander
3 tablespoons soy sauce
3 tablespoons sherry vinegar
juice of 1 lemon or lime

Prepare the pigeons by cutting off their heads, necks and claws and splitting them in half, lengthwise. Heat the oil in a deep-fryer or a large heavy-based frying pan to 175°C.

To make the spicy salt, mix all the remaining ingredients, except for the oil and lemon wedges, in a large mixing bowl. Add the pigeon halves to the bowl and toss in the spice mix until they are thoroughly coated. Fry them in batches until a glossy deep brown. If, like me, you like your pigeon rare, they'll need about 5 minutes. Cook them for longer if you prefer.

Remove the birds from the oil with a slotted spoon and drain on a wire rack.

Serve the pigeons hot, with lemon wedges, the spicy salt and dipping sauce and a few cold beers.

Serves 4

Roast pheasant with caramelised cherry and brandy glaze

As is often the case with game birds, the breast meat and legs need different cooking methods. I like to remove the legs, wings, undercarriages, necks and heads, leaving the breasts attached to the remaining carcass: this is what's known as the crown. The legs can be used to make Pheasant Pie (page 290) and the crown roasted separately.

I like to accompany this roast pheasant with sautéed spinach and Bread and Bacon Dumplings (page 302).

2 x 650 g pheasant crowns
salt
freshly ground black pepper
4 tablespoons olive oil

Caramelised Cherry and Brandy Glaze
(page 333)

Preheat the oven to 200°C.

Season the pheasant crowns with salt and pepper. Heat the oil in a heavy-based roasting tin and seal the pheasants over a medium heat, breast-side down, until golden brown. Turn the pheasants breast-side up and baste with the pan juices. Transfer to the oven and roast for 6–8 minutes. Transfer the birds to a warm platter, cover loosely with aluminium foil and leave to rest in a warm place for 10 minutes.

Warm the cherry glaze through in a medium saucepan. Slice the meat away from the breast bone and serve with a generous spoonful of sauce.

Serves 4

POULTRY

"A ROAST CHOOK IS THE MEAL I MOST LIKE TO COOK FOR THE FAMILY"

Poultry

Roast chicken was the very first meat that I ate, so it has a special place in my heart. In the early years of my childhood my father was a vegetarian and he insisted that my brother and I be brought up as vegos too. Family legend has it that for dinner one evening my nonna roasted a chook, and I, clearly not satisfied with the non-meat offerings, grabbed a drumstick from her plate.

Now I've always secretly suspected that Nonna might have edged that plate within my reach. She knew I wouldn't be able to resist, and true enough, that drumstick was gnawed and sucked clean. Shortly afterwards my dad gave up being a vegetarian. It seems that he, too, was seduced by the lure of a roast chicken. From then on my mother always had to cook two chickens for dinner to stop us boys and my dad fighting over it! To this day, a roast chook is one of my favourite meals, and the meal I love to cook most for the family. Nowadays it's my own three little boys who fight over it.

Technically speaking, any domesticated bird that is reared for the table comes under the heading of poultry. So as well as chicken and turkey, waterfowl such as duck and geese are poultry, while other birds, such as quail and pheasant are a little harder to categorise. I've decided to discuss them as game birds (Chapter 7), because although they are raised commercially, it is on a much smaller scale, and as such, more likely to be in conditions that mimic the wild.

We know that as early as the second millennium BC the Chinese were raising a wide variety of birds for consumption, and they gradually spread through Asia to the West. The Egyptians and Romans bred geese, ducks and chickens, while the Aztecs had domesticated the wild turkey centuries before the arrival of European explorers. There are many obvious reasons for the appeal of these birds: they are small (compared with beef cattle, say), easy to handle, have quick breeding cycles, and produce a vitally important by-product, the egg!

In the past, it was pretty common for most households (even in large cities) to have a few chickens fluttering around the backyard, but they were prized more for their regular supply of eggs, than as meat for the table. The bird itself was too valuable to be sacrificed for the cooking pot, unless a very special occasion required it.

Today things are very different. Over the last 50 years, demand for poultry – chicken in particular – has escalated dramatically, and to meet this demand most poultry birds are intensively farmed, the world over. The birds themselves look very different from their ancestors, and have been bred to put on weight rapidly, with minimum input from the farmer. What this means in many countries is that birds are raised in horrifically cramped conditions (to prevent them moving), and are fed high-protein diets and dosed with antibiotics. Millions of these miserable birds are slaughtered every year for the fast-food chains, the processed food industry and supermarkets, all of which exert continued and relentless pressure on the farmers to supply cheaper and cheaper birds.

In Australia the best that can be said for the broiler chicken (and turkey and duck, on a smaller scale) is that, at least it doesn't endure quite the same odious conditions as battery egg hens – these industries are quite separate and the poultry industry takes great pains to point out that it has strict regulations in place to safeguard the birds' welfare.

But although the large poultry producers would like to paint a rosy picture for us, insisting that chickens (and turkeys) are not raised in cages or fed hormones, and that they are free of antibiotics by the time they are slaughtered, these intensively reared birds still have lived horrible lives. It's worst of all for broiler chickens, which are raised indoors with up to 60,000 other birds (even free-range birds only have access to a limited amount of outdoor space), and although they are free to roam, by the time they are fully grown the available space for each bird is about the size of this book.

Selective breeding for accelerated weight gain means that by the time today's chooks reach slaughter weight (at around six to seven weeks of age) they cannot support the weight of their own bodies. As a result, they live in constant pain caused by kneeling in their own accumulated waste (which is generally not cleaned out over their lifespan), and suffer abnormally twisted limbs, hock burns on their knees and blisters on their breasts. Many die prematurely, while the rest endure considerable stress on the way to the slaughterhouse.

And if all that hasn't been enough to put you off your roast chicken, then think about what it actually tastes like. I'm fairly certain that many of our grandparents and parents will have a dim and distant memory of the days when chicken was actually tasty. But most of the younger generation have never experienced chicken as anything other than a pallid, bland and even tasteless meat, suited for little more than nuggets or chicken-in-a-bucket.

We do have a choice

Thankfully, many consumers these days are demanding birds that have been raised under more humane conditions. We just need to know what to look for.

Corn fed: This relates to taste rather than welfare. Corn-fed birds are raised conventionally, but receive a high level of corn in their diet. The corn itself is neither organic nor free of GMOs.

Chemical free: This relates to the way the meat is processed for the table, rather than to the way the bird is raised. It usually means that no chlorine has been used to wash the chickens.

Free-range: This means that once the birds are fully feathered (at around three weeks of age) they are allowed access to an outdoors run. Beak and toe trimming is not allowed. They must be fed 'natural foods' only and must not have been fed antibiotics at any stage during their life (unless under vet care). Currently, free-range chicken meat accounts for around 4 per cent of chicken produced in Australia, with roughly half of it also being organic.

Organic: The guidelines for raising organic birds are the most stringent. As well as being fed a diet free of antibiotics or vitamin or mineral supplements, insecticides or pesticides, they are generally allocated a greater area of space per bird than with other methods, and have outdoor access after 10 days of age. Beak and toe trimming is not allowed. Organic birds are slaughtered at 65–80 days of age, compared with 35–55 days for conventional and free-range birds.

POULTRY HYGIENE

Of all the meat we prepare and eat at home, we need to handle poultry especially carefully because it is very perishable. In addition to following the storage instructions above, do bear in mind the following points:

- Most food poisoning bacteria (such as salmonella) thrive between 20 and 60ºC, so keep poultry refrigerated at all times and never let it sit out at room temperature for more than 30 minutes.
- Store raw poultry in the coldest part of your fridge and don't let it come into contact with other foods.
- Defrost frozen poultry completely before cooking.
- Always use clean equipment (such as knives, boards, bowls and so on) when preparing poultry.
- Clean all equipment thoroughly after preparing poultry and before using again.
- Wash your hands thoroughly before and after handling raw poultry.
- Refrigerate any leftovers immediately.

HOW DO YOU KNOW WHEN IT'S COOKED?

Poultry needs to be thoroughly cooked, which is another reason why you must purchase a digital instant-read meat thermometer. It takes the guesswork out of determining doneness, and you can always be certain that your chicken or turkey will be perfectly cooked. A food thermometer inserted into the thickest part of the thigh should read 72ºC.

If you don't have a thermometer, there are some other tests to use. If you pierce the thickest part of the thigh with a skewer, the juices should run out clear and golden. If they are pink or red, it is not ready. Once the juices do run clear, wiggle the leg gently away from the body. If you feel it 'give', you can be quite sure the bird is cooked through.

CHICKEN

In Australia one out of three people eats chicken meat at least three times a week, with just about everybody eating it at least once a week. It's no surprise then that the chicken industry is huge, worth around $1.44 billion to our economy.

All modern breeds of chicken are descended from the wild red jungle fowl. In Australia the main chicken raised commercially for meat is the Cobb 500, which has been selectively bred for maximum weight gain in the shortest possible time. From a retail perspective, breed is not considered important; of more significance is the way the birds are raised and their diet.

The chicken industry in Australia is highly efficient and productive, with over 450 million chickens slaughtered all year round. Chickens are 'harvested' between 5 and 10 weeks of age, ranging in weight from around 1.2 kg (size 12) to 2.5 kg (size 25) and even more. At the other end of the scale, the poussin is a young chicken (three to four weeks of age, weighing 400–500 grams).

How to choose, store and cook chicken

Fresh and frozen chickens are widely available in supermarkets, poultry butchers and fresh produce markets. Fresh is always going to be a better option, with frozen mass-produced chickens being the lowest of the low in terms of quality. I've already talked about the available types of chicken, from conventional and corn-fed, to free-range and organic, and I strongly urge you to only buy good-quality, humanely reared chickens, wherever possible.

Chickens may be sold whole, or cut in various ways, depending on where you purchase them. In supermarkets you are most likely to find skinless chicken breasts, skinless chicken thighs, chicken wings and drumsticks. Elsewhere you will be able to buy chicken halves, breasts on or off the bone, chicken marylands (the thigh and leg attached), drumettes and wingettes. You will also be more likely to find chicken with the skin on.

Storing chicken

- Defrost frozen chicken overnight in the refrigerator. Once thawed, rinse and pat thoroughly dry. Cook within 24 hours.
- Unwrap and refrigerate fresh chicken immediately.
- Store chicken pieces in a Tupperware container, or sit them on a rack on a plate and cover with a tea towel.
- Whole chickens should be eaten within five days.
- Chicken pieces should be eaten within three days.
- Chicken mince should be eaten within two days.

Although I think there are few things to beat a roast chicken, one of the attractions of the meat is that it lends itself to so many different flavours and so many different ways of cooking. In fact every country and cuisine has its classic chicken dishes, from Indian curries, to French coq au vin, to Vietnamese salads. The breast and thigh meat are somewhat different, so as always you need to pick the appropriate cut for each dish.

Whole birds are ideal for roasting, pot-roasting and poaching. They can also be broken down into pieces for a casserole. Small whole chickens – especially poussins – may be split down the back and grilled or barbecued. One of my very favourite things to do with any whole bird – although it requires some good knife skills – is to bone it out completely, stuff it, roll and tie it before roasting. It makes a wonderfully economical dish, and everyone gets an equal share of meat and stuffing.

Chicken breast meat is pale and tender, as long as it isn't overcooked, when it can become dry and stringy. It lends itself brilliantly to poaching or baking in a foil package in the oven with herbs and a splash of wine. Cut into strips chicken breast meat makes terrific stir-fries, or can be skewered for grilled or barbecued kebabs.

Chicken thigh and leg meat is darker and more intensely flavoured than breast meat. These cuts can be roasted and grilled – and are especially good if marinated or rubbed with spice pastes and rubs before cooking. These cuts are also ideally suited to casseroles and braises, and are usually lightly browned first, before covering with an aromatic liquid and simmering until tender.

THINGS THAT LOVE CHICKEN
Butter, chilli, coriander, cream, garlic, ginger, leeks, lemon, lentils, lime, olive oil, onions, parsley, pepper, red peppers, red wine, rosemary, saffron, salt, smoked paprika, soy sauce, stuffings, tarragon, thyme, tomatoes, white wine

TURKEY

When the Spanish first landed in Mexico in the 16th century, they were greatly amused by a large, waddling, heavily plumaged bird with a curious gobbling call. This was the turkey, and it had been domesticated by the Aztecs for meat and eggs and for its gorgeous feathers. The Spanish introduced the turkey to Europe where it became very popular because of the generous amount of meat on its large body. But it was in North America that the turkey really came into its own. According to legend, the early Pilgrims ate turkey at the first Thanksgiving dinner, and it's been an annual tradition ever since. Today in the United States around 260 million turkeys are processed every year, and many of them go for the Thanksgiving dinner table.

Americans eat nearly 10 kg of turkey annually, compared with Australians, who eat a tiny 1 kg. Here in Australia it seems that we associate turkey firmly with Christmas and most of us don't really know what else to do with it. This is partly to do with the bird's reputation for being tricky to cook. The breast meat of our Christmas turkeys is renowned for being dry and flavourless, despite the processors' efforts to keep it moist with various 'self-basting' or 'pre-basted' techniques (which involve injecting the meat with water, fat and flavourings).

How to choose, store and cook turkey

In the weeks running up to Christmas the supermarkets begin stocking up on turkeys. You'll easily find whole turkeys (fresh and frozen) of various sizes, turkey 'buffets' (a whole breast for roasting), and stuffed turkeys rolls. But producers are making determined efforts to increase the appeal of turkey all year round, by making a wider range of cuts available to the consumer. So in many supermarkets you'll find cuts such as boned legs and whole breasts for roasting, thigh chops and strips, turkey mince, breast fillets, schnitzels and rolled breasts, and even turkey smoked ham.

Most of these birds come from the two large companies that control every aspect of Australia's small turkey industry – from breeding, to rearing and then processing the birds. The turkeys are intensively raised in sheds under similar conditions to conventional broiler chickens. These operations are similarly focused on economic production measures, aiming for quick-growing turkeys that can be pushed through to slaughter in the shortest possible time. These monster birds will be processed at anything from 9 weeks of age up to 18 weeks, depending on size demands.

Thankfully there is a growing number of enthusiastic small-scale turkey farmers in Australia. Their birds take up to 25 weeks to reach table weight and are reared in free-range and sometimes organic conditions. At this premium end of the market, producers also aim to get consumers interested in eating turkey all year round, and you should ask your butcher to try to source the cuts that you want.

Turkeys for roasting come in a range of sizes and you need to pick the appropriate size for the number of mouths you want to feed. Whole turkeys can weigh anything from 4 to 15 kilograms while turkey buffes range from 2.5 to 8 kilograms. In general, the larger the bird, the harder it is to cook satisfactorily – the breast will be overcooked and dry, the legs undercooked. As a rule of thumb, I would allow 250 grams per person for a buffet or rolled, stuffed turkey. Allow 300–350 grams per person from a whole bird.

Storing turkey

- Other than at Christmas time, whole turkeys are usually sold frozen.
- Defrost turkey overnight in the refrigerator. Once thawed, rinse and pat thoroughly dry. Cook within 24 hours.
- Store turkey cuts in a Tupperware container, or sit it on a rack on a plate and cover with a tea towel.
- Larger cuts of turkey should be eaten within five days.
- Small cuts should be eaten within three days.
- Turkey mince should be eaten within two days.

When roasting a turkey you will probably want to stuff one or both of the cavities (the main body or neck). Trussing the turkey holds the legs close to the body as it roasts and helps the bird cook evenly.

Turkeys are famously prone to drying out during roasting. There are several things you can do to prevent this: either stuff the breasts under the skin with butter or a moist stuffing, rub the breasts with liberal amounts of butter or drape them with slices of bacon, pancetta or even pork back fat.

DUCK

The best duck cooks in the world, in my view, are the Chinese (with the French coming a very close second) and if you want to be converted to this delicious bird, then I urge you to visit Chinatown. Many Asian restaurants will even have a selection of cooked ducks hanging in the window and you can buy them to take away for eating at home.

For most Australians, duck does tend to be something they prefer to eat in restaurants. It has a reputation for being very fatty and expensive – with one duck only providing enough meat to feed two people. But although it is something of a luxury item, duck can be a brilliantly rewarding bird to cook.

How to choose, store and cook duck

In different countries around the world there are many breeds of duck raised for the table. Some of the best known are famous English Aylesbury and Gessingham ducks, in France they prize the Nantais, Barbary and Rouennais breeds while in the USA they love their Long Island ducks. But for the most part, you'll have to go overseas to taste these beauties.

In Australia the most commonly bred eating duck is a cross between the Chinese pekin duck and the Aylesbury, with most going to the food service industry, rather than into shops. Nevertheless, farmed ducks are available, fresh and frozen, all year round. Some suppliers also provide muscovy ducks (which originally came from South America). These are bigger ducks, with a stronger flavour, but they do have a reputation for being a bit chewy.

There is a small number of free-range duck growers in some areas of Australia, which are often coss-bred from different varieties. These can be very exciting to try, if you have the opportunity, offering both tenderness and intense flavour.

THINGS THAT LOVE TURKEY
bacon, bread sauce, butter, cherry sauce, chestnuts, cornbread, cranberries, gravy, olive oil, onion, pepper, pumpkin, sage, salt, sausage meat, sweet potatoes,

THINGS THAT LOVE DUCK
Cherries, garlic, hoisin
sauce, honey, orange,
pepper, pomegranate,
quince, red cabbage, salt,
soy sauce, star anise,
turnips, vinegar.

Storing duck

- Defrost frozen duck overnight in the refrigerator. Once thawed, rinse and pat thoroughly dry. Cook within 24 hours.
- Unwrap and refrigerate fresh duck immediately.
- Store duck pieces in a Tupperware container, or sit them on a rack on a plate and cover with a tea towel.
- Whole ducks should be eaten within five days.
- Duck pieces should be eaten within three days.

Whole ducks are available (head on or off), and are great for roasting. The benefit of this high dry-heat method is that a lot of the fat that covers the breast renders down and keeps the meat moist.

Other readily available portions are duck breasts and whole duck legs. They each benefit from slightly different cooking methods and times. Duck breasts are best served when still a little pink; they are ideal for pan-frying, grilling and roasting. Duck legs need longer cooking as their dark meat tends to be tougher; they are wonderful for braising or turning into confit (page 255).

HOW DO YOU KNOW WHEN IT'S COOKED?

Because duck meat is darker than chicken or poultry, it lends itself more to cooking like beef or lamb. Different parts of the bird are suited to different types of cooking. The leg meat is tougher (because the leg muscles do more work), so it is ideal for longer, slowing cooking methods, such as braising.

Duck breasts can be treated more like beef or lamb steaks. In fact many people like to eat duck breasts very rare indeed. I recommend using a digital instant-read thermometer and following the cooking temperatures in the chart below, until the duck breast is cooked to your liking.

Remember that the reading will rise by about 5°C as the meat rests, so begin checking the temperature about 5 minutes before the end of the recommended cooking time.

rare	medium–rare	medium	medium–well	well done
35°C	45°C	55°C	65°C	75°C

The perfect roast chicken

More often than not this is the way I roast a chook, with a lovely herby butter stuffed beneath the skin, to keep the breast meat moist – to my mind the wings that go stickily crunchy and golden are the best bits. I serve it with Chunky-Cut Roasted Vegetables (page 307) and a simple sauce made from the pan juices.

1 x 2.4 kg free-range chicken
Herby Butter (page 349)
½ lemon
½ onion
2 garlic cloves, sliced

½ cup parsley leaves
4 sprigs thyme
salt
freshly ground black pepper
¼ cup olive oil

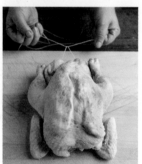

Preheat the oven to 180°C. Wipe the cavity of the chicken with paper towel and trim away any excess fat.

Hold the chicken firmly with one hand, and with the other, carefully insert your fingers under the skin that covers the breast meat. Gradually ease the skin away from each of the two chicken breasts to form a gap, being very careful not to tear the skin. Take knobs of the herby butter and gently ease it into the gap, as far in as you can, until it covers most of the breasts. Now pull the skin of the chicken breast gently forward, so that all of the meat is covered.

Stuff the lemon, onion, garlic and herbs inside the chicken's cavity and season with salt and pepper. Tie the chicken legs to the parson's nose as firmly as possible, then place it on a rack inside a large roasting tin. Use your hands to rub the olive oil into the skin of the chicken and season generously with salt and pepper.

Roast the chicken in the centre of the oven for 1¼–1¾ hours, although this is more of a guideline really; the actual cooking time will vary depending on your oven. Every 20 minutes or so during roasting, remove the chicken from the oven (not forgetting to close the oven door, to maintain the cooking temperature) and tip the roasting tin on an angle, so that the buttery juices pool in the corner. Baste the chicken all over with these juices, being a little careful, as the hot fat may sizzle and spit.

The chicken is cooked when the internal core temperature reaches 72°C. If you don't have a meat thermometer, insert a fork into the chicken's cavity and lift the bird up. Tilt it downwards and if the juices run clear the bird is cooked; if they're pink, then it needs more cooking.

Transfer the cooked chicken to a hot dish and leave it to rest for 15 minutes in a warm spot. To serve, use kitchen scissors to cut the bird into portions on the bone. To be honest, I'll do this any time, rather than carving it up into neat slices. Chicken tastes so much better when you can pick it up in your fingers and really get stuck in.

Serves 6, or 4 hungry blokes

Stir-fried chicken with Chinese mushrooms

There are endless versions of chicken stir-fries, and this is one of my favourites (although you can vary the ingredients any way you like). It may look like a long list of ingredients, but remember it will probably take you longer to assemble everything than to actually cook it.

Use fresh shiitake mushrooms if possible. If using dried shiitakes, remember that you'll need to reconstitute them by soaking them overnight in water (remove the stalks before slicing as they can be tough). And if you can't find shiitakes, then use Swiss browns instead.

For a really healthy stir-fry, you don't have to use much oil. Nor do you have to use the cornflour, although I really love the way it gives the chicken a lovely golden coating.

Marinade
1 teaspoon chopped garlic
1 teaspoon grated ginger
1 teaspoon finely chopped chilli
  (mild or hot, according to taste)
1 tablespoon sherry vinegar
1 tablespoon low-sodium soy sauce
1 teaspoon sesame seeds
¼ cup cornflour

400 g chicken breast fillets, skin removed
¼ cup vegetable oil, for frying
1 medium red onion, peeled and
  thinly sliced

1 garlic clove, crushed
1 x 4 cm piece ginger, thinly sliced
1 red chilli, finely chopped (mild or
  hot, according to taste)
1 red pepper, thinly sliced
150 g fresh or dried shiitake
  mushrooms, thinly sliced
150 g snow peas, trimmed and
  thinly sliced
½ cup chopped coriander
¼ cup chopped spring onions
2 tablespoons light soy sauce
2 tablespoons mirin

To make the marinade, combine all the ingredients, except for the cornflour, in a mixing bowl.

Cut the chicken into 1 cm x 6 cm strips. Add to the marinade and toss well so that the chicken is evenly coated. Cover, and leave to marinate in the refrigerator for 15–20 minutes while you prepare the ingredients for the rest of the dish.

When ready to cook, add the cornflour to the marinated chicken and mix well. It will all clump together to make a big sticky ball.

Heat the oil in a wok over a medium heat. Separate the chicken strips and fry in batches for about 1 minute, or until golden brown. Remove the chicken from the wok with a slotted spoon and drain on a wire rack.

When all the chicken has been cooked, tip off most of the oil from the wok, reserving about 2 tablespoons. Add the onion and stir-fry over a high heat for about 30 seconds, or until it starts to soften. Add the garlic, ginger and chilli and stir-fry for another 30 seconds, or until the garlic begins to colour. Add the red pepper, mushrooms and snow peas to the wok, one by one, so as to keep the temperature sizzling-hot. Stir-fry until the vegetables are just tender.

Return the chicken to the wok, add the coriander, spring onions, soy sauce and mirin and stir-fry for a further minute or so, or until the chicken is warmed through.

Serve immediately, hot from the wok, with steamed rice.

Serves 4

Southern-fried chicken

Southern-fried chicken is popular all over the USA, and it's usually cooked in a pressure-fryer, which is a miniature version of the ones used in fast food chains. The beauty of this method is that the chicken cooks very quickly, so it stays lovely and juicy. This is my version: the double coating of flour means that the batter is crisp and tasty, and the chicken within is tangy and moist.

Serve with Oven-Baked Organic Potato Chips (page 297) or sautéed potatoes.

1 x 2.4 kg chicken
2 teaspoons salt
2 teaspoons freshly ground
    black pepper
2 tablespoons sherry vinegar
vegetable oil for frying

Seasoned flour
1 cup cornflour
1½ cups plain flour
1 teaspoon salt
4 teaspoons freshly ground
    black pepper
1 teaspoon cinnamon

Egg wash
3 eggs
500 ml milk

Dipping sauce
¼ cup sherry vinegar
2 small red chillies, seeded
    and finely chopped

Use a sharp knife or poultry shears to joint the chicken, then cut into 12 smaller pieces and arrange them on a tray. Season generously and sprinkle on the vinegar, then set aside while you prepare the remaining ingredients.

Heat the oil in a deep-fryer or a large heavy-based frying pan to 180°C. Preheat the oven to 100°C.

Combine the seasoned flour ingredients in one bowl and the egg wash ingredients in another.

Dip the chicken pieces in the seasoned flour and shake off any excess. Dunk them into the egg wash and then back in the flour again. If you like a really crunchy coating, then you can repeat this process.

Cook the chicken in batches to maintain the temperature of the oil. If you overcrowd the fryer the temperature will drop and the batter won't be crisp. The chicken will take around 10–15 minutes to cook, and should be golden brown all over. Test for doneness by piercing a drumstick at the thickest part. If the juices run clear, the chicken is cooked. Remove the cooked chicken from the oil and drain briefly on paper towels. Transfer to a wire rack set in a roasting tin and keep warm in the oven while you cook the rest of the chicken.

Whisk together the vinegar and chilli to make a dipping sauce and serve.

Serves 4–6

Portuguese-style barbecued chicken skewers

I am a bit of a barbecue nut. I have several different barbecues at home – a Weber, a Tuscan grill, a table-top satay-griller and a classic gas-fired barbie – and think it's a great social way of entertaining. This Portuguese-style marinade is one of my favourites and I often use it for a whole chicken, poussins, or even quail, as well as chicken skewers. For a whole bird, whatever the size, I'll remove the backbone and flatten it out as outlined on page 156 to remove some of the bones. I then make deep slashes through the skin and flesh, which helps the marinade to penetrate the meat.

You can use metal or wooden skewers for this dish, but if you use wooden ones, remember to soak them for at least 30 minutes before threading on the marinated chicken.

1 x 1.2 kg skinless chicken breasts
2 tablespoons extra-virgin olive oil
4 garlic cloves, chopped
2 tablespoons smoked paprika
1 tablespoon finely chopped red chilli
   (mild or hot, according to taste)

1 teaspoon ground cumin
1 teaspoon dried oregano
juice of 1 lemon
¼ cup chopped coriander leaves
1 teaspoon salt
1 teaspoon freshly ground black pepper
lemon wedges to serve

Cut the chicken breast into 4 cm x 4 cm cubes. Place in a large mixing bowl with all the other ingredients, except the lemon wedges, and use your hands to toss well so the chicken is evenly coated. Cover with plastic wrap and leave to marinate in the refrigerator overnight.

When ready to cook, preheat your barbecue and if using bamboo skewers soak them for at least 30 minutes before threading on the marinated chicken.

Grill the chicken skewers over a high heat, turning frequently so that the flames don't burn the delicate meat.

Serve with a squeeze of lemon and your choice of salads – a Big Greek Salad (page 315) would be perfect.

Serves 6 (2 skewers each)

Sticky chicken wings with garlic and lemon

My nonna was born and raised in Egypt, and she often used to cook these tasty chicken wings for my brother and me when we were kids. They were an absolute favourite, and we could easily devour an entire platter within minutes. All that remained would be a pile of clean bones – and two little boys with sticky hands and smiling faces!

The wing comes in three parts, the mini drumstick (the thigh), the middle part (which has two skinny bones) and the small wing tip. There's very little meat on the wing tips, so I always cut them off and collect them in the freezer until I want to make stock (page 326–7).

2 kg chicken wings
¼ cup olive oil
10 garlic cloves, chopped
salt
freshly ground black pepper

juice of 3 lemons
½ cup roughly chopped parsley
1 tablespoon chopped thyme
lemon wedges to serve

Preheat the oven to 200°C.

In a large mixing bowl, mix the oil with the garlic, salt and pepper. Add the chicken wings and toss well, so they are evenly coated. Tip into a roasting tin and cover with aluminium foil. Bake for 20 minutes then remove the foil and pour on the lemon juice, parsley and thyme. Stir the wings around so they are all coated in the lemony-herb mixture, then return to the oven and bake for another 20 minutes, uncovered. By the end of the cooking time they should be a gorgeous golden brown and lovely and sticky.

Serve hot from the oven with lemon wedges and plenty of napkins.

Serves 6 as a snack, or 2 greedy boys

When I was living in London I had the pleasure of working with many Algerian chefs. They were all wonderful people, warm and friendly, and very passionate – whenever there was a scuffle in the kitchen, you could be sure one of the Algerian boys was in the middle of it. I loved their warmth and humour and really enjoyed learning about their country and their food. We had many a good Algerian-inspired 'staff' meal together, out in the back laneway, crouched between the garbage bins. This recipe was always a winner. Serve it with couscous or steamed rice, and perhaps a simple green salad.

Spicy Algerian chicken thighs

2 red peppers
4 tablespoons olive oil
2 small red chillies, finely chopped
1 onion, sliced
6 garlic cloves, chopped
1 teaspoon grated ginger
1 teaspoon cumin seeds, dry-roasted and ground
1 teaspoon coriander seeds, dry-roasted and ground
zest of 1 lemon

juice of 2 lemons
1 cup roughly chopped coriander (stalks and leaves)
¼ cup extra-virgin olive oil
6 x 250 g chicken marylands, skin on
salt
freshly ground black pepper
2 cups good-quality chicken stock or water
200 g green olives, pitted and halved

Halve the peppers lengthwise and rub them all over with 2 tablespoons of the olive oil. Grill, skin-side up, until black and charred. Transfer to a bowl and cover with plastic wrap. When cool enough to handle, peel off the skin and slice away the seeds and pith. Chop roughly and place in a blender with the chillies, onion, garlic, ginger, spices, zest and juice of 1 lemon and half the chopped coriander. Blitz on high to form a rough purée. Add the extra-virgin olive oil and blitz briefly to incorporate.

Use a sharp knife to trim away any excess fat from the chicken thighs. Slice 3 deep grooves into the flesh through the skin. Season generously with salt and pepper.

Heat the remaining 2 tablespoons of olive oil in a large, heavy-based casserole dish over a medium heat. Add the chicken marylands, skin-side down first, and sauté until brown all over. Pour on the purée then add the stock or water. Add the olives and stir everything together well. Cover the casserole and simmer very gently for 1–1½ hours, stirring frequently to ensure the sauce doesn't catch and burn. At the end of the cooking time, the chicken will be very tender and falling away from the bones.

When ready to serve, stir in the remaining lemon juice and chopped coriander. Taste and adjust the seasoning to your liking.

Serves 6

My wife often makes dumpling soups at home for our three small boys. They're a great way of sneaking in extra nutritional goodness to their diet in a way that they love. Adding dumplings to soup is an idea that crosses all kinds of food cultures, and it's got to be the best comfort food around. I was raised on tortellini in brodo, but today I'm just as likely to crave an Asian-style wonton soup, such as this one.

The heart of a good dumpling soup is the broth and in this recipe I roast half the chicken bones in the oven until they are a sticky dark brown. This makes the broth much richer in flavour as well as a deeper colour.

Asian-style chicken dumpling soup

Chicken broth
2 tablespoons vegetable oil
1 kg chicken carcasses
1 onion, chopped
2 large carrots, chopped
3 sticks celery, chopped
I head of garlic, cut in half
1 bunch coriander, roots only, scraped clean
4 tablespoons ketjap manis
3 tablespoons low-sodium soy sauce
1 tablespoon hoisin sauce
2 star anise
1 stick cinnamon

To serve
Asian Chicken Dumplings (page 303)
soy sauce
finely sliced red chillies
finely shredded spring onions
coriander leaves

To make the chicken broth, preheat the oven to 190°C. Drizzle the oil in a roasting tin. Roughly chop the chicken carcasses and add half of them to the tin. Roast for 15–20 minutes, stirring occasionally to stop them sticking and burning. When the bones are a deep golden brown remove them from the oven and tip into a colander to drain.

Transfer the roasted bones to a large saucepan or stockpot. Add a splash of water to the roasting tin and stir to scrape up any caramelised residue. Add to the saucepan with the rest of the chicken bones and all the remaining broth ingredients.

Cover with water and bring to the boil slowly. Skim away any scum and impurities as they rise to the surface. When the stock boils, lower the heat and simmer gently for 1½–2 hours, skimming frequently.

Remove the pan from the heat and leave to cool slightly before straining through a fine sieve into a bowl or jug. If not using immediately, cover and refrigerate for up to 4 days or freeze for up to 3 months.

When ready to eat, bring the broth to a gentle simmer and add the dumplings. Simmer for 5 minutes until the dumplings are cooked. Ladle into 6 serving bowls and serve, drizzled with soy sauce and garnished with chillies, spring onions and coriander leaves.

Serves 6

Nonna's chicken soup

This is another dish that takes me right back to my early childhood. When we visited my nonna, she nearly always had a big pot of chicken soup on the stove and the wonderful aroma would fill the house.

Nonna's soup is very easy to make, and is great to freeze for cold winter nights. When I make it I usually throw in a couple of wings and thighs, as well as the chicken carcasses. It's amazing how much meat you'll get. Feel free to use different vegies (I sometimes add a handful of spinach, or silverbeet from the garden), and add your choice of rice, vermicelli noodles, or alphabet pasta for the kids. When we make this soup at the restaurant we throw in off-cuts of fresh pasta. And please don't stress out too much about chilling the stock and skimming away every skerrick of fat. As far as I'm concerned it all adds to the flavour.

1½ kg chicken carcasses, plus a couple of wings and thighs
2 large carrots, cut into large chunks
3 sticks celery, cut into large chunks
2 tomatoes, halved
2 large onions, halved
10 garlic cloves, halved
2 bay leaves
4 sprigs thyme

5 stalks parsley
1 tablespoon salt
1 teaspoon freshly ground black pepper
½ cup cooked rice or pasta (optional)
2 eggs, lightly beaten
juice of 1 lemon
½ cup chopped parsley
freshly grated parmesan to serve

Put the chicken carcasses into a large stock pot and pour on enough water to cover. Bring to the boil slowly, skimming away any froth or scum that rises to the surface. Add the vegetables, garlic, herbs and seasonings, and bring back to the boil. Lower the heat and simmer gently, uncovered, for 1–1½ hours, skimming frequently.

Strain through a fine sieve into a clean saucepan. Tip the chicken bones and vegetables out onto a tray and leave to cool. When cool enough to handle, pick off the chicken meat, discarding the skin and bones. Chop the meat and vegetables into small pieces. Add them to the chicken stock and bring to the boil. Lower the heat to a simmer, and add the cooked rice or pasta, if using.

In a small bowl, whisk together the egg, lemon juice and parsley, and season lightly. Tip into the simmering soup and whisk gently with a fork. As it cooks, the whisked egg forms long 'rags'. Once they rise to the surface, remove the pan from the heat. Serve straight away with freshly grated parmesan and warm crusty bread.

Serves 6

Chicken, avocado and watercress salad with soft goat's cheese

Chicken breast meat is often dry and disappointing, but this poaching method ensures that it stays moist, juicy and tender. I love to serve this light summer salad with a chilled glass of riesling. It's just the thing for ladies who lunch.

600 g chicken breast fillets, skin removed
1 cup white wine
1 carrot, roughly chopped
1 stick celery, roughly chopped
½ onion, roughly chopped
1 bay leaf
3 sprigs thyme
1 teaspoon salt

Dressing
3 tablespoons lemon juice
3 tablespoons extra-virgin olive oil
1 tablespoon finely chopped dill
salt
freshly ground black pepper

Salad
1 bunch watercress, washed and leaves picked
1 small bunch frisée (curly endive), inner pale leaves only
1 cup parsley leaves
¼ cup chives, cut into 4 cm lengths
¼ cup dill, roughly chopped
200 g soft goat's cheese, roughly crumbled
100 g green olives, pitted
1 avocado, peeled and cut into 6 wedges

To poach the chicken, place all the ingredients in a heavy-based saucepan and add enough water to cover. Bring to the boil, then lower the heat and simmer gently for 8 minutes. Turn off the heat and leave the chicken to cool in the poaching liquid. When cold, remove the chicken from the liquid and refrigerate until ready to serve.

When ready to serve, slice the chicken into batons, around 1.5 cm x 6 cm. In a large mixing bowl, combine the dressing ingredients and whisk together well. Add the chicken pieces and toss gently.

In another large mixing bowl, combine all the salad ingredients, except for the avocado, and toss gently.

To assemble the salad, place a slice of avocado in the base of each of 6 shallow bowls. Divide the dressed chicken between the bowls, arranging it around the avocado. Top each with a generous handful of the salad and serve straight away.

Serves 6

Chicken ballottine

A ballottine is a piece of meat or a bird that has been boned out, stuffed and reassembled before cooking. I'm not going to pretend that this is a quick-and-easy dish to knock up for a weekday dinner, but it's a really good recipe to practise your boning skills on. In restaurant kitchens this job is usually given to an apprentice or trainee cook as their welcome to the world of butchery.

I really urge you to have a go at learning how to bone out various cuts of meat. In this recipe we start small, with a chicken maryland. Most of the work can be done way ahead of time, so it's a great dish to master for dinner parties. Serve with Red Wine Risotto (page 305) and a green leaf salad.

Stuffing
1 tablespoon butter
100 g wood mushrooms, roughly chopped
1 x 300 g chicken breast, roughly chopped
1 tablespoon thyme
¼ cup chopped parsley
100 g ham or smoky bacon, cut into 1 cm x 1 cm dice

1 tablespoon brandy
1 teaspoon Dijon mustard
1 tablespoon shelled pistachio nuts
1 teaspoon salt
1 teaspoon freshly ground black pepper

6 chicken marylands, skin on
olive oil
salt
freshly ground black pepper

To make the stuffing, heat the butter in a non-stick frying pan until it sizzles. Add the mushrooms and sauté for 3–4 minutes until softened. Set aside to cool completely.

Put the chopped chicken breast into the bowl of a food processor. Add an ice cube and pulse for 20–60 seconds to make a smooth paste. Scrape into a mixing bowl and add the remaining ingredients. Mix together well, then divide into 6 equal portions and refrigerate until needed.

Lay the chicken marylands on a chopping board, skin-side down. Use a small sharp boning knife to cut into the flesh to the start of the thigh bone. Cut along the bone to the knuckle, scraping the flesh away from the bone along its length. Continue from the knuckle to the end of the drumstick to expose the bones completely. Lift them up and away from the flesh and cut them free, taking care not to pierce the flesh.

Place each maryland on a large square of plastic wrap, skin-side down and season with salt and pepper. Place a portion of stuffing on each maryland and use the plastic wrap to help bring the chicken up around the stuffing. Twist the plastic wrap tightly to form a ball. Wrap each ballottine tightly in aluminium foil.

Place the 6 ballotines in a large saucepan of cold water over a medium heat. Just before the water boils, lower the heat to a gentle simmer. Cook for 15 minutes, then lift the ballottines out of the pan and transfer them to a bowl of iced water to cool down. When completely cold, unwrap the foil and carefully remove the plastic wrap. The ballotines can be prepared to this stage up to 3 days ahead of time.

Preheat your oven to 200°C. Place the ballottines on a rack inside a large roasting tin. Brush each ballottine lightly with oil and season. Roast for 12–15 minutes until cooked through and golden brown.

Serve a whole ballottine each, or cut into thick slices to show off the stuffing.

Serves 6

Chicken a la cacciatore

Cacciatore means 'hunter' in Italian, and the story goes that this tasty one-pot dish used to be made for the hunter to eat on his return from a hard day out in the forests and fields – using the spoils of his endeavours. It's often made using rabbit instead of chicken, and in my house we consider it the perfect dish for using up all those vegies that have been sitting in the crisper for a few days and may not be quite at the peak of perfection! And while I use sweet paprika here, to vary the flavour you could also use the wonderfully pungent Spanish smoked paprika.

This is a rustic dish and is best put straight onto the table so that everyone can help themselves. Serve with lots of crusty bread and a full-flavoured red wine.

1 x 2.4 kg free-range chicken, jointed
1½ tablespoons sweet paprika
2 tablespoons thyme, roughly chopped
2 teaspoons salt
2 teaspoons freshly ground black pepper
olive oil, for frying
2 red peppers
4 anchovies
2 red onions, sliced
6 garlic cloves, crushed

2 bay leaves
100 g black olives, pitted
3 large field mushrooms, thickly sliced
2 large carrots, sliced into rounds
6 sprigs thyme
1 sprig rosemary
2 cups red wine
1 cup chicken stock or water
3 cups tomato purée or tomato passata
¼ cup chopped parsley

Preheat the oven to 160°C.

In a large mixing bowl, combine the chicken pieces with the paprika, thyme, salt and pepper. Toss well so that they are evenly coated.

Heat a large, heavy-based casserole dish over a medium heat and add just enough oil to cover the base. When the oil is hot, brown the chicken in batches, so that the heat stays high. Transfer the browned chicken pieces to a plate and keep warm.

Halve the peppers lengthwise and rub them all over with a little more of the olive oil. Grill, skin-side up, until black and charred. Transfer to a bowl and cover with plastic wrap. When cool enough to handle, peel off the skin and slice away the seeds and pith. Chop roughly and place in a blender. Blitz on high to form a rough purée.

Add another splash of oil to the casserole and heat until it starts to sizzle. Add the anchovies, and using a wooden spoon, stir over a medium heat until they begin to disintegrate. Add the onions to the pot and sauté until they soften. Add the pepper pureé to the casserole with the garlic, bay leaves, olives, mushrooms and carrots and sauté for 3–4 minutes. Add the herbs – I like to tie them together with a piece of string, so I can fish them out at the end – then the red wine, stock and tomato purée. Season again to taste, then stir everything together well and bring to a gentle simmer.

Cover the casserole with a lid or aluminium foil, and bake in the oven for 2 hours. The vegetables should all cook down to a lovely rich, tomatoey sauce, and the chicken itself should fall from the bone easily.

When ready to eat, whip out the bundle of herbs, scatter on the parsley, and take to the table to serve.

Serves 6

This is a wonderful stuffing that is a bit savoury, a bit sweet, and a bit spicy. I like to put plenty of butter between the breast and skin, as it helps to keep the breast meat moist and adds lots of garlicky, herby flavour.

Roast turkey with pumpkin and pine nut stuffing

1 x 6.4 kg turkey
¼ cup olive oil
salt
freshly ground black pepper

Garlic and herb butter
300 g softened butter
1 teaspoon salt
1 teaspoon freshly ground black pepper
¼ cup chopped parsley
2 garlic cloves, finely chopped
2 tablespoons chopped thyme

Stuffing
400 g diced roasted pumpkin (choose Queensland blue or butternut, both of which stay quite firm when roasted)
½ small loaf sourdough, crusts removed and cut into 2 cm dice
2 eggs, lightly beaten
¼ cup pine nuts
100 g smoky bacon, cut into 1 cm dice
¼ cup runny honey
¼ cup chopped parsley
¼ cup chopped sage
¼ cup thyme leaves
1 tablespoon chopped rosemary
1 teaspoon ground cinnamon
1 teaspoon ground ginger or grated fresh ginger
1 tablespoon salt
1 tablespoon freshly ground black pepper

Preheat the oven to 180°C.

To make the garlic and herb butter, place the butter in a mixing bowl with the other ingredients and use your fingers to scrunch everything together well. This is a great job to give to the kids.

Hold the turkey firmly with one hand, and with the other, carefully insert your fingers under the skin that covers the breast meat. Gradually ease the skin away from each of the two breasts to form a gap, being very careful not to tear the skin. Take knobs of the butter and gently ease them into the gap, as far in as you can, until it covers most of the breasts. Now pull the skin gently forward over the turkey breast, so that all of the meat is covered.

To make the stuffing, place all the ingredients in a large bowl and mix together well. Pack the stuffing into the turkey's main cavity, filling it completely, but not too tightly. Any leftover stuffing can be baked in foil alongside the turkey.

Use a long piece of butcher's twine to tie the back legs to the parson's nose. Place the turkey on a rack inside a large roasting tin and rub all over with olive oil. Season with salt and pepper and cover loosely with aluminium foil. Roast in the centre of the oven for 2 hours, or until cooked. After 1½ hours, remove the foil and baste the turkey. Continue basting every 10 minutes or so, until cooked. If your bird doesn't have its own temperature gauge, and you don't have a meat thermometer, insert a fork into the turkey's cavity and lift the bird up. Tilt it downwards and if the juices run clear the bird is cooked; if they're pink, then it needs more cooking.

Transfer the cooked turkey to a hot dish and leave it to rest for 15 minutes in a warm spot. Use the pan juices to make Nanna's Gravy (page 330). Serve the turkey with all the trimmings.

Serves 8–10

Christmas turkey galantine

Every year as Christmas rolls around, my friends get on the phone and start begging me to make their annual turkey galantine. A galantine is a whole bird – in this case, a turkey – that's boned out, stuffed, and reassembled. All you need to do is stick it in the oven and roast it to a gorgeous golden brown. It's easy to carve, and everyone gets a bit of everything in one slice. It really is Christmas dinner made easy!

Ask your butcher to bone the turkey out completely for you, reserving the bones so you make stock for gravy.

1 x 5 kg turkey
olive oil
salt
freshly ground black pepper
1 onion, quartered
4 garlic cloves, unpeeled
1 large carrot, quartered
1 stick celery, quartered

Stuffing
2 tablespoons olive oil
1 onion, finely diced
6 garlic cloves, finely chopped
6 button mushrooms
750 g pork mince

100 g duck livers, chopped
½ cup diced smoked ham
½ cup breadcrumbs
1 egg
50 ml whisky
2 tablespoons Dijon mustard
100 g unsalted butter, cut into
   1 cm dice
2 tablespoons chopped thyme
1 teaspoon ground allspice
¼ cup chopped parsley
1 tablespoon salt
1 tablespoons freshly ground
   black pepper
olive oil

To make the stuffing, heat the olive oil in a large, non-stick frying pan. Add the onion and sauté gently until soft and translucent. Add the garlic and mushrooms and sauté for a few more minutes. Tip into a large mixing bowl and leave to cool.

Add all the remaining stuffing ingredients to the bowl and mix well, making sure the butter is evenly distributed.

Lay the boned turkey out on a work surface, skin-side down. Season with salt and pepper. Arrange the stuffing down the centre of the turkey, shaping it into a fat log. Bring the sides of the turkey up and over the stuffing and secure them through the skin and flesh with a long metal skewer. Tie the galantine securely with butcher's string at 6 cm intervals. Secure the openings at either end with skewers.

When ready to roast, preheat the oven to 190°C. Place the turkey, seam-side down, on a rack inside a large roasting tin. Rub all over with olive oil, season and cover loosely with aluminium foil. Roast for 1 hour, then remove the foil and baste. Continue cooking for another 2 hours, basting the turkey every 15 minutes or so. The galantine is cooked when the internal core temperature reaches 72°C. If you don't have a meat thermometer, then use a thin skewer to pierce the thickest part of the meat: if the juices run clear the galantine is cooked; if they're pink, then it needs more cooking.

Remove the cooked galantine to a warm serving platter and cover loosely with foil. Keep warm and allow to rest for 30–40 minutes in a warm place before serving with your choice of vegies and gravy.

Serves 8–12

Turkey frittata with balsamic syrup

After Christmas day, most people have a fridge full of turkey leftovers. This recipe is a great way to use them up, and you'll hardly know that you're eating turkey – yet again. In fact, the tangy balsamic syrup makes this frittata so tasty you'll find people coming back for seconds. Serve with a Watercress Salad (page 315) and warm crusty bread.

You'll need a large non-stick, ovenproof frying pan or oven tray to make the frittata. To make it really easy to serve, line the pan with baking paper so you can simply lift the frittata out and cut it into wedges.

15 free-range eggs
⅓ cup olive oil
2–3 cups chopped turkey leg meat, skin, sinews and gristly bits removed
2 cups diced vegetable leftovers (roast pumpkin, potatoes, onions, peas, beans and even leftover stuffing)

¼ cup chopped parsley
1½ teaspoons salt
1½ teaspoons freshly ground black pepper
Balsamic Syrup (page 347) to serve
parmesan cheese to serve

Preheat the oven to 200°C. Whisk the eggs in a large mixing bowl.

Heat half the oil in a large, non-stick, ovenproof frying pan or oven tray. Add the chopped turkey and vegetables and fry over a gentle heat, stirring from time to time, until warmed through. Add the parsley and season with salt and pepper.

Pour the egg mixture into the pan on top of the turkey and vegetables and stir gently for 3–5 minutes until it begins to set underneath. Transfer the pan to the oven for 15 minutes, or until the frittata is cooked through. The centre should be springy to the touch.

Cut into wedges and serve drizzled with balsamic syrup and sprinkled with a generous handful of parmesan.

Serves 6–8

Most people know that sour, tangy fruits, such as orange and cherries, go brilliantly with duck's rich, dark meat. I also like to use pomegranate, a slightly more unusual fruit, which has a distinctive sweet-sour tang and complements duck perfectly.

Don't worry about trying to get hold of fresh pomegranates. Pomegranate syrup (also called molasses) is available throughout the year from specialist food stores and Middle Eastern grocers. It's dark and sticky and is easy to make into a glaze. Because it caramelises quickly, don't start basting the ducks until about three-quarters of the way through the cooking time.

Substitute ripe nectarines for the pears, when they are in season.

Roast duck with pomegranate glaze

2 x 1.8 kg ducks
salt
freshly ground black pepper
1 onion, quartered
1 orange, quartered
4 garlic cloves, sliced

1 bunch thyme
5 tablespoons pomegranate molasses
4 tablespoons olive oil
2 bunches watercress, leaves picked
4 ripe pears, sliced
½ quick-pickled red onion
   (see page 346 for method)
pomegranate seeds (optional)

Preheat the oven to 200°C.

Remove the ducks' necks (if still attached) and trim away any loose fat. Cut off the first wing joints and remove any giblets from inside the birds. Season each cavity generously with salt and pepper. Divide the onion, orange, garlic and thyme evenly between the birds, tucking them snugly inside the cavities. Drizzle 1 tablespoon of pomegranate molasses into each bird then use a long piece of butcher's string to tie the back legs to the parson's nose. This will seal the cavity and flavour the bird from the inside.

Place the ducks on a rack inside a large roasting tin and rub them all over with olive oil. Season generously and roast in the centre of the oven for 1–1½ hours, depending on your oven.

Every 15 minutes or so during roasting, remove the ducks from the oven (not forgetting to close the oven door, to maintain the cooking temperature) and tip the roasting tin on an angle, so that the fat pools in the corner. Baste the ducks all over, being a little careful, as the hot fat may sizzle and spit.

Three-quarters of the way through the cooking time, carefully tip off about ¼ cup of the hot duck fat and mix it with the remaining 3 tablespoons of pomegranate molasses to make a glaze. Stir well and brush onto the ducks. Repeat several times until the ducks are cooked a rich dark brown, reserving a little of the glaze for serving.

Transfer the cooked ducks to a hot plate and leave them to rest for 10 minutes in a warm spot. To serve, use kitchen scissors or a cleaver to cut the birds into portions on the bone.

Pile the duck pieces onto a large serving platter and top with the watercress, pears and onion. Drizzle with a little of the reserved pomegranate glaze and scatter on a few pomegranate seeds.

Serves 4

Seared duck breast with red cabbage, apple and caraway

These days it is fairly easy to find duck breasts at the market and butcher's shops. I particularly like muscovy ducks, as they are larger, and their meat is darker and tastier.

This is one dish where you really must leave the skin on. It cooks to a lovely golden crispness and helps to keep the meat moist in the high heat of the oven.

4 muscovy duck breasts, skin on
salt
freshly ground black pepper

1 tablespoon extra-virgin olive oil
Red Cabbage with Apple and Caraway
(page 310)

Preheat the oven to 200°C.

Season the duck breasts all over with salt and pepper. Heat the oil in a heavy-based, oven proof pan. Add the duck breasts to the pan, skin-side down. Sear over a medium–high heat for 4–5 minutes, until the skin is golden brown. Turn the duck breasts over and transfer to the oven for 6–8 minutes, which will cook them rare. Increase the time, if you prefer them more thoroughly cooked. Remove the duck from the oven and leave to rest for 5 minutes.

While the duck is cooking, prepare the red cabbage following the method on page 310. By the time the cabbage is tender, the duck will be nicely rested.

To serve, spoon the cabbage onto plates. Slice each duck breast on an angle and arrange on top.

Serves 4

Shredded duck with mushrooms, lemon thyme and papardelle pasta

This is a wonderful and slightly unusual way of using confit duck. Of course you could always use leftovers from a cooked duck, instead.

At La Luna Bistro we make our own fresh pasta flavoured with saffron for this dish. These days there is a wide choice of fresh and dried gourmet pasta to choose from, so be as adventurous as you like. And if you feel inspired to make your own ... then go for it!

¼ cup extra-virgin olive oil
1 onion, finely sliced
3 garlic cloves, finely chopped
100 g butter
200 g mixed mushrooms (Swiss brown, shiitake and oyster)

500 g papardelle pasta
2 tablespoons chopped lemon thyme
¼ cup chopped parsley
400 g Confit Duck Leg (page 255), shredded
grated parmesan to serve

Heat the oil in a heavy-based frying pan. Add the onion and garlic and sauté for 5–8 minutes until golden brown. Add the butter to the pan and heat until it begins to foam. Add the mushrooms and stir everything together well. Sauté for 5 minutes or so, or until the mushrooms are tender.

Meanwhile, cook the pasta in a large pan of boiling, salted water. Then drain well.

When ready to serve, add the thyme, parsley and duck to the sautéed mixture. Tip the cooked papardelle into the pan and toss everything together well. Serve straight away with plenty of freshly grated parmesan.

Serves 6

Duck crêpes with pears, walnuts and curly endive

Duck and pancakes partner each other proudly in Chinese cookery. This recipe is much more 'French Bistro', but the marriage is just as good.

Crêpes
1 cup plain flour
pinch salt
1 tablespoon chopped thyme
1 tablespoon chopped parsley
1 egg
2 cups milk
melted butter or olive oil, for
  cooking the crêpes

Duck stuffing
400 g Confit Duck Leg (page 255)
1 onion, finely chopped, sweated
  and cooled
1 tablespoon chopped thyme
¼ teaspoon salt
¼ teaspoon pepper
2 tablespoons chopped parsley
splash of lemon juice

Salad
2 ripe pears, thinly sliced
1 small bunch frisée (curly endive),
  inner heart only
½ bunch chives, cut into 3 cm batons
¼ cup toasted walnuts
juice of 1 lime
3 tablespoons extra-virgin olive oil
salt
freshly ground black pepper
Balsamic Syrup (page 347), to serve
  (optional)

To make the crêpes, put all the dry ingredients in a large mixing bowl and mix together. Make a well in the flour and crack in the egg. Work in some of the flour to form a paste. Gradually pour in the milk, whisking all the time, until the mixture is very smooth and has the consistency of thin cream. Cover with a tea towel and leave for 30 minutes to rest.

Heat a large, non-stick frying pan and brush lightly with butter or oil. Ladle in some batter and swirl the pan so that the batter covers the base thinly and evenly. Cook for 1 minute over a medium heat. When the underside is golden brown, flip the pancake over and cook for another 30 seconds until just cooked. Transfer to a plate and cover with a tea towel. Repeat with the rest of the batter, which should be enough to make around 20 crêpes. The crêpes can be made ahead of time.

To make the duck stuffing, put all the ingredients into a blender or food processor, and blitz for 5–10 seconds to form a rough paste.

Preheat the oven to 180°C and lightly oil a baking tray.

Lay the crêpes out on your work surface. Spread one half with a generous spoonful of the duck stuffing and fold over to enclose. Fold in half again to form a triangle. Arrange the stuffed crêpes on the prepared baking tray and cook in the oven for 5–10 minutes until warmed through and slightly crisp around the edges.

To make the salad, combine all the ingredients, except for the balsamic syrup, in a large mixing bowl and toss gently to combine.

To serve, arrange 2 crêpes on each plate and drizzle with balsamic syrup if using. Place a mound of salad on the side and serve straight away.

Serves 6

OFFAL

9

"...FAR FROM BEING SCARY, A PIG'S HEAD IS A JOY."

Offal

Offal definitely falls into the 'love it or loathe it' category of foodstuffs. There are no prizes for guessing which camp I belong to – especially since I've devoted an entire chapter to the stuff! But as well as finding these more unusual parts of the animal quite delicious, I also believe that we humans have a responsibility not to waste any part of the animals that die in order that we might live. And that means eating every little bit of them.

To be honest, I don't really understand why some people have such strong objections to eating offal. If you think about it logically, why is it so much worse to eat an animal's ear, or its tongue, than it is to eat the muscles in its thigh, or in its bum? (What did you think the rump was?) It's all about what you're used to, I suppose, which is going to be quite different, depending on when, where and how you grew up.

So while most people in the wealthy West won't even consider eating offal, in many more countries around Asia, the Middle East and Europe it is prized as a delicacy. Think of how the Spanish love their blood sausages and bull's testicles, or the Italians their calf's liver alla Veneziana. In France they adore pig's trotters and fricassées made from kidneys or sweetbreads. The Turks turn tripe into a soup that is widely eaten as a hangover cure, and grilled intestines are a popular street snack. And throughout the Middle East and China you'll see offal butchers selling everything from camel's heads to ox tendons to monkey's brains. There is even a strong offal tradition in Britain – think of brawn, chitterlings, faggots and potted hough, not to mention the Scots' devotion to black pudding and haggis.

So what exactly is offal? The word itself supposedly comes from the 'fall off' in the abattoir – which conveys quite vividly the way the guts and intestines spill out of the suspended carcass onto the floor. As well as the animal's internal organs, offal also extends to the extremities: the head (and everything inside it), the feet, ears, nose and tail.

Offal and nutrition

Offal is a rich source of nutrients. It is high in protein, low in carbohydrate and contains less fat than much of the meat that comes from animal muscle. In general, offal products are also richer than lean meat in many vitamins, minerals and trace elements – in particular vitamin A, the B vitamins, iron, folate and zinc.

On the downside, most offal (except for heart) is high in cholesterol and also contains high levels of purines, which you should avoid if you suffer from gout. Pregnant women are also advised to avoid offal – especially liver, which is particularly high in vitamin A, which can cause birth defects in early pregnancy.

How and where to buy offal

The aversion to offal has intensified in recent years – especially in the UK and in the USA – because of health scares such as BSE (bovine spongiform encephalopathy) and scrapie (a similar degenerative disease in sheep). In the UK, abattoirs are required by law to remove all parts of cattle or sheep that might carry BSE – which means that brains are definitely off the menu.

While we are free of these diseases in Australia, it is still really important to buy offal from a reliable source. Many of these soft organs and glands play an important role in the body's defence mechanisms. They are responsible for filtering out toxins, waste and infections, so they are especially vulnerable to a build-up of chemicals and damage caused by disease or stress. An understanding of the animal's diet and lifestyle is therefore even more important than with other meat.

Furthermore, freshness is absolutely essential when you are buying offal. Because offal cuts are 'soft', and because of the job they do in the body, they deteriorate much more quickly than other types of meat.

In Australia most offal is exported to countries that appreciate it more than we do. Some offal is virtually impossible to find here and you are certainly extremely unlikely to be able to buy it in your local supermarket. Your own butcher should be able to buy most offal in for you, but if you are after a good range of different cuts then you should go to a specialist butcher. Butchers that sell to Asian, Greek, Turkish or Arab communities will be a good bet – you'll almost certainly find a good turnover in sheep products in halal butchers.

So what should you look for? Fresh offal should look super-fresh. It should be firm and glossy, not dry and shrivelled around the edges. And if there is even the faintest whiff about it, then you should avoid it.

PIG'S HEAD
Far from being scary, a whole pig's head is a joy – and it is something that you should be able to source relatively easily, as long as you give your butcher a bit of notice. At La Luna Bistro we use the whole head to make brawn (page 259), but we also break it down and use the specific parts to make Cotechini (page 270) and sausages.

BRAINS
People seem to be particularly squeamish about the thought of eating brains. I suspect this has something to with the fact that they look so much like what they are. And many people are unable to get beyond the thought that they are our 'gray matter'! It's a great shame, because brains have a mild, slightly sweet flavour and a rich creamy texture.

Calf's brains are virtually impossible to buy in Australia, although lamb's brains are pretty easy to find. All brains need to be soaked before cooking, to remove any small blood clots. They must then be briefly poached before further cooking. Sometimes they are still covered with a thin membrane, which needs to be carefully peeled away after poaching. I think they are most delicious when sautéed in butter or fried in a crunchy coating.

PIG'S EARS
Most us only ever see pig's ears in pet shops, where they are sold as treats for the family dog. But they are very popular in French country cooking, where they can be stuffed and baked or fried until crisp. They are as tough as they look, so you'll need to poach them for a few hours to make them tender. But through the magic of slow-cooking they become soft and tasty.

STORING OFFAL
- Unwrap and refrigerate all offal immediately.
- Store it in a Tupperware container, or sit it on a rack on a plate and cover it with a tea towel.
- Ideally, use offal on the day you buy it. It will keep for one to two days – but only if very fresh.
- Some offal items come pickled or preserved, in which case follow your butcher's instructions.

TONGUE

Tongues come in all shapes and sizes, from the tiny duck's tongues that are popular in Chinese cooking, through to hefty ox tongues. Your butcher is most likely to be able to find you lamb's, calf's or ox tongues – and they are all delicious.

I do understand that raw tongues look a bit confronting, with their dense muscular texture and bumpy skin that needs to be peeled away. But if you can get over your squeamishness you'll find that they make brilliant eating. They are very easy to cook, and their flesh becomes soft, rich and creamy.

Many Continental butchers have pickled ox tongue as a matter of course. Pickling keeps it nice and pink and intensifies the flavour but it is not essential. If you want fresh tongue – of any animal – you'll probably have to order it specially.

CHEEK

This is sometimes sold as 'jowl' meat, but I think cheek sounds so much nicer.

The cheek meat from pigs and beef has become increasingly popular on modern restaurant menus – and rightly so. When cooked slowly it becomes rich, gelatinous and tasty, and is meltingly tender enough to flake with a fork.

SWEETBREADS

The name 'sweetbread' is a terrific euphemism, because they have nothing to do with bread, and neither are they sweet. Sweetbreads are actually two different glands – one that sits near the throat, the other near the heart. They might not sound like something you want to eat, but in many countries sweetbreads are considered a real treat. They are similar to brains, with a creamy, soft texture and a very delicate flavour. In Australia, most sweetbreads – like nearly all our offal – are reserved for the lucrative export market. You'll definitely need to order them from your butcher well in advance, but as true offal-lovers will know, it's well worth it.

As is the case with brains, sweetbreads need a bit of preparation. First they need to be soaked for a few hours in several changes of water, then simmered quickly in a poaching stock before cleaning and trimming. Once that bit's done, then off you go with the recipe of your choice!

DUCK'S NECKS

This is a part of the bird that is usually completely ignored, but it makes a wonderful natural sausage casing! You can often buy ready-prepared duck necks from a poultry butcher (or of course you can chop them off whole ducks yourself, before roasting).

You need to peel the skin down and away from the internal vertebrae so you end up with a tube. Then you turn it inside out to see if there are any small tubes or glands still attached. If there are, trim them neatly away, being careful not to cut through the skin. Although it sounds a bit daunting, it's easy enough to do.

GIZZARDS

In the good old days you could buy chickens with the giblets tucked neatly inside the body cavity. What you'd get was the neck, heart, liver and the gizzard, and they were ideal for boiling up to make a quick stock for your gravy. Nowadays you have to order this sort of thing specially from your butcher.

The gizzard is a funny piece of hard-working muscle that sits at the top of the bird's stomach and grinds the food as it passes through. It's usually overlooked, but is very meaty and tasty. These days, most butchers will sell you gizzards already cut and cleaned. Like all offal, they need to be washed and blanched before cooking.

HEART

As is the case with a great deal of offal, hearts are a bit of a rarity these days. I think it's a great shame, because they are really tasty. To my mind, heart should either be cooked quickly and eaten a bit pink, or cooked long and slow until it tenderises.

You'll most likely be able to find lamb's, sheep's or pig's hearts. Ox hearts can be a bit tough and too strongly flavoured for some people. All hearts can be sliced for grilling or diced and marinated in olive oil and garlic, and threaded onto skewers for barbecuing. But I think they are especially good when you fill their natural cavity with a good flavoursome stuffing (or simply cut them in half lengthwise and pack the stuffing in).

LIVERS

Nearly everyone has tried liver, but sadly, some people never go back for seconds. There is no doubt in my mind that the reason for this is that it is so often very badly cooked. Just so you know, liver shouldn't be tough and chewy and full of gristly bits. When properly cooked – above all, not overcooked – liver is wonderful. It has a soft, smooth texture and a much milder flavour than you might think.

Liver is probably easier to find than any other offal. Chicken livers and lamb's liver are fairly widely available, although calf's liver, which is the most prized, will probably have to be ordered in specially for you. Pig's liver has quite a strong flavour (which I love) and it is perhaps best used in small amounts. I like to use it in terrines, for instance.

Buy whole livers, wherever possible, rather than slices of liver. They should look lovely and shiny, and have a vibrant deep reddish colour. To prepare lamb's, calf's and pig's liver, first peel away the delicate outer membrane, being careful not to crush the delicate flesh. Trim away any bits of tube before cutting into slices. Chicken livers need to be carefully inspected all over, and any greenish bits removed before cooking.

KIDNEYS

I'm sure the reason most people reject kidneys out of hand is because they associate them with urine! And to be honest, they do sometimes have a faint smell. But as is always the case with offal, freshness is everything. They also have quite a distinctive flavour, which varies from mild (in the case of lamb's kidneys) to quite strong (in the case of pig's kidneys).

Kidneys differ depending on which animal they come from. Ox and calf's kidneys have several lobes that are attached to a central fatty core. Lamb's and pig's kidneys come as one single lobe. In the olden days, kidneys used to be sold still in a thick layer of solid, creamy fat (suet), but these days this is the exception, rather than the rule.

To prepare kidneys they must first be skinned and then sliced in half lengthwise to snip out the tough inner core. The kidneys from young animals are best cooked briefly so they are still a little pink inside. Pig or ox kidneys are best braised for a long time, to soften them.

BLOOD

Although they don't sound immediately appealing, many countries have their own versions of blood sausages. There is the rich, cinnamon-scented Spanish morcilla, soft and creamy French boudin noir and of course Scottish black pudding. They can use the blood of any animal, although pig's blood is the most usual.

As governments around the world take ever-increasing control over the food we eat, it is becoming harder for the average person to get hold of top-quality fresh pig's blood. And more's the pity, I say. You will probably have to come to terms with the fact that you just won't be able to buy it, so I am not including recipes that use it in this book. But thankfully there are still a few small goods manufacturers left who are licensed to make real blood sausage. Michael Frederick of Morrison Street Butcher in Wodonga makes the best blood sausage that I have ever tasted – and I've tasted plenty.

TRIPE

Tripe is the lining of the stomach from cud-chewing animals – which usually means from an ox. It's really very versatile, and can be eaten on its own, or it can be stuffed – in fact sheep's tripe is stuffed to make the famous Scottish dish haggis (see page 229). If you've ever seen tripe at the butcher's you'll know that there are different types, depending on which of the cow's four stomachs it comes from. Honeycomb tripe (from the second stomach) is probably the most widely available, while the tripe from the third stomach is generally considered to have the finest texture and flavour.

All tripe has to be treated by bleaching and blanching (pre-cooking) before being sold – although you might be lucky enough to find some unblanched tripe at certain specialist butchers. Unblanched tripe will need to be cooked at home for about 8 hours, but aficionados insist that the flavour is superior.

There's no doubt that tripe is one of the more challenging cuts of offal, but anyone who's holidayed in France, Italy or Asia will know how delicious it can be.

INTESTINES AND STOMACH

These provide natural casings that lend themselves brilliantly to stuffing. In the case of intestines, they are widely used for making gourmet and homemade sausages. In France they love to turn them into a strongly flavoured sausage known as andouillette, in which they form both the casing and the stuffing itself. Intestines can sometimes be found fresh, but they are more likely to come salted. They need to be thoroughly rinsed and soaked before using.

The stomach is really just a big bag, so is ideal for filling with a tasty stuffing. It's most famously used in the Scottish dish, haggis.

TESTICLES

These are more likely to be sold under the name 'fries' (aka hanging beef, prairie oysters and cowboy caviar) and they are a rare delicacy. They are not available all that often, and when we put them on the menu at La Luna Bistro, they are gobbled up very quickly. They must be treated gently (as any bloke will tell you), and need an initial poaching before being skinned and sliced. Like brains and sweetbreads, I think they are best fried in a crunchy coating. They have a delicate flavour and their texture is pretty much what you might expect – soft and creamy, yet a little chewy.

TAIL

Of all the animals we eat, in my view, only the ox has a tail big enough to bother with. And although they are pretty bony, and are full of fat and connective tissue, oxtails are surprisingly meaty, too. All of which makes them perfect for long, slow cooking, which transforms them into something rich and lip-smackingly good.

TROTTERS

Because trotters are packed full of wonderful gelatine, they are often cooked with other cuts of meat where richness and body is required, or where you want to make sure your cooking stock will set to a jelly when cold. But I think they are also well worth cooking as a dish in their own right.

Although most fancy restaurants prefer to bone and stuff trotters before roasting or braising them (think of a classic Italian zampone), they are just as delicious when cooked whole. The Chinese seem to have a particular fondness for trotters – perhaps because they really understand the appeal of sucking and slurping away on all those soft, sticky bones.

MARROW

As anyone who loves osso buco knows, there's a hidden delight tucked inside those meaty veal bones: it's the juicy, meltingly soft and sticky marrow.

Although the main use of marrow bones is for making a rich beef stock, they can also be simmered for one to two hours or roasted in a hot oven to soften the marrow to a jelly-like softness. The hot marrow is then sprinkled with salt flakes and smeared onto toast for a wonderful old-fashioned treat.

CAUL

This is the lacy skein of fatty membrane that encases an animal's stomach. It is used to wrap around lean meats or patties to add lubrication and to hold them together. It melts away in the heat of the oven and helps to crisp the surface of the dish to a gorgeous golden brown.

Caul fat generally comes from pigs and can be sold fresh or frozen. Either way, rinse it thoroughly under cold running water then transfer to a container of heavily salted water (500 g salt per litre water). They will keep in the refrigerator for up to a month. Give them a quick rinse before using.

Crumbed lamb's brains with aïoli dipping sauce

If you've never tried brains before, then this recipe is a great introduction to their delicate flavour and creamy texture. And who can resist a crunchy crumb coating? They are wonderful on their own, served with lemon wedges and garlicky Aïoli (page 340) as a dipping sauce. But you could also serve them with some peppery rocket or watercress to make a more elegant starter or a light lunch.

12 sets lamb's brains (around
   100 g each)
3 eggs
¼ cup milk
plain flour for dusting
1 cup homemade breadcrumbs
1 tablespoon chopped thyme
salt
freshly ground black pepper
vegetable oil, for frying
lemon wedges to serve
Aïoli (page 340) to serve

Poaching stock
1 onion, roughly chopped
1 carrot, roughly chopped
1 stick celery, roughly chopped
1 leek, roughly chopped
1 garlic clove, halved
1 bay leaf
1 cup wine
2 litres water
1 tablespoon salt

Soak the brains in cold salted water for 1 hour.

Place the ingredients for the poaching stock in a large, heavy-based saucepan. Add the soaked brains and bring to the boil. Lower the heat and simmer very gently for 4 minutes. Use a slotted spoon to carefully lift the brains out of the stock and transfer them to a tray lined with a clean tea towel. Refrigerate until completely cold. If they are still covered with a thin membrane, peel it away carefully. Slice out any tiny bone shards.

Whisk the egg with the milk in a shallow dish. Set up a little production line of 3 dishes containing flour, the egg mixture and the breadcrumbs. Split the brains in half and dip them into the flour first, then into the egg mixture and then into the breadcrumbs so they are evenly coated.

Heat the oil in a heavy-based frying pan and shallow-fry the crumbed brains for about 5 minutes until golden brown all over. Drain briefly on a wire rack.

Serve hot from the pan with lemon wedges and garlicky aïoli as a dipping sauce.

Serves 6 as a starter or light meal

Some people are a bit resistant to the idea of eating pig's ears. But if any dish will win them over, it will be this one. The long cooking turns the ear soft, silken and succulent. And who can argue with a crunchy crumb coating?

Crisp pig's ear salad

Poaching stock
1 onion, roughly chopped
1 carrot, roughly chopped
1 stick celery, roughly chopped
1 garlic clove
1 teaspoon salt

6 x pig's ears (about 570 g total weight)
flour for dusting
1 egg
½ cup milk
1 cup dried breadcrumbs

Salad
200 g baby spinach leaves
¼ cup parsley leaves
¼ cup chives, cut into 4 cm batons
4 roma tomatoes, sliced
1 Lebanese cucumber, peeled
    and sliced
2 Granny Smith apples, sliced thinly
    (leave the skin on)

Dressing
2 tablespoons tarragon vinegar
salt
freshly ground black pepper
1 garlic clove, crushed
1 tablespoon mustard
3 tablespoons extra-virgin olive oil

Place the ingredients for the poaching stock in a large, heavy-based casserole dish. Add the pig's ears and cover generously with water. Bring to the boil, then cover the casserole and simmer very gently for 2½ hours. Check every 30 minutes or so and turn the ears in the poaching stock. When cooked they should be very tender. Remove the casserole from the heat and leave the pig's ears to cool in the stock.

When cold, remove from the stock and pat thoroughly dry. Sandwich the ears between two sheets of baking paper. Set a small chopping board on top of the ears and weight it down (tins from the pantry will do the job). Transfer to the refrigerator and leave overnight.

When ready to assemble the salad, combine all the ingredients in a large mixing bowl. Whisk the dressing ingredients together.

Cut the pig's ears into thin strips. Whisk the egg with the milk in a shallow disk. Set up a little production line of 3 dishes containing the flour, egg mixture, and breadcrumbs. Dip the strips in the flour first then dip them into the egg mixture and then the breadcrumbs so they are evenly coated.

Heat the oil in a heavy-based frying pan and shallow-fry the crumbed strips for 4–5 minutes until crisp and golden brown all over. Drain briefly on a wire rack.

To serve, pour the dressing onto the salad and toss lightly. Scatter on the crispy pig's ear strips and serve straight away.

Serves 6

Pickled lambs' tongues with cos heart and watercress salad

Pickling the lambs' tongues in a simple brine keeps them a lovely rosy pink. They are then poached to tender softness, sliced wafer-thin and scattered into a tangy salad.

10 x lambs' tongues
1 litre Basic Brine (page 246)

Poaching stock
1 onion, roughly chopped
1 carrot, roughly chopped
1 stick celery, roughly chopped
1 garlic clove, halved
1 bay leaf

Salad
2 cos hearts, leaves separated
1 bunch watercress, leaves picked
¼ cup cornichons
¼ cup sun-dried tomatoes
¼ cup chopped chives
¼ cup picked parsley
4 tablespoons tarragon vinegar
2 tablespoons grain mustard
4 tablespoons extra-virgin olive oil
salt
freshly ground black pepper

Place the lambs' tongues in a non-reactive container (i.e. not aluminium) that is just large enough to contain them snugly. Pour on the brine so that the tongues are completely covered. Sit a plate on top of the tongues and weight it down (tins from the pantry will do the job). Refrigerate for at least 2 days. Discard the brine and pat the lambs' tongues dry.

To poach the tongues, place them in a large saucepan with the onion, carrot, celery, garlic and bay leaf. Pour in enough cold water to cover and bring to the boil. Lower the heat and simmer very gently, covered, for 1½ hours, or until the tongues are tender. The water should barely simmer and the tongues should always remain covered with water. Check the pan from time to time and top up with more water if needed. Remove from the heat and leave to cool in the cooking liquid. When cool enough to handle, carefully peel away the skin and pull off any excess fat. Return the tongues to the cooking liquid and leave to cool overnight in the refrigerator.

Remove the cold tongues from the cooking liquid and pat dry. Use a sharp knife to trim back the root end of the tongues, slicing away any gristle or fat. Cut into wafer-thin slices and keep chilled until ready to serve.

To make the salad, combine the cos lettuce, watercress, cornichons, tomatoes and herbs in a large mixing bowl and toss together gently. In a separate bowl whisk together the vinegar, mustard and oil to make a dressing. Season to taste with salt and pepper. Scatter the lambs' tongues slices onto the salad and drizzle on the dressing. Toss gently so that everything is lightly coated with the dressing and serve with crusty bread and a glass of chilled riesling.

Serves 6

Warm salad of ox tongue, potato and gherkins

Ox tongue is one of those things that really polarise people. For some, it is just too large and confronting to be edible. For aficionados like me, it is an amazingly dense meat: rich and gelatinous when served hot, but surprisingly delicate and creamy when chilled. Ox tongue is fairly easy to find in good butcher's shops, either raw, pickled or ready-cooked. Pickled tongue is a nice rosy pink colour, whereas raw tongue tends to look a bit lifelike! They are equally delicious and either can be used for this recipe.

1 x raw ox tongue (around 1 kg)
1 onion, roughly chopped
1 carrot, roughly chopped
1 stick celery, roughly chopped

1 garlic clove, halved
1 bay leaf
1 kg Potato Salad (page 298)

Place the tongue in a large saucepan with the onion, carrot, celery, garlic and bay leaf. Pour in enough cold water to cover and bring to the boil. Lower the heat and simmer very gently, covered, for 2½ hours, or until the tongue is tender. The water should barely simmer and the tongue should always remain covered with water. Check the pan from time to time and top up with more water if needed. Remove from the heat and leave to cool in the cooking liquid. When cool enough to handle, carefully peel away the skin and pull off any excess fat. Return the tongue to the cooking liquid and leave to cool overnight in the refrigerator.

Remove the cold tongue from the cooking liquid and pat dry. Use a sharp knife to trim back the root end of the tongue, slicing away any gristle or fat. Chop the tongue into small dice or slice it thinly. Keep chilled until ready to serve.

Prepare the potato salad as described on page 298. While it is still warm, add the diced ox tongue and toss gently to combine. Serve warm or chilled with warm crusty bread.

Serves 6

Pig's cheeks are fairly fatty, there's no getting away from it. So this is a dish you'll want to eat once in a while, rather than every day! As it is rich, serve it with a Fresh Herb Salad (page 314) and warm crusty bread to mop up the sauce.

Braised pig's cheeks with tomatoes and borlotti beans

6 pig's cheeks, fat and skin intact
salt
freshly ground black pepper
¼ cup extra-virgin olive oil
100 g butter
2 onions, roughly chopped
10 garlic cloves, flattened with
  the back of a knife
2 sticks celery, finely chopped

1 carrot, finely chopped
1 tablespoon fennel seeds
1 tablespoon chilli powder
2 bay leaves
1 cup basil leaves
2 cups red wine
1 litre tomato passata
1 cup cooked borlotti beans
¼ cup snipped chives

Preheat the oven to 160°C and season the pig's cheeks all over with salt and pepper.

Heat the oil in a large casserole dish over a medium heat. When it sizzles, add the cheeks, two at a time, and sauté until browned all over. Remove the cheeks from the casserole and set aside.

Add the butter to the same casserole dish and heat gently until it begins to sizzle. Add the onions, garlic, celery and carrot and sweat for 5 minutes, or until just softened. Add the fennel seeds, chilli powder, bay leaves and half of the basil leaves. Stir well and sweat for 2 minutes. Add the wine to the pan and increase the heat to high. Bubble vigorously for 5 minutes, until slightly reduced, then add the tomato passata and stir well.

Return the pig's cheeks to the casserole dish, making sure they are covered with the sauce. Braise in the oven, uncovered, for 2½ hours. Check every 30 minutes or so and turn the cheeks around in the sauce. When cooked, the cheeks should be very tender – you should be able to flake the meat easily with a fork.

Ten minutes before the end of the cooking time, stir in the borlotti beans. Remove the bay leaves and scatter with the rest of the basil and chives just before serving.

Serves 6

Golden sautéed sweetbreads

Sweetbreads have a delicate creamy texture, similar to brains. Some people like to serve them in a creamy sauce, but I think they are better when fried in a crisp coating. This seasoned flour is lighter than breadcrumbs, but just as delicious.

1 kg veal or lamb sweetbreads
½ cup plain flour
1 tablespoon chopped thyme
1 teaspoon salt
¼ teaspoon freshly ground
   white pepper
¼ teaspoon cayenne pepper
oil for frying
lemon wedges

Poaching stock
1 onion, roughly chopped
1 carrot, roughly chopped
1 stick celery, roughly chopped
1 garlic clove, halved
1 bay leaf

Soak the sweetbreads for 3 hours in cold water, changing it at least twice.

Place the sweetbreads in a large saucepan with the poaching stock ingredients and pour in enough cold water to cover. Bring to the boil then lower the heat and simmer very gently for 5 minutes. Drain straight away and leave to cool. When cool enough to handle, carefully peel away the skin and trim away any bits of gristle, sinew or fat. Transfer the sweetbreads to a tray lined with a clean tea towel and chill until ready to use, but no longer than 3 days.

In a mixing bowl, combine the flour and seasonings. Coat the sweetbreads in the seasoned flour.

Heat the oil in a heavy-based frying pan and shallow-fry the sweetbreads for about 5 minutes until golden brown all over. Drain briefly on a wire rack.

Serve hot from the pan with lemon wedges, herb salad, aïoli, and plenty of buttered bread.

Serves 6

The roasted 'sausage' is wonderful – all crisp and golden – and it looks very impressive when carved into slices. Because it is fairly rich, I think it's best served with a tangy or peppery salad. Cabbage, Apple and Tarragon Salad (page 318), Fresh Herb Salad (page 314) or White bean, Blood Orange and Watercress Salad (page 318) are all good choices.

Stuffed duck's neck sausage

6 duck neck skins
3 tablespoons olive oil
salt
freshly ground black pepper

Stuffing
300 g minced pork
300 g minced duck
150 g diced ham
¼ cup shelled pistachios
¼ cup chopped parsley
2 tablespoons chopped thyme
30 ml brandy
1 teaspoon salt
½ teaspoon freshly ground
   black pepper

Turn the duck necks inside out and trim away any glands or tubes. Turn them back the right way and season lightly all over.

Combine the stuffing ingredients in a large mixing bowl and use your hands to mix everything together thoroughly. Divide the stuffing mixture into 6 portions.

Carefully fill the duck necks with the stuffing mixture to form a fat sausage, making sure you leave some excess skin at either end. Lay each sausage on a square of plastic wrap and roll up tightly. Twist the ends and secure with butcher's string. Now wrap each sausage again in aluminium foil. This double-wrapping is important, as it helps the sausage to maintain a good firm shape while it's poaching.

Place the sausages in a large pan of cold water. Bring to a gentle simmer and poach the sausages for 35 minutes. Lift them out carefully and place them in a bowl of iced water. When cold, remove from the water and pat dry on a tea towel. Keep the sausages in their wrappings until ready to roast. They can be prepared to this stage up to 4 days ahead of time.

Preheat the oven to 180°C. Arrange the sausages on a wire rack in a roasting tin and roast for 8–10 minutes, turning from time to time, until evenly coloured and cooked through. Remove from the oven and rest for a few minutes before slicing and serving.

Serves 6

Chicken gizzards with onions, lemon and parsley

Although they sound rather Shakespearian, gizzards are surprisingly meaty. This is a tasty and unusual sauce to serve with pasta or with hot buttered toast.

1 kg fresh chicken gizzards
salt
100 g butter
2 large onions, thinly sliced

6 garlic cloves, crushed
juice of 1 lemon
1 cup chopped parsley
linguine pasta to serve

To prepare the gizzards, slice them open and rinse them thoroughly under cold running water. Trim away any sinews then rinse them again. Put them in a large saucepan and cover generously with cold water. Add 1 tablespoon of salt and bring to the boil.

Strain the gizzards then return them to the saucepan and cover with fresh cold water and a pinch of salt. Bring to the boil, skimming away any foam that rises to the surface, then lower the heat and simmer gently for 2 hours or until tender.

Heat the butter in a heavy-based frying pan. Sweat the onions and garlic for 5 minutes until soft but not coloured. Add the gizzards and increase the heat to medium. Cook for 20 minutes, then add the lemon juice and parsley.

Serve with freshly cooked linguine pasta or with hot buttered toast.

Serves 4–6

To prepare the hearts you first need to trim away any blood vessels leading to the heart, but leave the fat (it will render down during cooking and baste the meat as it cooks). Next, make a long incision along the length of the heart and open it out. You'll see a natural cavity, which is ideal for stuffing. Slice away the ventricles and season lightly with salt and pepper before stuffing.

Two of my favourite stuffing recipes follow.

Stuffed lamb's hearts

6 fresh lamb hearts, trimmed and butterflied
salt

freshly ground black pepper
olive oil

Tomato, basil and caper stuffing
2 tablespoons olive oil
1 onion, diced
3 garlic cloves, finely chopped
6 tomatoes, peeled, seeded and diced
¼ cup chopped parsley
¼ cup chopped basil

1 tablespoon capers, chopped
1 tablespoon green peppercorns, chopped
¼ cup extra-virgin olive oil
1 teaspoon salt
1 ½ cups homemade breadcrumbs

Preheat the oven to 200°C.

To make the stuffing, heat the oil in a heavy-based frying pan and sweat the onion and garlic gently until soft but not coloured. Tip into a large mixing bowl and leave to cool.

Stir the remaining ingredients into the onions until well combined. Pack the stuffing into the hearts. Brush them lightly with olive oil, then arrange them in a roasting tin and roast for 10 minutes.

Serves 6

Bacon and mushroom stuffing
2 lamb hearts
2 tablespoons olive oil
1 onion, diced
3 cloves garlic, finely chopped

100 g mushrooms, finely diced
120 g bacon, finely diced
½ cup breadcrumbs
¼ cup chopped parsley

Preheat the oven to 200°C.

Trim the hearts of any blood vessels then slice them open and cut away the ventricles. Mince them fairly finely and set aside.

Heat the oil in a heavy-based frying pan and sweat the onion and garlic gently until soft but not coloured. Increase the heat and add the minced heart to the pan. Sauté for a few minutes until the meat begins to colour. Add the mushrooms and bacon to the pan and sauté for a few more minutes. Tip into a large mixing bowl and cool before stirring in the breadcrumbs and parsley.

Pack the stuffing into the hearts. Brush the stuffed hearts lightly with olive oil, then arrange them in a roasting tin and roast for 10 minutes.

Serves 6

This is a bit like a breakfast mixed grill, with everything cooked together on a skewer! As well as adding flavour, the smoky bacon also keeps the delicate liver and kidney moist, and protects them from the heat of the grill.

Kidney, liver and bacon brochettes with olive oil and lemon

300 g lamb's kidney
300 g, calf's liver
3 tablespoons olive oil
juice of 1 lemon
2 garlic cloves, crushed, plus 16 cloves
   extra for the skewers

1 tablespoon thyme leaves
salt
freshly ground black pepper
32 fresh bay leaves (optional)
100 g smoky bacon rashers,
   thinly sliced

Carefully peel the membranes away from the kidneys and liver and neatly slice away any tubes. Cut into 3 cm chunks.

Combine the oil, lemon juice, garlic and thyme in a mixing bowl with plenty of salt and pepper. Toss the kidney and liver pieces in the marinade and leave for 30 minutes for the flavours to infuse.

When ready to cook, preheat your grill or barbecue to medium–high. Thread alternating pieces of kidney, liver, garlic cloves and bay leaves (if using) onto the skewers, then carefully twist a slice of bacon around each brochette.

Grill the brochettes over a medium heat, turning frequently so the flames don't burn them. Serve with grilled tomatoes.

Serves 4 (8 skewers)

Chicken liver parfait with cognac

This parfait is soft, creamy and wickedly rich. You can make it with duck livers or even rabbit livers – each of which have their own distinct flavour. As the mixture is very soft – almost like thick cream – it is best to make it in little ramekin dishes, or a larger terrine mould.

This makes a very indulgent starter or lunch, served with thin slices of toast and Pickled Quinces (page 347).

700 g chicken livers (cleaned weight of 600 g)
3 eggs, at room temperature
600 unsalted butter, at room temperature
300 ml cream, at room temperature

1 teaspoon salt
1 teaspoon freshly ground white pepper
60 ml brandy or cognac
melted butter, to seal

Prepare the livers by trimming away any sinews and greenish bits. Preheat the oven to 175°C.

When making this parfait, it is important to have all your ingredients at a uniform blood temperature. Before you even begin, you should make sure you bring the various ingredients to room temperature. Next, fill your sink with warm water, as close to blood temperature (37°C) as you can manage. Sit the various ingredients (in containers, where appropriate) in the water for 5–10 minutes, stirring from time to time to ensure everything is evenly warmed through.

Put the chicken livers into the bowl of a food processor and blitz to a smooth purée Use a wooden spoon or the back of a ladle to push the purée through a fine sieve into a mixing bowl which will remove any lingering bits of sinew. Add the eggs, one at a time, beating them in well. Next beat in the melted butter, followed by the cream, until you have a very smooth, creamy mixture. Add the seasoning and beat in the brandy.

Divide the parfait into 3 x 500 ml ramekins and sit them in a deep roasting tin. Pour in enough hot tap water to come half way up the sides. Cook in the oven for 45 minutes. If using a meat thermometer (which I strongly recommend), the internal core temperature should reach 72°C.

Carefully lift the ramekins out of their water bath and leave to cool. When completely cold, cover and refrigerate overnight before serving and eat within 7 days. Over time the exposed surface of the parfait will oxidise and discolour, so you may like to seal the surface with a layer of melted butter – or duck or goose fat, if you have any to hand.

Serves 6–8

Rabbit livers with PX sherry, caramelised onions and brioche toast

While they might seem a bit esoteric, rabbit livers are in fact really delicious. You will sometimes find them attached to a whole rabbit, but all too often they are thrown out when the animal is skinned. For this reason you'll need to order them in advance from your butcher. Pedro Ximenez sherry is sweet and syrupy with muscat-like flavours, and it goes brilliantly with liver's rich, dark flavour. Served like this, on toasted brioche slices, rabbit livers make a really lovely lunch dish, or a rich starter on a cold winter's night.

Caramelised onions
2 tablespoons olive oil
2 onions, thinly sliced

100 g butter
1 garlic clove, finely chopped
600 g rabbit livers, cleaned
¼ cup PX sweet sherry
½ cup Jus (page 331) (or 1 cup good
   quality beef stock, reduced to ¼ cup)
salt
freshly ground black pepper
6 slices brioche, lightly toasted
2 tablespoons chopped parsley
1 tablespoon snipped chives

To make the caramelised onions, heat the olive oil in a large, heavy-based frying pan or casserole. When it begins to sizzle, add the onions and turn them around in the oil. Cook for 5–10 minutes, or until the onions turn a deep caramel brown. Stir frequently, so they colour evenly. Set aside until ready to use.

Melt the butter in a large heavy-based frying pan. When it begins to sizzle, add the garlic and sweat for a few minutes until it softens and begins to colour. Add the rabbit livers to the pan with the caramelised onions and sauté for 3–4 minutes. Increase the heat and add the sherry and jus to the pan. Let it bubble vigorously for a minute or so, then season with salt and pepper.

Spoon the livers over lightly toasted brioche slices and serve sprinkled with parsley and chives.

Serves 6

Calf's liver with apples and calvados

Calf's liver is a real treat. It has a smooth, fine texture and a delicate flavour. It really only needs to be cooked very simply, and I think this apple and calvados sauce complements it brilliantly. Calf's liver should be cooked quickly so it is still pink in the centre; overcooking it is a crime.

600 g calf's liver
2 Granny Smith apples
75 g butter
½ onion, thinly sliced

¼ cup calvados
salt
freshly ground black pepper
1 tablespoon thyme leaves

Carefully peel the membranes away from the liver and neatly slice away any tubes. Cut into slices around 5 mm thick.

Peel and core the apples and cut them into eighths.

Heat half the butter in a heavy-based frying pan and sweat the onions for 8 minutes, or until very soft and starting to colour. Add the apples to the pan and cook for a further 5 minutes, or until they are soft, but not mushy. Tip the onion-apple mixture onto a warm plate and set aside.

Add the remaining butter to the pan over a medium–high heat until it begins to sizzle. Cook the calf's liver slices for 1 minute on each side, or until lightly browned – you really just want to seal it at this stage. Return the onions and apples to the pan and carefully add the calvados – be careful as it may flame up. Season generously and add the thyme. Cook for a further minute on each side.

Serve straight away with hot buttered toast.

Serves 4

I like to use a Scottish-style black pudding for this dish. It will be firmer than a Continental-style blood sausage, which makes it ideal for slicing and frying in butter for breakfast.

Black pudding on sourdough toast with poached egg and thick-cut bacon

1 teaspoon white wine vinegar
8 free-range eggs, at room
   temperature
1 tablespoon olive oil
8 thick-cut rashers smoky bacon

small knob of butter
12 x 2.5 cm thick slices Scottish
   black pudding
4 thick slices crusty sourdough bread
4 sprigs parsley to garnish

Preheat the oven to 150°C and put 4 plates on the lowest shelf to warm.

Bring a large saucepan of water to a gentle boil and add the vinegar. Stir the simmering water vigorously, to form a sort of whirlpool. Carefully slip in an egg and allow the swirling water to shape it into a neatish ball. Poach for 3 minutes, or until the white is completely set. Remove the egg carefully and transfer it into a bowl of iced water to stop it cooking further. Lift onto a clean tea towel. The eggs can be poached to this stage ahead of time. Reheat them in a pan of gently simmering water for 30–60 seconds just before you serve them.

Heat the oil in a large, non-stick frying pan and fry the bacon until crisp and golden brown. Transfer to an ovenproof platter and put in the oven to keep warm.

Add the butter to the residual bacon fat left in the pan and heat until it begins to foam. Add the black pudding slices and fry on both sides until brown and crisp. Transfer to the platter in the oven.

Toast the bread slices to your liking and when they are done, butter them lightly. While the toast is cooking, reheat the poached eggs.

To serve, divide the bacon, black pudding and toast between the warmed plates. Top with 2 poached eggs and garnish with parsley. Serve straight away with Dijon mustard, HP sauce and a strong Bloody Mary.

Serves 4

Blood sausage with roasted mushrooms, soft polenta and truffled pecorino

When it comes to mushrooms, I like a free-form natural look! I tend to cut them fairly large and chunky, according to their shape and size, while smaller mushrooms can be left whole. I usually roast them in a foil bag, as I find it keeps them moist and you end up with plenty of tasty cooking juices.

Soft polenta
50 g butter
1 onion, finely diced
2 garlic cloves, finely chopped
1 tablespoon fresh thyme
1 litre good-quality chicken stock
150 g instant polenta
50 g grated parmesan
1 tablespoon chopped parsley
1 tablespoon chopped thyme
1 tablespoon chopped coriander

Roasted mushrooms
250 g mixed mushrooms,
   roughly chopped
3 sprigs thyme
1 garlic clove, thinly sliced
salt
freshly ground black pepper
50 g butter

6 blood sausages
2 tablespoons chopped parsley
75 g truffled pecorino (or ordinary
   pecorino)
Red Wine Reduction (page 332)
   (optional)

Preheat the oven to 180°C.

To make the polenta, melt the butter in a heavy-based saucepan. Add the onion, garlic and thyme and sweat gently for 5 minutes until the onion is soft, but not coloured. Add the stock to the pan and bring it to the boil. Pour in the polenta in a slow, steady stream, whisking all the while. Keep whisking vigorously until the mixture begins to boil, then lower the heat to a brisk simmer. Cook for 5–10 minutes, stirring with a wooden spoon from time to time, until the mixture thickens and becomes smooth and creamy. Remove the pan from the heat and stir in the cheese and chopped herbs. Taste and adjust the seasoning if needed. Cover and keep warm while you cook the mushrooms and sausages.

In a large mixing bowl, toss the mushrooms with the thyme and garlic and season lightly. Place them on a large rectangle of aluminium foil and sit the butter on top. Fold the sides over and in to make an airtight bag. Transfer to a baking tray and roast for 8–10 minutes, or until the bag puffs up.

While the mushrooms are roasting, bake the blood sausages for 6 minutes, or until they are warmed through.

To serve, place a spoonful of polenta on each plate and top with a blood sausage. Divide the mushrooms and their cooking liquor evenly between the plates and sprinkle with the parsley and shavings of pecorino. Spoon on the red wine sauce, if using, and eat straight away.

Serves 6

Slow-cooked pork offal

This dish is for true offal-lovers only! It was inspired by a meal I ate in Beijing a few years ago. I was out late one night with a mate and we stumbled across an offal-soup stall tucked away in a small alleyway. The dish that caught my fancy was chock-full of various intestines and internal organs and thickened with blood. I scoffed it down – much to my friend's horror.

Pig's liver and kidney are both strongly flavoured, and some people might prefer to substitute calf's or lamb's offal instead. But if you're going to attempt it at all, you'll probably want to go the whole way!

salt
freshly ground black pepper
400 g pig's kidney, skinned, cored and cut into 5 cm pieces
400 g pig's liver, trimmed and cut into 5 cm pieces
400 g pork belly, diced
¼ cup extra-virgin olive oil
4 onions, diced
8 garlic cloves, crushed

2 bay leaves
3 sprigs thyme
1 fresh chilli, halved
1 cup white wine
¼ cup chicken stock or water
6 small potatoes, peeled and halved (around 700 g)
¼ cup chopped parsley
big squeeze of lemon

Preheat the oven to 175°C.

Season the kidney, liver and belly and keep them separate.

Heat the oil in large, heavy-based casserole dish. Add the onions and garlic and sauté over a low heat until golden brown. Add the bay leaves, thyme and chilli and sauté for a few more minutes. Add the kidney, liver and pork belly to the casserole and stir well. Pour in the wine and stock then add the potatoes. Bring to the boil then cover the casserole and transfer to the oven.

Cook for 45 minutes then remove the lid and cook for a further 45 minutes. You may need to add a more stock if it all evaporates. Remove from the oven and serve with a sprinkling of chopped parsley and a squeeze of lemon juice.

Serves 6

This recipe is a classic Italian dish that I serve with lots of parmesan cheese and sourdough toast. There are many of my customers at La Luna that find it quite irresistible.

Tripe alla Romana

1 kg bleached and blanched
  honeycomb tripe
150 g butter
2 onions, sliced
10 garlic cloves, crushed
3 medium carrots, sliced
4 sticks celery, sliced
1 cup red wine
1.5 litres tomato passata

1 cup basil leaves
2 bay leaves
salt
freshly ground black pepper
½ cup chopped parsley
grated parmesan to serve
slices of sourdough baguette,
  toasted or grilled

Cut the tripe into strips around 1.5 cm wide.

Heat the butter in a heavy-based casserole dish. When it foams, add the onion and garlic and sauté over a medium heat until golden brown. Add the carrots and celery and sauté for 5–8 minutes until they start to soften. Add the tripe and stir for 2 minutes until it starts to colour. Stir in the wine and tomato passata then add the basil and bay leaves and season with salt and pepper. Bring to the boil, then lower the heat and simmer, uncovered, for 2 hours, stirring from time to time as the sauce thickens.

Serve the tripe straight away with plenty of parsley and grated parmesan and sourdough toast.

Serves 4–6

I'm not going to sugar-coat it: this recipe requires a brave heart to make, and a strong stomach to eat! However, plenty of people (including me) think that haggis is a wonderful thing. You should find it quite easy to source sheep's stomachs from your butcher – as long as you give him a bit of advance warning. The pluck may be a bit harder to come by, but a nod and a wink to your butcher may do the job.

Haggis is traditionally brought to the table to the sound of bagpipes. To serve, slice it open lengthwise and scoop out the spicy contents. As most people probably know, the proper accompaniments for haggis are 'neeps and tatties' (mashed swede and potatoes) and a wee dram of whisky.

Haggis

Classic haggis

3 cups oatmeal
1 large onion, skin on (about 250 g)
1 sheep's pluck (which comes as heart, lungs and liver, joined together as one)
300 g minced lamb
200 g beef or lamb suet, grated (this is easier to do when frozen)
⅓ cup good whisky
2 teaspoons white pepper
2 teaspoons salt
½ tablespoon cayenne pepper
1 sheep's stomach

Preheat your oven to 180°C.

Scatter the oatmeal onto a baking sheet and toast in the oven for 15–20 minutes, shaking from time to time, until evenly coloured. On a separate tray, roast the onion for about 20 minutes, until nicely soft and golden. When cool enough to handle, peel away the skin and chop the onion finely.

Meanwhile, put the pluck into a stockpot or large saucepan and pour on enough cold water to cover. Bring to the boil, then lower the heat and simmer fairly vigorously for 20 minutes. Drain and leave to cool. When cool enough to handle, cut away the windpipe and chop or mince the organs.

Put the chopped pluck into a large mixing bowl with all the remaining ingredients, except for the sheep's stomach. Use your hands to mix everything together very thoroughly.

Stuff the mixture into the sheep's stomach until it's about three-quarters full – you need to leave room for the oatmeal to expand. Squeeze out as much air as possible then sew or tie the stomach bag securely. Use a pin to prick the haggis randomly a few times, which allows the steam to escape during the cooking and stops it bursting. You can make the haggis to this stage in advance. If you vacuum-pack it (and your butcher will probably oblige with this), it will keep in the freezer for up to 3 months.

To cook the haggis, defrost it slowly, if frozen, and leave in its vacuum-pack. Sit it on an upturned saucer in a saucepan that contains it snugly and pour on boiling water to cover. Return to a rolling boil, then lower the heat and simmer gently for 2½–3 hours. Top up with boiling water, if need be, so that it remains completely covered.

Remove from the poaching water and leave to rest for a few minutes before removing from the vacuum-pack and serving.

Serves 8–10

If you develop a taste for haggis, you might like to try a few flavour variations. To the classic recipe, I sometimes add the following:

300 g minced ham
2 cups chopped parsley
6 garlic cloves, roasted
4 tablespoons chopped thyme
1 tablespoon dried oregano

or

300 g minced ham
2 cups chopped parsley
6 garlic cloves, roasted
grated zest of 1 orange
8 cloves, roughly crushed
1 teaspoon cinnamon
1 teaspoon nutmeg
1 tablespoon freshly ground black pepper

229

Prairie oysters with polenta crumbs and garlic mayonnaise

For this recipe you can use lamb's or pig's testicles instead of bull's testicles, depending on what your butcher can find for you. These only need to be poached for about 10 minutes, as they are smaller, and haven't done as much work as those of the mighty bull!

3 sets bull's testicles
salt
1 tablespoon white vinegar
1 egg
¼ cup milk
plain flour

coarse polenta
vegetable oil for frying
Aïoli (page 340), to serve
lemon wedges, to serve

Soak the testicles in very lightly salted cold water for 24 hours, to soften the outer skin. Drain and soak for 1 hour in fresh cold water to which you've added 1 tablespoon of vinegar. Drain again.

Place the testicles in a large saucepan and cover with cold water. Bring to the boil slowly, skimming away any impurities that float to the surface. Lower the heat and poach very gently for 35 minutes. Turn off the heat and leave the testicles to cool down in the water. When cool enough to handle, use a small sharp knife to peel away the outer skin. Cover with a damp tea towel and refrigerate until ready to cook.

Cut the cold testicles into slices about 1 cm thick. Whisk the egg with the milk in a shallow dish. Set up a little production line of 3 dishes containing plain flour, egg wash and an equal mixture of plain flour and polenta. Dip the testicle slices in the flour and shake off any excess. Dunk them into the egg wash and then in the flour-polenta mixture. Refrigerate for 15 minutes.

Pour the oil into a heavy-based frying pan to a depth of about ½ cm. Heat until the oil sizzles, then fry the crumbed slices for 2–3 minutes until golden and crunchy. Serve hot from the pan with aïoli and lemon wedges.

Serves 6

Oxtail soup

My favourite way of cooking oxtail is in a sticky, full-flavoured soup. I like to throw in a pig's trotter or an ear while the oxtails are cooking, as they enrich the soup even more, and add a lovely sheen to the soup.

2 tablespoons olive oil
2 kg oxtails, cut into small chunks
salt
freshly ground black pepper 2 medium carrots, roughly chopped
2 sticks celery, roughly chopped
1 parsnip, peeled and chopped
150 g butter
4 onions, sliced
6 garlic cloves, sliced
1 cup red wine

1 cup port or Madeira
1 pig's trotter or pig's ear (optional)
6 sprigs thyme
1.5 litres good-quality beef or chicken stock
¼ cup chopped parsley

Heat the oil in a heavy-based casserole dish until it sizzles. Season the oxtails. Brown them all over, then transfer them to a plate. Add the carrots, celery and parsnip to the casserole and sauté over a medium heat until they begin to colour.

Add the butter to the casserole and when it begins to sizzle add the onions and garlic. Sweat over a medium heat until the onions begin to soften and turn a pale golden brown. Deglaze the pan with the red wine and port then return the oxtails to the pan.

Add the pig's trotter and thyme to the casserole then pour on the stock. Bring to the boil, then lower the heat to a simmer. Cover the casserole and simmer gently for 3 hours, or until the meat is very tender.

When cool enough to handle, pick all the meat from the oxtails and pig's trotter and discard the bones. Return the meat to the soup, taste and adjust the seasoning to your liking and serve garnished with parsley.

Serves 6

This simple braise is less fancy than stuffed trotters but it makes a wonderfully tasty and satisfying once-in-a-while treat.

You can also use this recipe for cooking boned pig's hocks.

Roast pig's trotters with borlotti bean braise

4 pig's trotters
salt
freshly ground black pepper
2 tablespoons olive oil
1 medium onion, roughly chopped
½ leek, roughly chopped
4 garlic cloves, crushed
2 sticks celery, roughly chopped
1 carrot, roughly chopped
4 sprigs thyme
2 bay leaves
1½ litres good-quality chicken stock
caul fat, for wrapping

Borlotti bean braise
3 tablespoons olive oil
1 medium onion, finely diced
2 medium zucchini, cut into large dice
6 garlic cloves, finely diced
1 x 400 g can borlotti beans
4 tomatoes, skinned, seeded and chopped
½ cup reduced poaching stock (see method below)
salt
freshly ground black pepper
¼ cup chopped parsley
¼ cup basil leaves, roughly torn
extra-virgin olive oil to serve

Scrape or singe away any hairs from the trotters. Season generously with salt and pepper.

Heat the oil in a heavy-based saucepan or stockpot. Add the chopped vegetables and garlic and sweat over a low heat until they start to soften. Add the herbs and the pig's trotters to the pan and sweat for a few more minutes. Pour on the stock and bring to the boil. Lower the heat and simmer gently, covered, for 2½ hours, by which time the trotters should be soft and gelatinous.

Strain the poaching stock into a clean saucepan, reserving the pig's trotters and discarding the vegies and herbs. Bring the stock to the boil, then simmer until reduced by half. Set aside until ready to make the sauce.

When the trotters are cool enough to handle, use a small sharp knife to carefully ease the skin away from the bone and peel it down to the toe, as if you're taking off a long glove. Cut through the bone, leaving the toe in place (be careful not to cut through the skin), then roll the skin back up, forming a long pocket. Preheat the oven to 180°C. Season the trotters all over with salt and pepper. Cut the caul fat into 4 pieces, about double the size of a trotter. Wrap each trotter firmly – there's no need to secure it – and arrange in a lightly oiled roasting tin. Roast the trotters for 10–12 minutes.

To make the braise heat the oil in a heavy-based saucepan. Add the onion, zucchini and garlic and sweat gently for 5 minutes until soft, but not coloured. Add the borlotti beans and chopped tomatoes to the pan, together with the reduced poaching stock. Simmer for 5 minutes then season with salt and pepper and scatter in the parsley and basil.

To serve, place a spoonful of the braise on each plate and top with a roasted trotter. Drizzle with extra-virgin olive oil and serve immediately with warm crusty bread.

Serves 4

Roasted bone marrow with red onion salad

Fergus Henderson of St John Restaurant in London has made roasted bone marrow served with a parsley salad famous. You definitely need to serve it with something robust and sharp to cut through the richness and this red onion salad also works brilliantly.

Sumac is a Middle Eastern berry with a sharp, lemony flavour. You can find ground sumac in Middle Eastern grocers and specialty food stores.

Red onion salad
3 red onions, thinly sliced
1 teaspoon salt
¼ cup red wine vinegar
1 cup parsley leaves
½ cup coriander leaves
3 tablespoons extra-virgin olive oil
1 tablespoon ground sumac
½ teaspoon freshly ground
  black pepper

olive oil
12 beef shin bones (12–14 cm long)
sourdough bread or toast to serve
coarse salt flakes to serve

To make the salad, place the sliced onions in a small bowl. Mix the salt and vinegar together and pour on the onions. Leave to soak for 2 hours, which will reduce their sharpness.

Meanwhile, preheat the oven to 200°C and lightly oil a roasting tin. Arrange the beef bones in the tin so they are standing up. Roast for 15 minutes until the bones are well browned and the marrow is soft and bubbling.

Drain the onions thoroughly and place in a mixing bowl with the fresh herbs. Pour on the extra-virgin olive oil and sprinkle with sumac and black pepper. Toss together lightly.

To serve, arrange 3 bones on each plate, together with a generous mound of onion salad. You can sometimes find long spoons, specially designed for scooping out the marrow. Failing this, provide your guests with a chopstick or skewer to prize out the precious marrow. The idea is to spread the hot marrow onto the sourdough bread and eat it sprinkled with salt and a few salad leaves. Be warned ... it is very rich!

Serves 4

CHARCUTERIE

10

MAKING MEAT
GO
FURTHER

Charcuterie

If I had a big enough backyard, I think I'd like to keep a pig, as my nonno's family did in the northern Italian village where he grew up. When my brother and I were very young, Nonno would tell us stories of his childhood there, and lots of them would revolve around his animals and their place in the rhythm of daily life.

In small rural communities all around Europe, it was normal to grow your own vegetables and keep animals for food. The household pig was especially important for providing families with food through the long cold winter months, because just about every part of it could be used, from the nose right down to the tail. Nonno had vivid descriptions of the local butcher's visits to his house every autumn. He'd help the men of the family slaughter the pig, and then move on to the next house in the village. The entire household would then set about converting the pig into food. A few tasty morsels would be set aside for a spot of celebratory feasting, but most of the choice cuts would be put into a brine solution for curing. Other fatty cuts were turned into fresh sausages or set aside for making air-dried salamis; blood was turned into blood pudding; the head was cooked long and slow to make brawn – nothing at all was wasted.

These were the days when there were no freezers or fridges to help prevent fresh food from spoiling, so it was vitally important to process and preserve as much food as possible for eating through the winter. Many of the preserving techniques we use today date back to ancient times, when people first realised that removing moisture from meat stopped it going mouldy or decaying. The earliest and simplest methods of preserving involved hanging meat in the air to dry and salting it to draw out the juices. Other techniques include smoking and pickling in brine, vinegar or alcohol.

In addition to these preserving methods there are also various ways of processing meat that can help to extend its 'use-by' date. This category, which technically is known as charcuterie, includes a huge range of sausages, potted meats, pâtés and terrines, galantines, ballottines and confits, which will often involve cooking the meat first before preserving it in fat or gelatine.

I love this thrifty approach to food and to cooking, which really does make the most of every part of the animal, and it's something that we do a lot of at La Luna Bistro. If you visit my dry-store and cool-room on any given day, you'll see our own range of salamis, air-dried hams, fresh sausages and blood puddings, as well as the more usual restaurant fare of pâtés, terrines and confits. While some preserving techniques involve a fair bit of science, there are many that are really simple for the home cook and I hope you'll try some of the recipes that follow.

DRY-CURING

Dry-curing is one of the oldest and simplest preserving techniques known to man. The ancient Egyptians were one of the earliest societies to work out that salt absorbs the moisture in meat, which prevents bacteria growing. This key discovery was one of the main reasons why salt became such a vital commodity around the world. It led to new trade routes, the creation of empires and was even the cause of wars.

At its simplest, dry-curing involves rubbing salt into meat and leaving it to draw out the moisture. It's especially effective with pork, which is the reason there are such a vast number of different bacons, hams, and cured sausages to be found in countries all around the world.

Here in Australia you will be able to recognise a good butcher by his range of traditionally dry-cured products, and if you're lucky, he may even make his own. Similarly, a butcher worth his salt (no pun intended) will also be able to supply you with good old-fashioned dry-cured bacon, rather than the mass-produced flabby stuff that crops up everywhere.

Dry-curing is also an essential precursor to other preserving methods, such as air-drying and smoking (both on page 241).

I'm not going to suggest that you cure your own hams and bacons at home (although you could attempt it if you can find a farmer who'll sell you some really first-class fresh pork). At the very least, though, I do think it's well worth hunting out traditional dry-cured products from small producers. You'll really notice the difference.

WET-CURING

Wet-curing is simply another way of curing meat in salt, but it uses a salt solution called brine, instead of dry salt to remove the moisture. Traditional wet-curing involves completely immersing the meat in brine, and it can take a week or more, depending on the size of the cut. Today most mass-produced ham and bacon is 'wet-cured' by injecting the meat with a brine solution. It's a much faster technique, which not only gets the product out onto the shelves faster, but has the benefit to the manufacturer of increasing the water content. For the consumer, this is the reason why so much bacon seems to shrivel disappointingly in the frying pan in a puddle of liquid.

Wet-curing your own ham and bacon at home can be a bit tricky, as you do have to be careful about the ratio of salt to water. But I would like to encourage you to experiment with some quick brines (page 246). These are not going to prolong the lifespan of your meat by a very long time, but they do have a couple of major benefits.

The first benefit of a quick brine is that it keeps your meat lovely and pink and moist. Second, brines are a great way of adding flavour to the meat, as you can add all sorts of aromatics to the mix. Some brines are predominantly salty, others are sweet or have an acid tang, while various herbs and spices add different flavours.

As with any recipe using vinegar (or a lot of salt), make sure you use a non-reactive saucepan – i.e. one that isn't made out of aluminium.

AIR-DRYING

This is not strictly speaking a preservation method, but rather, it is a way of maturing or aging meat that has already undergone some sort of curing process, either in salt or in a salt solution.

Some of the most famous dry-cured hams come from Europe, and include Spanish Serrano ham, speck, Bayonne ham and prosciutto. These are all cured in a salt rub before being aged for anything between 10 months for Bayonne ham, 18 months for a good Serrano or prosciutto, and up to 36 months for a true jamon Iberico.

At La Luna Bistro we make the Italian classic air-dried beef called bresaola, which also incorporates two types of preserving methods. The meat – in this case beef, rather than pork – is first wet-cured in brine before being air-dried for four to six weeks in a cool environment. This dries it a little more and develops the flavour, transforming it into a tasty treat for your antipasto plate.

SMOKING

Smoking meat (or fish, of course) is a brilliant way of adding flavour, as well as improving its lifespan. But as with air-drying, the meat needs to be cured first by undergoing an initial salting process.

The traditional method of smoking was simply to suspend a piece of meat in the chimney space of a fireplace (well away from the direct heat of the flames). It would be left there for anything from a few hours up to many months. Extra flavour could be added to the smoke by throwing in aromatic branches or pinecones.

Modern smoking methods do essentially the same thing, which means that it is still something of a craft. Don't confuse the 'smoky' flavour that has been sprayed onto mass-produced foodstuffs with true artisan-smoked products. You'll be able to find a wide range of smoked products in Continental butchers that specialise in this technique. All sorts of items can be smoked, from pork hocks, hams and bacon, to sausages, chicken breasts, venison and even kangaroo.

PRESERVING IN FAT

This technique of cooking and preserving meats in fat is especially popular in France, but is also how the English make their potted meats. The French have their own potted meat called rillettes, made from shredded seasoned pork that is cooked and preserved in its own fat.

Another well-known technique is the confit – which is actually the French word for preserving. To make a confit, meat such as pork, goose or duck is cooked very slowly in its own rendered fat until very tender. The finished confit is then stored in earthenware pots or jars and completely covered with a layer of liquid fat. When the fat solidifies it acts as a sort of protective layer. In the days before refrigeration a confit would keep quite happily over the long winter months, to be enjoyed when fresh meat was not so easy to come by. This preserving method makes the texture of the meat beautifully soft and tender.

PRESERVING IN JELLY

I've talked elsewhere about the beauty of gelatine. Some cuts of meat, such as calves' feet, oxtails, pigs' trotters and the pig's head, are chock-a-block full of connective tissue, bone and skin – all of which create a wonderful gelatine-rich liquid after long, slow cooking.

When this liquid is poured over chunks or shreds of the cooked meat, it sets to a brilliant shimmering jelly that not only looks beautiful, but is amazingly tasty. The recipe for brawn on page 259 is a fantastic example of this technique, and I really love the contrast between the slippery smoothness of the jelly, and the coarse texture of the meat. If you're not sure you can deal with a whole pig's head, then try the recipe for Jambon Persillé (page 260).

TERRINES

Terrines (and their smoother cousins, pâtés) are simply meatloaf by a fancier name! But this shouldn't in any way detract from the complexity of their flavour and their wonderful texture.

Don't be fooled into thinking they're difficult to make. Although some terrines involve some fancy layering, most simpler versions require nothing more tricky in the way of technique than a bit of chopping or mincing. You'll want to use a mixture of lean and fatty meats (to keep it moist), then add a few aromatics and seasonings and pack the mixture into a terrine mould. Some terrines require you to line the mould with bacon rashers, but again, this isn't difficult – and it does look brilliant when you unmould the finished terrine. However they are put together, all terrines are then cooked very gently in a water bath, to ensure they cook through thoroughly.

Terrines usually benefit from being left to mature for three to four days, so the flavours develop and intensify.

SAUSAGES

Sausage-making is a regular activity at La Luna Bistro, but it's also something I do at home with my boys. They love the whole idea of it – and of course they love the end result too.

Even though there are plenty of good-quality gourmet sausages around the place these days, I do think there's nothing that quite beats making them yourself. You can get by without any special equipment, although there are a few items that make life easier. First, a mincer makes the whole job faster, is indispensable for finer-textured sausages, and does a good job of mixing together the lean and fatty meats. Second, a sausage-filling attachment for the mincer makes the somewhat fiddly job of filling the casings much easier. If you don't have a mincer, then ask your butcher nicely to do the hard work for you.

It's really not difficult to make your own sausages as long as you follow a few simple principles concerning the ratio of meat to fat to seasoning – and these are the same, whichever type of sausage you make.

- **Meat:** Don't think you can do what the big sausage manufacturers do and bung in any old bits and pieces. To make great sausages you need to start with good-quality fresh meat. Keep your meat as cold as possible throughout the process. Start by trimming off as much of the sinew, gristle and tendons as you can, then dice the meat into small pieces or mince it. Texture is up to you, but personally I prefer a coarser texture, rather than too smooth a sausage.

- **Fat:** As far as I'm concerned, there's no such thing as a low-fat sausage. Fat content is vitally important because it helps carry the flavour of the meat and keeps the sausages juicy and moist. Fat is important for 'mouth feel' – the way something feels while you're chewing it. You need to aim for 20–30 per cent fat which means either using a fatty cut of meat or adding it (usually in the form of finely chopped pork back fat).

- **Salt:** This is a key flavour enhancer and an important preserver, so don't skimp. Make sure you add 1.5 per cent of the total weight of the sausage mixture – i.e. 15 g per kilo of sausage mixture.

- **Flavour:** This is your opportunity to be creative. Depending on the meat, you might like to add pepper, chilli, fennel, rosemary, cooked garlic, thyme – in fact anything you think would work! Just a word of caution, don't add too many different ingredients: keep it simple!

- **Casings:** The best sausage skins are made from natural casings, which means animal intestines. They come in various sizes and lengths, depending on exactly which section of the intestine they are from. In general, ask for lamb or pig casings for making regular sausages and ox-bung casings for larger sausages, such as cotechino or salami. You'll need to order the casings from your butcher – they usually come packed in salt and need to be thoroughly soaked and rinsed before using.

- **Filling the casings:** Attach a sausage-making attachment to the mincer. Carefully ease the entire length of a casing over the nozzle, leaving about 6 cm dangling. Fill the mouth of the mincer with a good wodge of sausage mixture, packing it in carefully to avoid any pockets of air. Turn the handle of the mincer until you see the mixture start to appear in the casing, and tie a knot to seal the end. Hold the casing in the palm of your left hand, and keep turning the handle of the mincer with your right hand. Try to maintain a steady rhythm, so that the casing fills evenly and smoothly. Add more sausage mixture to the mincer as needed, and when the casing is filled to within 6 cm of the end, carefully detach it from the mincer and tie a knot at the end to seal. Arrange the whole sausage out on your work surface and, if necessary, use your hands to roll it gently to distribute the filling evenly.

  For anyone who doesn't have a sausage-making attachment, here's a handy tip: a builder's caulking gun does the trick beautifully!

- **Forming links:** To form links, twist the sausages a complete 360-degree turn, at even intervals. Twist each alternate link the opposite way, which will stop them unwinding again. If you like, you can tie them neatly with butcher's string at each join. Transfer the sausage links to the refrigerator until ready to use. They will keep up to four days in the fridge or up to three months in the freezer.

Dry-curing
Big egg and bacon sanga

This sandwich should be so big that you can hardly get your mouth around it. Enjoy with a cold beer!

12 thick-cut rashers smoky bacon
8 thick slices sourdough bread
butter
Homemade Tomato Sauce (page 343)
your favourite mustard
your favourite barbecue sauce

4 slices cheese
2 hard-boiled eggs, sliced
1 small cos lettuce, shredded
4 tomatoes, sliced
salt
freshly ground black pepper

Grill or fry the bacon until it's crisp and golden brown.

Butter the bread and smear a little tomato sauce and mustard onto 4 slices and a little barbecue sauce onto the rest.

Now start building your sandwiches. I like to sit 3 slices of hot bacon onto the bread spread with barbecue sauce, then top it with slices of cheese, followed by slices of egg. Top with a handful of lettuce and finish with the tomato. Season it all generously with salt and pepper and top off with the rest of the bread. Squish the sandwiches together firmly and get stuck in.

Serves 4

Dry-cure mix for the enthusiast

The ideal mix for making your own streaky bacon.

1.5 kg coarse salt
350 g freshly ground white pepper
100 g fennel seeds

1 tablespoon dried chilli flakes
1 whole pork belly, around 2 kg, cut
   into 4 pieces

In a large mixing bowl, combine the salt with the pepper, fennel seeds and chilli flakes.

Work a generous handful of the dry-cure mix into each piece of pork belly then stack them on top of each other in a non-reactive container (plastic, enamel or glass is perfect). After 24 hours drain off the liquid that has leached out of the meat and rinse and dry the container. Rub a fresh handful of dry-cure mix into the pork belly pieces and stack them back into the container. Repeat this process every 24 hours for between 5–8 days.

Once cured, the pieces of bacon should be rinsed well and patted thoroughly dry. Suspend them from a hook in a cool, well-ventilated place and cut off slices as you need them. The bacon will keep for up to 6 months.

This is the sort of breakfast you want to cook at the weekend, when you've got a long lazy day stretching ahead of you filled with nothing more energetic than the newspapers or watching the footy.

You can fry the sausages and bacon, or grill them if you prefer. And obviously you can fry, scramble or poach the eggs, depending on how virtuous you want to pretend you are. This sort of meal is really more an exercise in organisation than about fancy techniques. You need to get all your ingredients ready and then keep them warm in the oven as you go. Obviously you'll prepare your toast and eggs at the last minute, but none of the other things will suffer too much from being kept warm for 10–15 minutes.

Dry-curing
La Luna 'fat boy' breakfast special

olive oil for frying
4 big fat sausages
4 big field mushrooms
4 big tomatoes, halved
3 tablespoons extra-virgin olive oil
salt
freshly ground black pepper
few sprigs thyme

1 garlic clove, finely chopped
butter for frying
12 thick-cut rashers smoky bacon
2 large cooked potatoes, sliced
4 thick slices sourdough bread
8 free-range eggs
¼ cup chopped parsley leaves

Preheat the oven to 150°C and put 4 plates on the lowest shelf to warm.

Heat a little of the olive oil in a large, non-stick frying pan and fry the sausages until cooked and golden brown. Transfer the sausages to an ovenproof platter and put them in the oven to keep warm.

While the sausages are cooking, brush the mushrooms and tomatoes all over with the extra-virgin olive oil. Season liberally with salt and pepper. Place them all, cut-side down, in a small roasting tin and sprinkle the mushrooms with thyme and garlic. Transfer to the top shelf of your oven – they'll take around 12 minutes to cook.

Add a tiny knob of butter to the frying pan and fry the bacon until crisp and golden brown. Transfer to the platter in the oven.

Add a splash more oil and a little more butter to the pan and sauté the potatoes until golden brown and crunchy all over – about 5 minutes. Transfer to the platter in the oven.

Now you're into the home stretch, with just the toast and eggs to go. Pop the bread in the toaster and when it's done, butter it generously.

Melt a bit more butter in the pan and when it's sizzling, fry the eggs the way you like them.

Now bring everything else out of the oven and start assembling. Divide the tomatoes, mushrooms, sausages, bacon and fried potatoes evenly between the 4 warmed plates. Slide the eggs onto the plates and scatter generously with parsley. You'll want to serve this breakfast special with a pot of strong tea – and then go and have a lie down!

Serves 4

Wet-curing
Basic brine

This brine works brilliantly with pork and I think it's particularly good for chops, which can dry out and be a bit tough. After brining, barbecue or grill the chops on a medium heat and turn them frequently: the sugar in the brine can caramelise and burn very quickly.

1 litre water
100 g salt
100 g brown sugar
1 teaspoon juniper berries

1 teaspoon black peppercorns
1 bay leaf
5 sprigs thyme
1 clove

To make the brine, combine all the ingredients in a large non-reactive saucepan or casserole dish and heat gently until the salt and sugar have dissolved. Increase the heat and boil vigorously for 2 minutes. Remove from the heat and leave to cool overnight before using.

Makes 1 litre

Sweet spiced brine

This is a great brine for sweeter meats, such as pork or chicken.

800 ml water
200 ml tarragon vinegar
50 g salt
100 g brown sugar

1 long red chilli
1 bay leaf
1 teaspoon black peppercorns
3 sprigs thyme

To make the sweet pickling solution, combine all the ingredients in a large non-reactive saucepan or casserole dish and heat gently until the salt and sugar have dissolved. Increase the heat and boil vigorously for 5 minutes. Remove from the heat and leave to cool overnight before using.

Makes 1 litre

Red wine brine

It is strong in colour and flavour and works particularly well with dark red meats, such as beef. This is the brine I use to cure girello for making Bresaola (page 251).

1.25 litres red wine
2 cups water
150 g salt

1 tablespoon black peppercorns
1 tablespoon allspice berries
2 bay leaves

To make the brine, combine all the ingredients in a large non-reactive saucepan or casserole dish and heat gently until the salt has dissolved. Increase the heat and boil vigorously for 2 minutes. Remove from the heat and leave to cool overnight before using.

Makes 1.25 litres

This is what I call a good old-fashioned dish. We serve it at La Luna Bistro from time to time and it's always the first dish on the menu to be sold out. Serve it with hot crusty bread to mop up the lovely buttery broth.

The silverside will make the poaching stock very salty, but it's fantastically tasty and shouldn't be wasted. I strain the stock and then dilute it with an equal amount of fresh stock or even water. It can then be used for braising the vegies that accompany the silverside.

Wet-curing

Corned beef with mustard and parsley

1 kg corned silverside

Poaching stock
2 medium onions, thickly sliced
2 medium carrots, thickly sliced
2 sticks celery, thickly sliced
6 cloves
1 tablespoon fennel seeds
2 bay leaves
2 cups white wine
1 tablespoon black peppercorns

Vegetable braise
up to 2 litres chicken or vegetable
  stock
400 g white cabbage, finely sliced
400 g pumpkin, peeled and diced
6 small potatoes
2 parsnips, peeled and diced
2 medium leeks, sliced
100 g butter
2 tablespoons Dijon or English mustard
¼ cup chopped parsley

Put the silverside into a large casserole dish and add the poaching stock ingredients. Pour on enough cold water to cover generously and bring to the boil. Lower the heat and simmer, uncovered, for 2½ hours.

Lift the silverside out of the braising liquid and transfer it to a deep dish, just large enough to hold it snugly.

Strain the braising stock and add an equal amount of the fresh chicken or vegetable stock. Taste to check that it is not too salty. Pour a little of the diluted stock onto the silverside – just enough to keep it moist – and pour the rest into the rinsed-out casserole dish. Add the cabbage, pumpkin, potatoes, parsnips and leeks and bring to the boil. Lower the heat and simmer for 20–30 minutes, or until the vegetables are tender.

Carve the corned beef into thick slices and add them to the casserole. Simmer gently until the beef is just warmed through then stir in the butter, mustard and parsley and serve with hot crusty bread.

Serves 6

This is a great pork dish; the meat takes on the flavour of the caraway and sweetness of the honey. Just be careful when you're grilling the chops as the honey can burn very easily. Serve with Red Cabbage with Apple and Caraway (page 310) or Cabbage, Apple and Tarragon Salad (page 318).

6 x 300 g pork chops
1 litre Basic Brine (page 246)
1 tablespoon caraway seeds
3 tablespoon chopped coriander

1 teaspoon freshly ground black pepper
2 spring onions, chopped
¼ cup honey
juice of 2 lemons

Place the pork chops in the brine, making sure they are completely submerged. You might want to place a weighted plate on top to keep them immersed. Refrigerate for a minimum of 12 hours and for up to 24 hours. Discard the brine after using.

When ready to cook the chops, preheat your barbecue or grill to medium. Mix the caraway, coriander, pepper, spring onions, honey and lemon juice to a paste and brush all over the chops. Cook the chops for 8–10 minutes, depending on thickness, basting with more of the paste and turning frequently. Remove from the heat and leave in a warm place to rest for a few minutes before serving.

Serves 6

Wet-curing

Barbecued pickled pork chop with honey and caraway

Wet-curing

Sweet-pickled lamb breast with pumpkin, fennel and cabbage

This is one of the most popular dishes at La Luna Bistro and it's really easy to make. We use lamb (or sometimes mutton) that has been pickled in a sweet brine for several days, which gives it a wonderful sweet-savoury flavour and a lovely rosy pink colour. The pickled lamb is simmered gently with pumpkin, fennel and cabbage – which all seem to bring out the underlying sweetness of the meat – and the broth cooks down to a gorgeous thick sauce.

1 x 2 kg leg of lamb, bone removed,
    trimmed and butterflied
1 litre Sweet Spiced Brine (page 246)
½ white cabbage, chopped into
    6 cm squares
4 onions, quartered
1 carrot, cut into 6 cm lengths
1 stick celery, cut into 6 cm lengths
10 garlic cloves
2 tablespoons fennel seeds

2 cups white wine
2 litres good-quality chicken stock
    or water
500 g pumpkin, peeled and cut
    into big chunks
salt
freshly ground black pepper
100 g butter
½ cup chopped parsley
2 tablespoons extra-virgin olive oil

Place the lamb in the brine, making sure it is completely submerged. You might want to place a weighted plate on top to keep it immersed. Refrigerate for a minimum of 24 hours and for up to 48 hours. Discard the brine after using.

Remove the lamb from the brine and cut it into 6 cm cubes. Put into a large casserole dish or heavy-based saucepan with the vegetables, garlic and fennel seeds. Pour in the wine and enough of the stock or water to cover generously.

Bring to the boil, skimming away any scum or impurities. Lower the heat to a gentle simmer and cook for 30 minuites, uncovered, skimming every now and then. Add the pumpkin to the casserole and cook for 1 further hour. You may need to add a little more liquid if it begins to dry out. By the end of the cooking time the meat will be wonderfully tender and the pumpkin will have disintegrated to form a lovely sweet, rich sauce. Taste and adjust the seasoning to your liking.

Stir in the butter and parsley and serve with a drizzle of extra-virgin olive oil.

Serves 6–8

Girello is one of the muscles that sit next to the silverside at the back of the animal's thigh. It's a muscle that gets a lot of use, so really needs long, slow cooking to tenderise it. Alternatively, you can turn it into the classic Italian cured beef called bresaola.

As with other European air-dried smallgoods, such as prosciutto di Parma, jamòn de Serrano and jambon de Bayonne, girello is sliced wafer-thin and eaten raw. I like to drizzle it with extra-virgin olive oil and sprinkle it with salt flakes before serving with Pickled Cherries (page 247) and crunchy grilled croutons.

Air-drying

Bresaola – air-cured girello in red wine brine

1 x 1.5 kg beef girello

1.25 litres Red Wine Brine (page 246)

Trim the girello of any fat or sinews. Place it in the brine, making sure it is completely submerged. Place a weighted plate on top to keep it immersed. Cover and refrigerate for 7 days, turning it around in the brine every day. Discard the brine after using.

Remove the girello from the brine and pat it dry. Tie it up with string and hang it in a cool, dry spot with good air circulation. (If you live in a temperate climate, then the garage is an ideal place!) Leave it for 4–6 weeks, by which time much of the moisture will have evaporated from the meat. It will feel hard to the touch and you may see a white mould forming on the surface. Don't worry, this is good mould, not bad mould.

To serve, slice the girello as finely as you can and arrange in overlapping layers on a large serving plate. Drizzle with extra-virgin olive oil and sprinkle with sea salt before serving.

Makes 1 bresaola

Smoking

Glazed baked pork hocks

The hock is the lower part of a pig's front leg. It often doesn't look to be much more than a big bone covered in lots of tough skin. But like other tough-but-tasty cuts, the hock cooks to a lovely juicy tenderness, and all that skin and connective tissue render down to add plenty of gelatine and flavour.

Hocks are sometimes sold fresh, but you're more likely to find them smoked. The following recipe is a wonderful way to cook smoked hocks as the sweet sticky glaze is brilliant against the rich smoky flavours and is just the thing on a cold winter night.

The secret to this dish is to cook the hocks just long enough so that the meat becomes meltingly tender, but is not completely falling off the bone. You'll have plenty of delicious stock left over, which you can strain and freeze, or use for making soups, or for braising beans or lentils with some vegies and a slug of wine.

Serve with plenty of Creamy, Buttery Mash (page 296) and Garlicky Green Beans (page 308).

4 x 700 g smoked pork hocks
1 onion, quartered
1 carrot, cut into chunks
2 sticks celery, cut into chunks
2 bay leaves
1 cinnamon stick
4 cloves
peel of 1 orange

Glaze
¼ cup Marsala
200 g softened butter
¼ cup raw sugar
splash of brandy

Ask your butcher to remove the knuckle end of the hock and to 'french' the bones for a neat presentation.

Put them in a stockpot or large casserole dish with the remaining ingredients and cover generously with cold water. Bring to the boil, skimming away any impurities that rise to the surface, then lower the heat and simmer, uncovered, for 1½ hours. The meat needs to be very soft, but not falling from the bones. Remove the pan from the heat and leave the hocks to cool in the stock.

When the hocks are completely cold, lift them out of the stock (which you can strain and re-use), and pat dry. Remove the skin and trim away any thick fatty bits (they'll make a great treat for your dog).

Preheat the oven to 190°C. Use a fork to beat the Marsala into the butter. Smear it all over the hocks and sprinkle them with sugar. Arrange the hocks in a deep roasting tin and pour in reserved stock to a depth of about 2 cm. This stops the hocks from sticking to the tin, keeps them moist and reduces down to make a lovely sauce. Bake in the oven for 20 minutes, until the butter and sugar form a shiny dark glaze.

Remove the hocks from the roasting tin and keep warm while you make a quick sauce. Add a splash of brandy to the roasting tin and bubble vigorously over a high heat. Serve the glazed hocks with the sauce and heaps of mashed potatoes.

Serves 4

Pork rillettes with bruschetta and shaved fennel

The key thing when making rillettes is to have the correct 80:20 ratio of lean meat to fat. Tell you butcher that you are making rillettes and that you need a good fatty piece of pork belly. Once you've separated the lean meat from the fat, weigh it, and if necessary, make up the fat content with pork back fat.

Rillettes makes a great appetiser to serve with pre-dinner drinks. Use a sourdough baguette to make small slices, or serve on larger slices as a starter. As a variation, make a salsa from chopped cornichons, pickled onions, green olives and parsley, tossed with lemon juice and extra-virgin olive oil. The main thing is to use strong salty and acidic flavours to cut through the richness of the pork fat.

Rillettes

1 kg pork belly, neck or shoulder
up to 250 g pork back fat, diced
3 sprigs thyme
1 bay leaf
2 allspice berries, crushed
1 star anise
1 teaspoon salt
½ teaspoon freshly ground
   black pepper
750 ml apple cider (or white wine
   or beer)

1 small bulb fennel
juice of 2 lemons
salt
freshly ground black pepper
big slug extra-virgin olive oil
½ cup roughly chopped parsley
4 slices sourdough loaf or baguette
olive oil

To make the rillettes, separate the pork belly meat from the fat and cut both into small chunks. Weigh meat and fat separately and if necessary, add enough pork back fat to make up the 20 per cent ratio. Place both the fat and the lean meat in a heavy-based saucepan and add the herbs and spices. Season with salt and pepper and pour in the cider. Cover the pan and heat gently until the liquid starts to boil. Skim away any foam that rises to the surface then lower the heat to the barest simmer. Cover with a lid and cook gently for 3–4 hours, stirring from time to time. By the end of the cooking time the meat should be completely tender and immersed in fatty juices.

Strain, reserving both the meat and cooking juices, but discarding the aromatics. Return the cooking juices to the pan and bring to the boil. Cook until reduced by half, then remove from the heat.

Use a fork to break the meat into shreds, or for a smoother consistency, pulse it briefly in a food processor. Stir in some of the reduced cooking liquid, reserving enough to seal the surface, then tip the mixture into 6 x 6 cm ramekins. Pack in fairly well, to ensure there are no air pockets. Spoon the remaining liquid over the surface then cover with plastic wrap and refrigerate. As long as the surface of the rillettes is covered by a thick layer of fat, it will keep in the fridge for up to seven days.

Slice the fennel as finely as you can. Place in a mixing bowl and toss thoroughly with the lemon juice. Season generously and toss with the oil.

Preheat your grill or a griddle plate on your stovetop. Brush the sourdough slices on both sides with olive oil and season. Grill on both sides until golden brown.

To serve, spread the hot toast with rillettes and top with a small mound of fennel salad. Finish with a drizzle of oil and a sprinkling of salt and pepper.

Serves 4–6

Preserving in fat
Confit duck leg

This is the classic French method of cooking and preserving meats such as duck, goose or pork in their own rendered fat.

6 duck legs
1 tablespoon salt
1.5 kg duck fat (or olive oil)
6 allspice berries

6 cardamon pods
1 bay leaf
6 black peppercorns

Lay the duck legs out on a clean tea towel and sprinkle all over with the salt. Leave for about 1 hour, to allow the salt to draw out moisture from the skin. If you are planning to store the confit duck, instead of eating it straight away, then salt for 24 hours. This helps preserve the duck for longer.

Wipe the salt off and pat the duck legs dry with paper towels.

Heat the duck fat or olive oil in a large heavy-based saucepan until it just starts to bubble. Add the legs, one at a time. Bring back to the boil then lower the heat to a very gentle simmer. Cook for 50 minutes, skimming from time to time.

When the duck meat is very tender but before it begins to come away from the bone, remove the pan from the heat. Transfer to a sink of iced water to chill as quickly as you can. Add the remaining ingredients and stir into the duck fat. When cold, refrigerate until ready to use. If you plan to keep the confit duck (for up to 1 month) then transfer the duck legs to a shallow earthenware dish and ladle on enough fat to cover them completely. Refrigerate until needed.

When ready to eat, bring the confit duck to room temperature and preheat the oven to 200°C. Place the duck in the oven for 1 or 2 minutes, just until the fat liquefies, then remove the duck legs from the fat and place them on a rack in a roasting tin. Heat for 10 minutes until the skin is crisp and the duck warmed through.

Serves 6

Preserving in fat
Cassoulet

This is the famous dish from southern France and there are endless different versions, depending on which village or even which family you ask. The constants, though, are white beans, pork and duck or goose, cooked to a rich and filling stew. Some people throw their hands up in horror at the inclusion of tomatoes; others are dismayed by a breadcrumb topping – I love both!

500 g dried white haricot beans, soaked overnight in cold water
1 onion, diced
1 carrot, sliced
2 sticks celery, sliced
1 leek, sliced

6 garlic cloves, roughly chopped
2 bay leaves
3 sprigs thyme
1 litre chicken stock
1 cup white wine

6 thick-cut rashers smoky bacon or gammon, cut into chunks
6 Toulouse sausages (or another thick, rustic, pure-meat sausage), cut into chunks
4 tomatoes, skinned, seeded and chopped
4 Confit Duck Legs (page 255), halved
salt
freshly ground black pepper
1 cup breadcrumbs
¼ cup chopped parsley

Preheat the oven to 175°C.

Drain the beans and put them in a large casserole dish or a deep earthenware pot. Add just enough cold water to cover the beans and bring to the boil. Add the onion, carrot, celery, leek, garlic and herbs, then stir in the stock and the wine. Return to the boil, skimming away any impurities that rise to the surface.

Add the bacon and sausages to the casserole, tucking them in among the beans. Cover and transfer to the oven. Cook for 1 hour, then add the tomatoes and the pieces of confit duck. Taste and adjust the seasoning to your liking. Scatter the breadcrumbs over the surface and return to the oven, uncovered. Cook for a further 30 minutes, until the breadcrumbs have formed a golden brown crust. Sprinkle with parsley as you serve.

Serves 6–8

Preserving
in jelly

Classic jellied brawn

This is an old-fashioned English dish of chopped cooked meats set in jelly. Traditionally, brawn uses the whole pig's head – yes, all of it – and I like to throw in a couple of pig's trotters too. Trotters and head both contain lots of gelatine, which is released by long gentle poaching. The poaching liquid is reduced, then used to set the chopped meat into a delicious jellied glaze.

Serve the brawn as part of a charcuterie or antipasto selection, with pickles, greens and warm crusty bread or crunchy toast.

1 pig's head
2 pig's trotters
2 onions, sliced
1 carrot, sliced

3 sticks celery, sliced
2 bay leaves
1 tablespoon salt
½ cup chopped parsley

To prepare the pig's head and trotters, first remove any hair with a razor or blowtorch. Place them all in a large stockpot or casserole dish. Add half the vegetables and the bay leaves and cover with cold water. Add the salt and bring to the boil then lower the heat and simmer gently, covered, for 3 hours. At the end of the cooking time the meat should be very soft and falling away from the bones.

Remove the pig's head and trotters from the pot and strain and reserve the poaching liquid. Add the rest of the vegetables to the strained liquid and boil vigorously until reduced by three-quarters, skimming from time to time. Remove from the heat and leave to cool.

Once the head and trotters are cool enough to handle, remove all the bones and discard them. Use your fingers to break the meat into smallish chunks – retain as much of the skin and eyeballs as you can bear. Mix the parsley into the meat.

Line a 1 litre terrine or circular mould with several layers of plastic wrap, leaving a big overhang. Scatter the shredded meat and parsley in, pressing gently as you go, so there are no air pockets. Pour in enough of the reduced poaching liquid to reach the top of the meat. Bring up the overhang of plastic wrap and fold neatly to cover the surface of the terrine, place a weighted plate or board on top and put in the refrigerator to set.

To serve the brawn, turn it out of its mould onto a platter and cut into slices. Peel away the plastic wrap before serving and accompany with a selection of your favourite pickles.

Serves 6–8

Terrines

Jambon persillé

A specialty of French delicatessens, this pressed terrine is very pretty with its layers of pink ham and bright green parsley. It's a good recipe for using up any leftover Christmas ham, or you can use good meaty ham hocks.

Serve with a peppery rocket or watercress salad to make an elegant starter.

2 pig's trotters
2 ham hocks or 800 g ham off the bone
1 onion, chopped
2 sticks celery, chopped
1 leek, sliced and chopped
2 bay leaves

6 peppercorns
3 sprigs thyme
1 cup chopped parsley
salt
freshly ground black pepper

To prepare the pig's trotters, first remove any hair with a razor or blowtorch.

Place the trotters and ham hocks in a large stockpot or casserole dish. Add half the vegetables, the bay leaves, peppercorns and thyme and cover with cold water. Bring to the boil then lower the heat and simmer gently, covered, for 2½ hours. At the end of the cooking time the meat should be very soft and falling away from the bones.

Remove the trotters and ham hocks from the pot and strain and reserve the poaching liquid. Add the rest of the vegetables to the strained liquid and boil vigorously until reduced by three-quarters. Cool to room temperature. Taste the poaching liquid and adjust seasoning if necessary.

Once the trotters and hocks are cool enough to handle, remove all the bones and discard them. Use your fingers to break the meat into smallish chunks.

Line a 1 litre terrine mould with several layers of plastic wrap, leaving a big overhang. Scatter the shredded meat and parsley in – the more higgledy-piggledy the better. Press gently as you go, so there are no air pockets. Pour in enough of the reduced poaching liquid to reach the top of the meat. Bring up the overhang of plastic wrap and fold neatly to cover the surface of the terrine, place a weighted plate or board on top and put in the refrigerator to set.

To serve the terrine, turn it out of its mould onto a platter and cut into slices. Peel away the plastic wrap before serving with lightly dressed rocket or watercress leaves.

Serves 8–10

Terrines

Pork and liver terrine with crisp garlic toast

Some people find pig's liver has too strong a flavour for their liking, in which case calf's liver – or even chicken or duck livers – can be substituted. If you do use pig's liver, make sure you clean and peel it before using.

Pork and liver terrine
2 tablespoons olive oil
1 medium onion, finely diced
2 garlic cloves, crushed
350 g pork belly
350 g pork neck
200 g smoky bacon
350 pig's liver (or veal, chicken or duck livers), cut into chunks
½ teaspoon ground allspice
2 tablespoons brandy
2 tablespoons Dijon mustard
1 tablespoon chopped thyme
¼ cup chopped parsley
2 teaspoons freshly ground black pepper
½ tablespoon salt
1 egg

1 small loaf sourdough bread
garlic cloves, to rub
extra-virgin olive oil, to drizzle
cornichons to serve

Preheat the oven to 175°C and lightly oil a 1 litre terrine mould.

Heat the oil in a heavy-based frying pan and sweat the onion and garlic gently until soft but not coloured. Tip into a large mixing bowl and leave to cool.

Chop the pork belly, pork neck and bacon roughly then mix them together and push through a mincer. Add to the mixing bowl with the remaining ingredients and use your hands to mix everything together evenly. Tip the mixture into the prepared terrine mould, packing it well into the corners to prevent air bubbles. Bang the mould on your work surface a few times to help it settle.

Transfer the terrine to a deep oven tray and pour in enough hot water to come halfway up the sides. Cover the terrine mould with its lid or aluminium foil and cook for 1½ hours. The terrine is cooked when the internal core temperature reaches 72°C or when the juices run clear.

Remove the terrine from the water bath and place a weighted board or plate on top. When cool, transfer to the refrigerator and leave overnight before removing the weights. Terrines are usually better after a few days, as the flavours mature and improve.

To serve, toast slices of sourdough bread then rub each side with garlic and drizzle on a little oil. Cut the terrine into slices and serve with the crisp garlic toast and cornichons.

Serves 8–10

Terrines

Country-style terrine

I love to serve this chunky terrine as part of a ploughman's lunch. Add some good cheddar cheese, pickles and slices of apple and serve with crusty bread.

20 long rashers smoky bacon, rinds removed
2 tablespoons olive oil
1 onion, finely diced
1 garlic clove, crushed
500 g minced lean pork (or veal)
500 g minced pork belly (or shoulder or neck)
¼ cup diced ham

2 tablespoons Dijon mustard
3 tablespoons brandy
3 tablespoons green peppercorns
2 tablespoons chopped thyme
2 tablespoons chopped parsley
½ cup pistachio nuts
½ tablespoon salt
1 teaspoon freshly ground black pepper

Preheat the oven to 175°C and lightly oil a 1 litre terrine mould. Line the mould crosswise with the bacon rashers, leaving enough of an overhang to bring up and over the top of the terrine.

Heat the oil in a heavy-based frying pan and sweat the onion and garlic gently until soft but not coloured. Tip into a large mixing bowl and leave to cool.

Add the remaining ingredients to the bowl and use your hands to mix everything together evenly. Tip the mixture into the prepared mould, packing it well into the corners to prevent air bubbles. Bang the mould on your work surface a few times to help it settle then bring the ends of the bacon rashers over the top of the terrine.

Transfer the terrine to a deep oven tray and pour in enough hot water to come halfway up the sides. Cover the terrine mould with its lid or aluminium foil and cook for 1½ hours. The terrine is cooked when the internal core temperature reaches 72°C or when the juices run clear.

Remove the terrine from the water bath and place a weighted board or plate on top. When cool, transfer to the refrigerator and leave overnight before removing the weights. Terrines are usually better after a few days, as the flavours mature and improve.

Serves 8–10

Sausages

Classic Italian pork and fennel sausages

This is a classic Italian combination of pork with fennel and a hint of chilli – although you can make them hotter or milder if you prefer.

My favourite way of serving these sausages is with Nonno's Cake (page 299) and lots of freshly grated parmesan. Traditionally, the polenta would be poured out onto a clean wooden table and the sausages piled on top – sometimes in a spicy tomato sauce. It's the perfect dish for festivals and other special occasions, when everyone gets stuck in together!

See pages 242–3 for tips on making sausages.

1 kg lean pork belly, neck or shoulder
300 g pork back fat
2 garlic cloves, sliced
2 tablespoons fennel seeds
1 teaspoon dried chilli flakes
1 teaspoon ground allspice

2 tablespoons freshly ground black pepper
1½ tablespoons kitchen or table salt (not rock salt or salt flakes)
½ cup chopped parsley
3–4 metres of natural sausage casings

To prepare the sausage mixture, first trim away any connective tissue and sinews from the meat, then dice both meat and fat into 5 cm cubes. Transfer to a large mixing bowl and add the remaining ingredients. Use your hands to mix everything together well, so that the fat and flavourings are evenly distributed. At this stage, I like to cover the bowl and refrigerate the sausage mixture overnight, which allows all the flavours to develop, but you can proceed straight away to making the sausages if you prefer.

When ready to make the sausages, remove the mixture from the refrigerator and feed it through a mincer fitted with a medium blade, until you achieve the consistency you like. I prefer a coarser texture.

Fill the sausage casings and twist to form links. Transfer the sausage links to the refrigerator until ready to use, but at least overnight.

Makes around 1.3 kg sausages

Sausages

Lamb, rosemary and roasted garlic sausages with a splash of pinot

This is another of my favourite sausage recipes, which combines lamb with all its traditional partners. Instead of using raw garlic, which can be a bit fierce, I simmer it gently in oil first. This keeps the garlic moist and mellows the flavour. You can add a splash of oil in the sausage itself, or keep it to make salad dressings.

See pages 242–3 for tips on making sausages.

10 garlic cloves
½ cup olive oil
1 kg lamb leg meat
200 g pork fat
2 tablespoons chopped rosemary
¼ cup pinot noir, or another light
  red wine

1 teaspoon ground allspice
1 scant tablespoon kitchen or table salt
  (not rock salt or salt flakes)
1 tablespoon freshly ground black
  pepper
3–4 metres of natural sausage casings

Peel the garlic cloves and put them into a small saucepan with the olive oil. Heat gently until it begins to simmer. Lower the heat and cook very gently – you just want the odd bubble to pop up to the surface, rather than a vigorous simmer – until the garlic softens. After 15–20 minutes, or when the garlic cloves are tender, remove them from the oil.

Trim away any connective tissue and sinews from the lamb, then dice both meat and pork fat into 5 cm cubes. Transfer to a large mixing bowl and add the remaining ingredients. Use your hands to mix everything together well, so that the fat and flavourings are evenly distributed. At this stage, I like to cover the bowl and refrigerate the sausage mixture overnight, which allows all the flavours to develop, but you can proceed straight away to making the sausages if you prefer.

When ready to make the sausages, remove the mixture from the refrigerator and feed it through a mincer fitted with a medium blade, until you achieve the consistency you like. I prefer a coarser texture.

Fill the sausage casings and twist to form links. Transfer the sausage links to the refrigerator until ready to use, but at least overnight.

Makes around 1.3 kg sausages

This sausage has achieved legendary status around Victoria, and has even been listed by the Slow Food movement's list of endangered foodstuffs! It's a traditional *salsiccie* – sausage – brought by Swiss-Italian migrants to the Australian goldfields in the 19th century. The bull-boar acquired its name because it uses a mixture of beef and pork. It's a robust, spicy sausage flavoured with lots of garlic and red wine.

See pages 242–3 for tips on making sausages.

Daylesford bull-boar sausages

500 ml red wine
6 garlic cloves, chopped
1 kg beef, leg or shoulder
1 kg fatty pork, from the neck or shoulder
¼ cup fennel seeds
1 tablespoon chopped dried chillies

1 teaspoon ground allspice
½ cup chopped parsley
1½ level tablespoons kitchen or table salt (not rock salt or salt flakes)
2 tablespoons freshly ground black pepper

Place the red wine and garlic in a heavy-based saucepan. Bring to the boil, then simmer vigorously until reduced by three-quarters. Remove from the heat and leave to cool completely.

Trim away any connective tissue and sinews from the beef and pork, then dice both into 5 cm cubes. Transfer to a large mixing bowl and add the remaining ingredients and the cold wine-garlic reduction. Use your hands to mix everything together well, so that the fat and flavourings are evenly distributed. Cover the bowl and refrigerate the sausage mixture overnight, which allows all the flavours to develop.

When ready to make the sausages, remove the mixture from the refrigerator and feed it through a mincer fitted with a medium blade, until you achieve the consistency you like. I prefer a coarser texture.

Fill the sausage casings and twist to form links. Transfer the sausage links to the refrigerator until ready to use, but at least overnight.

Makes around 2 kg sausages

Sausages

Elk sausages with juniper and green peppercorns

I am lucky enough to have a farmer friend who supplies me with elk meat to make these sausages. I really like the flavour, which is similar to venison. Elk are a type of deer that are native to North America and parts of eastern Asia. They are being bred in New Zealand, and in smaller numbers here in Australia, but may well be hard to find. You can, of course, use venison meat instead, which is fairly readily available.

The meat of both elk and venison is very lean – which is one of the reasons for its increased popularity with health-conscious diners. But for sausages, you do need to have a good amount of fat content, to keep the meat moist, and sadly, the fat from deer has a rather unpleasant flavour. I add pork cheek to the mixture, which has a brilliant flavour, and its high fat content adds the necessary moisture to the mix.

See pages 242–3 for tips on making sausages.

---

1 kg elk or venison (leg or neck)
300 g pork cheek
1 tablespoon juniper berries, crushed
1 tablespoon green peppercorns

¼ cup chopped parsley
1 level tablespoon kitchen or table salt
  (not rock salt or salt flakes)
2–3 metres of natural sausage casings

Trim away any connective tissue and sinews from the elk or venison, then dice both meat and pork cheek into 5 cm cubes. Transfer to a large mixing bowl and add the remaining ingredients. Use your hands to mix everything together well, so that the fat and flavourings are evenly distributed. At this stage, I like to cover the bowl and refrigerate the sausage mixture overnight, which allows all the flavours to develop, but you can proceed straight away to making the sausages if you prefer.

When ready to make the sausages, remove the mixture from the refrigerator and feed it through a mincer fitted with a medium blade, until you achieve the consistency you like. I prefer a coarser texture.

Fill the sausage casings and twist to form links. Transfer the sausage links to the refrigerator until ready to use, but at least overnight.

Makes around 1.3 kg sausages

I created this recipe when a friend of mine gave me a couple of pheasants that were too damaged to sell as whole birds for the table. Sausages were the perfect solution, and I really loved their delicate flavour.

As is the case with all game birds – especially ones that are shot in the wild – the meat is very lean. I didn't want to compromise the flavour by adding pork fat, so instead I decided to mince up the skin of the bird, which has a subcutaneous layer of lovely creamy fat, and add that to the mixture. It worked a treat.

See pages 242–3 for tips on making sausages.

To cook these sausages, fry them very gently in butter.

Pheasant sausages with whisky and thyme

2 pheasants
50 ml good scotch whisky
2 tablespoons chopped thyme
2 teaspoons kitchen or table salt
 (not rock salt or salt flakes)
1 teaspoon freshly ground white
 pepper
2 tablespoons chopped parsley
2–3 metres of natural sausage casings

Skin the birds and pick off as much fat from the meat as you can. Chop it all roughly, then put it into a food processor and blend to a purée.

Remove all the meat from the bones (which you can keep to make stock) and discard any bits of sinew and tendon. Dice the meat roughly.

Transfer both the meat and puréed skin to a large mixing bowl and add the remaining ingredients. Use your hands to mix everything together well, so that the meat, skin and flavourings are evenly distributed. At this stage, I like to cover the bowl and refrigerate the sausage mixture overnight, which allows all the flavours to develop, but you can proceed straight away to making the sausages if you prefer.

When ready to make the sausages, remove the mixture from the refrigerator and feed it through a mincer fitted with a medium blade, until you achieve the consistency you like. I prefer a coarser texture.

Fill the sausage casings and twist to form links. Transfer the sausage links to the refrigerator until ready to use, but at least overnight.

Makes around 800 g sausages, depending on how much meat you get from the pheasants

Sausages
Cotechino with onions and mushrooms

Cotechino is an Italian boiling sausage with a distinctive sticky, gelatinous texture that comes from adding pig's skin to the mix. In fact it gets its name from *coteca*, the Italian word for 'skin'. You can buy good cotechino sausages from specialist smallgoods manufacturers, but like me, you might relish the chance of making your own.

For this recipe you'll really benefit from having made friends with your butcher! Ask him to do the hard work for you in preparing the pig's head and tongues. You might also ask him to mince the cotechino mix for you, too, once you've prepared it. Most domestic mincers will struggle to process the tough skin, but your butcher's machine will (if you'll pardon the pun) make mincemeat of it! You'll also need to ask him for an ox 'bung' casing, which will make a nice fat sausage.

I always cook my cotechino in its vacuum-pack (or plastic wrap). It is less likely to burst and, because it cooks in its own juices, the flavours intensify. Use these juices to add extra flavour to the onion and mushroom braise.

Cotechino is traditionally served with Salsa Verde (page 344) or with braised lentils, and it is also one of the key ingredients in the Italian dish, bollito misto. Here I serve it with earthy mushrooms and onions, both of which work well with its rich spicy flavour.

Cotechino sausage
1 boned pig's head (remove the ears)
2 pigs' tongues, peeled and trimmed
3 garlic cloves, crushed
1 teaspoon cinnamon
2 teaspoons ground allspice
1 teaspoon ground ginger
1 teaspoon ground cloves
¼ cup chopped parsley
zest of ½ orange
1 tablespoon freshly ground black pepper

kitchen or table salt (not rock salt or salt flakes)
1 ox bung casing

Onions and mushrooms
50 g butter
2 tablespoons extra-virgin olive oil,
3 onions, thickly sliced
2 garlic cloves, roughly chopped
200 g mushrooms, sliced

Check over the boned pig's head and if there is any residual cartilage attached to the ear, nose or throat, trim it away. Chop the remaining meat and skin into 3 cm cubes.

Chop the pigs' tongues into 3 cm cubes.

Mix the diced meat with all the remaining ingredients except for the salt. Weigh the mix and calculate 1.5 per cent of the amount. Measure out this quantity of table salt and add to the mixture. Use your hands to mix everything together well, so that the flavourings are evenly distributed. At this stage, I like to cover the bowl and refrigerate the cotechino mixture overnight, which allows all the flavours to develop, but you can proceed straight away to making the cotechino if you prefer.

When ready to make the cotechino, remove the mixture from the refrigerator. and feed it through a mincer fitted with a very sharp blade, until you achieve the consistency you like. I prefer a coarser texture. Alternatively, take the mixture to your butcher and ask him to mince it for you.

Fill the ox bung with the cotechino mixture and tie the end securely with string. Sit the cotechino on a wire rack so the air can circulate around it and refrigerate overnight. At this stage the cotechino may be vacuum-packed or wrapped tightly in plastic wrap and frozen for up to 3 months.

To cook the cotechino, place the unopened package in a pan of cold water and bring it to the boil. Lower the heat and simmer very gently for 4 hours, topping up with water as needed. Remove the cotechino from the pan and drain it briefly on a tea towel. Cool in iced water. When cold the cotechino will firm up and set hard, which makes it much easier to slice. When ready to serve, open the vacuum-pack and remove the cotechino (use the jelly for braising vegetables or lentils). Grill or or pan-fry the cotechino in a little olive oil until golden brown all over.

To prepare the vegetables, melt the butter and olive oil in a heavy-based frying pan. When it starts to sizzle, add the onions and garlic then lower the heat and sweat gently until soft, about 10 minutes. Add the mushrooms to the pan and stir them into the softened onion mixture. Sauté until the mushrooms are soft, about 8 minutes. Increase the heat and allow to bubble away until most of the liquid in the pan has reduced. Stir in the chopped parsley and top with slices of grilled cotechino.

Serves 6–8

Sausages

Cotechino with onions and mushrooms

PIES

11

Pies

As any of the chefs in my restaurant kitchen will tell you, I am serious about pies. So serious, that I insisted on having a whole chapter devoted to them.

In my view a pie is the perfect package of meat, vegies and starch all in one compact dish. Even better, you don't need a knife and fork to eat a pie, so you can use the other hand for holding your beer (or glass of wine); and pies are the ideal meal to have on the run, or when you're cheering on your team at the footy!

When you think about it, a pie is really nothing more than a casserole with a flaky pastry lid (and sometimes a pastry base, too). Which means you can make them with all sorts of different fillings. You can be as traditional as you like (think beef and burgundy, steak and kidney, chicken and leek) or as inventive as you like (bacon and egg, curried vegetable, pheasant and wild mushroom). And you can breathe new life into yesterday's stew by crowning it with a golden pastry hat.

Different pies call for different pastries, from light and crispy puff, to crisp shortcrust, tender suet and delicate yoghurt pastry. I've included recipes for all these in the pages that follow.

And as well as giving recipes for my favourite pies, I've also included some other tasty pastry items, such as sausage rolls and little empanadas, that will be a big hit with the kids. And though it doesn't have a pastry lid, I couldn't resist slipping in a recipe for everyone's home-cooked favourite, a shepherd's pie.

Savoury shortcrust pastry

This is a lovely rich, short pastry that I use for all my savoury pies and tarts. The quantity given is enough to make 2 tarts, but you can freeze half for future use. Similarly, any off-cuts can be rolled together and refrigerated or frozen for future use.

500 g plain flour
a pinch of salt
300 g butter, roughly chopped

1 whole egg
2 egg yolks
40 ml water

Combine the flour, salt and butter in a food processor and blitz to form sandy crumbs. Lightly beat the egg with the egg yolks and add to the flour mixture. Pulse until incorporated. With the motor running, slowly drizzle in the water until the mixture starts to come together to form a big ball. Tip out onto a lightly floured work surface and knead briefly to form a smooth pastry ball.

Divide the pastry into 2 portions, wrap them both in plastic wrap and refrigerate for at least 1 hour before using. When ready to use, roll the pastry out on a lightly floured work surface and then use to line a tart tin or pie dish. Refrigerate again for 1 hour before baking.

The pastry will keep in the fridge for up to 4 days or in the freezer for up to 3 months.

Makes around 850 g

Yoghurt pastry

This soft, tender pastry is virtually foolproof and can be made with yoghurt or sour cream. Either way, it cooks to a lovely crisp and light crust, and makes a great base for pizzas.

Any off-cuts can be rolled together and refrigerated or frozen for future use.

600 g plain flour
a pinch salt

1 egg, lightly beaten
500 g yoghurt

Sift the flour and salt onto a work surface. Make a well in the flour and pour in the beaten egg. Use your fingers to gradually work in the flour. Add the yoghurt and mix with your hands until it's all incorporated. Knead gently to form a smooth, very soft pastry.

Divide the pastry into 2 portions, wrap them both in plastic wrap and refrigerate for at least 1 hour before using. When ready to use, roll the pastry out on a lightly floured work surface and line a tart tin or pie dish. Refrigerate again for at least 2 hours before using.

The pastry will keep in the fridge for up to 4 days or in the freezer for up to 3 months.

Makes 1 kg

Rough puff pastry

True puff pastry is something of an art, and is probably best left to the professionals. This 'cheat's' version, known as 'rough puff', is much easier for the home cook to master, and it does come fairly close to the real thing: light, flaky and golden.

One of the keys to success is leaving the butter a bit lumpy. The less the butter is worked into the flour, the more water you'll need – and it is the water that creates steam during the baking, which in turn makes the pastry rise.

Once you've made this rough puff a few times, you'll get the hang of it. It can be made well ahead of time and stored in the freezer. I usually roll it out to about 1 cm thick and freeze it on a flat tray. Let it defrost at room temperature for 30 minutes before using.

500 g butter
500 g plain flour, sifted

a pinch of salt
1½ cups iced water

Remove the butter from the fridge about 45 minutes before using, so it is firm, but not rock-hard. Cut it into cubes and place in a mixing bowl with the flour and salt. Use your fingertips to rub the butter into the flour, leaving it a bit lumpy, rather than uniform sandy crumbs.

Add the iced water, a little at a time, (you may not need all of it), and work it into the flour mixture until it comes together as a dough. You should be able to see clearly defined little flecks of butter in the pastry. Wrap in plastic wrap and refrigerate for 1 hour.

Roll the pastry out on a lightly floured work surface, to form a long rectangle, about 20 cm x 40 cm x 5 mm thick. Fold the 2 short ends in upon each other to make 3 thick layers. Rotate the pastry a quarter-turn and roll it away from you again, to form a long rectangle, the same dimensions as before. Fold into thirds again. Wrap in plastic wrap and refrigerate for 30 minutes.

Repeat this rolling, turning and folding process again, then refrigerate for 30 minutes before using. Alternatively, the pastry can be wrapped tightly in plastic wrap and kept in the refrigerator for up to 4 days or in the freezer for 3 months.

Makes 1 kg

It may be out of favour with health fanatics, but suet pastry is indispensable for making steamed puddings – savoury or sweet. It actually has a bit of a dual personality: when steamed, it is pale, soft and spongy; when baked, it is golden, flaky and crisp.

You can buy suet from your friendly butcher. It should be stored in the freezer and will keep for 3 months. Use it straight from the freezer as it's easier to grate.

Suet pastry

350 g frozen suet
700 g plain flour, sifted

1 teaspoon salt
up to 400 ml cold water

Grate the suet onto your work surface and sprinkle on about 100 g of the flour. Use a long, sharp knife to chop the suet with the flour; this prevents it from becoming sticky.

Transfer the suet to a large mixing bowl and stir in the remaining flour and salt. Use your finger tips to rub the suet into the flour, but leave it a little rough and lumpy; it helps it to rise.

Add the water, a little at a time, until the mixture just comes together. Knead for 2–3 minutes, until elastic and springy. Wrap in plastic wrap and refrigerate for 30 minutes before using. When ready to use, roll the pastry out on a lightly floured work surface and line a tart tin or pie dish. Unlike other pastries, suet pastry doesn't need to be blind-baked.

The pastry will keep in the fridge for up to 4 days or in the freezer for up to 3 months.

Makes around 850 g

Family-size chicken, leek and mushroom pie

Nothing beats a big family-size pie, with all your meat and veggies in the one dish, covered with a buttery, flaky pastry. This is a very simple recipe. I use chicken because it cooks really quickly, but you can substitute your favourite filling. When I make this pie for my family there is never anything left over.

600 g boned chicken thighs, skinned and roughly diced
salt
freshly ground black pepper
50 g butter
2 tablespoons olive oil
1 medium onion, finely diced
4 garlic cloves, crushed
3 medium leeks, thoroughly washed and sliced into rounds
200 g button mushrooms, sliced or halved

1 cup white wine
2 cups chicken stock
4 tablespoons cornflour, mixed to a paste with a little water
½ cup cream
¼ cup chopped parsley
2 tablespoons chopped thyme
2 tablespoons chopped dill

500 g Rough Puff Pastry (page 276)
1 egg yolk, beaten with 2 tablespoons milk

Heat the olive oil in a heavy-based saucepan or casserole. Season the chicken liberally. When the oil is sizzling, brown the chicken in batches then transfer to a plate.

Add the butter to the pan and sweat the onion and garlic until they soften. Add the leeks and mushrooms to the pan and sauté for 5–8 minutes, or until soft. Add the wine and chicken stock and bring to the boil. Lower the heat and simmer for 10 minutes. Add the browned chicken to the pan and simmer for 15 minutes. Stir in the cornflour paste, cream and herbs and simmer for a few minutes.

When ready to bake the pie, preheat the oven to 200°C and spoon the chicken filling into a large shallow pie dish.

Roll the pastry out to a large circle, around 1 cm thick. You need it to be a few centimetres larger than the pie dish. Lift the pastry onto the pie dish and brush all over with the egg wash. Don't trim the overhang as the pastry will probably shrink as it cooks. Bake for 15–20 minutes, or until the pastry has puffed up to a lovely golden brown and the filling is bubbling up around the edges.

Serves 6

The great Aussie meat pie

The great Aussie pie is an Aussie icon, and I don't know many people who can resist its charms – especially when homemade. I always top my meat pies with puff pastry, but will sometimes use suet pastry for the base instead of shortcrust as it is so easy to work with. And I always add a little cornflour to the filling, as I like it to be very thick.

These quantities will make 6 x 12 cm pies or 1 x 27 cm pie.

1 kg rump or gravy beef, cut into
  1 cm dice
2 teaspoons salt
1 teaspoon freshly ground black pepper
1 teaspoon cayenne pepper
4 tablespoons olive oil
2 onions, finely diced
4 garlic cloves, finely chopped
2 medium carrots, thinly sliced
2 sticks celery, finely diced
4 cups beef stock (the better quality
  stock you use, the better the pie)

3 tablespoons cornflour mixed to
  a paste with a little water
2 tablespoons chopped parsley

500 g Savoury Shortcrust Pastry
  (page 275) or Suet Pastry (page 277)
500 g Rough Puff Pastry (page 276)
2 egg yolks, lightly beaten with
  4 tablespoons milk

Place the diced beef into a large mixing bowl with the salt, pepper and cayenne and toss well so it is evenly coated.

Heat half the oil in a heavy-based saucepan or casserole dish over a medium heat. When the oil is sizzling, brown the beef in batches, so that the heat stays high. Transfer the browned beef to a plate.

Add the rest of the oil to the pan and sweat the onions, garlic, carrots and celery for 5 minutes, or until the onion starts to soften and colour. Return the beef to the casserole and sauté for 2–3 minutes. Add the beef stock and stir well. Bring to the boil, then lower the heat and simmer, uncovered, for 45 minutes, stirring from time to time.

Stir in the cornflour paste and parsley and simmer for another 3 minutes. Remove from the heat and leave to cool.

When ready to bake the pies, preheat the oven to 200°C and lightly grease 6 x 12 cm pie tins.

Divide the shortcrust pastry into 6 even portions and roll out to circles around 5 mm thick. Use to line the pie tins, leaving about a 2 cm overhang. Spoon in the filling until the tins are three-quarters full.

Roll the puff pastry out and cut into 6 x 12 cm circles to form the pie lids. Lightly brush the rim of the pies with egg wash and place the lids on top. Press the edges firmly to seal, then roll with a rolling pin to trim off any surplus pastry. Make a small cut in the pastry lid so that the steam can escape as the pies bake. Brush with a little more egg wash and bake for 20 minutes until the pastry is cooked on the underside and the top has puffed up to a lovely golden brown. One large pie will probably take 25–30 minutes.

Serve the pies with lots of tomato sauce, a few cold beers and a good game of footy.

Makes 6 pies

Traditional recipes for steak and kidney pudding simply pile the raw ingredients into the suet-lined basin before steaming. I prefer to cook the mixture first so that I can taste and adjust the seasoning to my liking.

Steak and kidney pudding

400 g rump steak, cut into small dice
400 g ox or veal kidneys, skinned, cored and cut into small dice
salt
freshly ground black pepper
3 tablespoons olive oil
200 g smoky bacon, roughly diced
50 g butter
2 onions, finely diced
4 garlic cloves, crushed

1 stick celery, finely diced
100 g button mushrooms
1 bay leaf
3 sprigs thyme
2 good-quality beef stock
3 tablespoons cornflour, mixed to a paste with a little water
½ cup chopped parsley

1 kg Suet Pastry (page 277)

Season the beef and kidneys generously with salt and pepper. Heat the oil in a heavy-based frying pan until sizzling. Sauté the beef, kidney and bacon in batches, until lightly coloured, then tip into a large mixing bowl.

Add the butter to the pan then lower the heat and sweat the onion, garlic and celery for a few minutes until soft, but not coloured. Add the mushrooms to the pan, together with the bay leaf, thyme and stock. Return the browned meats to the pan and stir in the cornflour paste. Simmer gently for 5 minutes then remove from the heat and leave to cool before skimming away any surface fat. Stir in the parsley.

Grease a 1½ litre pudding basin. Set aside a quarter of the pastry for the lid of the pudding. Roll out the rest to form a large circle, no more than 1 cm thick, and use it to line the pudding basin. Spoon the filling into the pudding, packing it in fairly firmly. Roll out the pastry lid. Wet the edges and set it on top of the pudding. Press to seal well. Cover with a double sheet of aluminium foil, pleated to allow room for expansion while cooking. Tie securely under the lip of the pudding basin (if it has one), and if you want to be clever, make a little handle with a loose loop over the top of the pudding.

Place the pudding in a steamer, or if you don't have a steamer, sit it on a rack or small upturned plate in a saucepan. Pour in boiling water to come two-thirds up the side. Cover the steamer or saucepan with a tight-fitting lid and steam over a low–medium heat for 3½ hours. You will probably need to top up the water level from time to time.

Carefully lift the pudding out of the water and leave for 5–10 minutes to rest before serving at the table. If you want to be traditional you can wrap the pud in a snowy-white napkin.

Serves 6

This is another uniquely Australian pie – this time from Adelaide in South Australia. There's really nothing elegant about a pie floater, which is a meat pie, doused in tomato sauce, sitting in a puddle of vivid green mushy peas. Floaters are sold from pie carts and are best enjoyed as a late-night snack after a big evening out. The mash and gravy are additional refinements!

Little meat pie floaters

1 kg rump or gravy beef, diced small
salt
freshly ground black pepper
4 tablespoons olive oil
1 medium onion, finely diced
3 garlic cloves, finely chopped
1 medium carrot, fine diced
2 sticks celery, finely diced
3 cups beef stock
¼ cup port
3 tablespoons cornflour, mixed to a
   paste with a little water
2 tablespoons chopped parsley

1 kg Suet Pastry (page 277)
2 egg yolks, lightly beaten with
   4 tablespoons milk
Minted Peas (page 308)
Creamy, Buttery Mash (page 296)
1 cup Nanna's Gravy (page 330)

Season the beef generously with salt and pepper. Heat half the oil in a heavy-based saucepan or casserole dish over a medium heat. When the oil is sizzling, brown the beef in batches, so that the heat stays high. Transfer the browned beef to a plate.

Add the rest of the oil to the pan and sweat the onion, garlic, carrot and celery for 5 minutes, or until the onion starts to soften and colour. Return the beef to the casserole and sauté for 2–3 minutes. Add the beef stock and port and stir well. Bring to the boil, then lower the heat and simmer, uncovered, for 45 minutes, stirring from time to time.

Stir in the cornflour paste and parsley and simmer for another 3 minutes. Remove from the heat and leave to cool.

When ready to bake the pies, preheat the oven to 200ºC and lightly grease 6 x 12 cm pie tins.

Roll out the suet pastry to around 5 mm thick. Cut circles to line the pie tins, leaving about a 2 cm overhang. Spoon in the filling, so the pies are three-quarters full. From the remaining pastry cut 6 x 12 cm circles to form the pie lids. Lightly brush the rim of the pies with egg wash and place the lids on top. Press the edges firmly to seal, then trim off any surplus pastry. Make a small cut in the pastry lid so that the steam can escape as the pies bake. Brush with a little more egg wash and bake for 20 minutes until the pastry is cooked on the underside and the top is a lovely golden brown.

Crush the minted peas with a fork or blitz to make a coarse purée. Serve each pie on a generous spoonful of mushy peas with mash and gravy on the side. Douse in tomato sauce and enjoy.

Makes 6 pies

These little lamb turnovers are irresistibly spicy and make a great snack or canapé to serve at a drinks party. Your kids will love them too.

Before baking, the empanadas are quite soft and fragile, so I place the pastry circles onto the prepared baking trays before filling and folding them. These quantities will make between 20 and 30 small empanadas. You can reduce the quantities by half, although they do freeze very well.

Lamb empanadas

3 tablespoons olive oil
1 onion, finely diced
3 garlic cloves, crushed
1½ teaspoons cumin seeds,
   toasted and ground
½ teaspoon allspice
1 tablespoon paprika
1 kg minced lamb
salt
freshly ground black pepper

2 cups tomato passata
½ cup chopped coriander leaves
chilli powder to taste (optional)

1 kg Yoghurt Pastry (page 275)
2 egg yolks lightly beaten with
   4 tablespoons milk

Heat the oil in a heavy-based saucepan. Add the onion and garlic and sweat gently until soft and translucent. Add the spices and the minced lamb and stir well to combine. Add the tomato passata and stir well. Simmer over a medium heat until the lamb is cooked and the sauce is lovely and thick. Tip into a mixing bowl and leave to cool. When completely cold, fold in the coriander.

When ready to make the empanadas, preheat the oven to 200ºC and lightly oil a baking tray.

Cut the pastry into 60 g portions. Roll each piece of dough out on a lightly floured work surface to a 10 cm circle. Lift the pastry circles onto the prepared baking tin and place a generous spoonful in the centre of each. Brush the edge of each circle with a little egg wash and fold over to enclose the filling. Press to seal.

Bake for 20 minutes, until the empanadas are crisp and golden.

Makes 20–30

Chicken and vegetable Cornish pasties

With its semicircular shape and crimped edge, the Cornish pasty must be one of the best known pies in the world. Legend has it that they were first eaten by tin miners, who had to spend long days down in the mines without returning to the surface for lunch. The crimped edge acted as a sort of handle, and the miners could munch away at the rest of the pasty and discard the handle that had come into contact with their dirty (sometimes arsenic-contaminated) hands.

Traditional Cornish pasties are made from beef, onion and potato, but these days they come with all sorts of funky fillings. These chicken pasties are not strictly authentic, but they are light and tasty. I think the shortcrust pastry is much nicer than the traditional tough pastry. You won't want to throw any of it away.

1 medium potato, peeled and finely diced
1 medium carrot, finely diced
1 medium parsnip, finely diced
2 tablespoons olive oil
1 onion, finely diced
2 garlic cloves, crushed
1 leek, finely diced
1 stick celery, finely diced
½ cup peas
400 g chicken breast, cut into small dice
¼ cup chopped parsley
¼ cup homemade breadcrumbs
salt
freshly ground black pepper

1 kg Savoury Shortcrust Pastry (page 275)
2 egg yolks lightly beaten with 4 tablespoons milk

Preheat the oven to 200°C and lightly oil a baking tray.

Bring a small saucepan of water to the boil. Add the potato, carrot and parsnip and return to the boil. Turn off the heat and leave to stand for 10 minutes before draining.

Heat the oil in a heavy-based frying pan and sweat the onion, garlic, leek and celery for 5 minutes, or until they soften. Add the potato, carrot, parsnip, peas and chicken, and stir well. Fold in the parsley and breadcrumbs and season generously.

Roll the pastry out on a lightly floured work surface to 0.5 cm thickness. Cut into 15 cm circles and place a generous spoonful of filling in the centre of each. Brush the edge of each circle with the egg wash and fold over to enclose the filling. Press to seal then crimp the edges together. Use the sharp point of a knife to make a small incision in each pasty to let out the steam. Brush with egg wash then lift the pasties onto the prepared baking tray. Bake for 20 minutes until crisp and golden.

Makes 10

When I make these at home for my kids I put in a little less meat and a few more vegies. It's a great way to get them to eat more healthy stuff, and they'll never know how sneaky you're being. Freeze the uncooked sausage rolls if you like, and defrost them slowly on an oven tray before baking.

Sausage rolls

Filling
800 g minced pork neck or shoulder
1 onion, very finely diced
1 carrot, grated
2 garlic cloves, crushed
1 tablespoon chopped thyme
2 tablespoons chopped parsley
2 tablespoons homemade
   breadcrumbs
½ tablespoon salt
½ tablespoon freshly ground
   black pepper

750 g Rough Puff Pastry (page 276)
1 egg, beaten with 2 tablespoons milk

Preheat the oven to 210°C and lightly oil a baking tray.

To make the filling, combine the ingredients in a large mixing bowl. Use your hands to scrunch everything together so that the onion, carrot, breadcrumbs and seasonings are evenly mixed in. Divide the mixture in half and form each into a long sausage, around 30 cm long.

Roll out the pastry on a lightly floured work surface to form a 30 cm x 40 cm rectangle, around 0.5 cm thick. Cut in half lengthwise, to form 2 strips and arrange 1 long sausage along the centre of each. Brush one edge of each strip with the beaten egg mixture and fold the pastry over to enclose the filling. Press the edges together with a fork to seal. Cut each filled pastry strip into desired lengths to form sausage rolls.

Arrange the sausage rolls on the prepared baking tray and brush the tops lightly with the egg mixture. Bake for 15–20 minutes, or until golden brown.

Makes 10–12

Lamb and spinach filo pie dusted with icing sugar and cinnamon

Instead of making shepherd's pie with your leftover roast lamb, why not try making these exotic Moroccan-inspired filo pies instead? They are wonderfully warming and spicy, and the Danish feta makes them nice and creamy. I especially love the way the crisp filo pastry crunches in your mouth. I know that dusting a savoury pie with icing sugar and cinnamon sounds a bit weird, but I think the sweetness is a great counterpoint to the savoury spiciness of the filling. Try serving them as an elegant canapé or make larger pies, and serve them with a Fresh Herb Salad (page 314) as a starter.

Lamb and spinach filling
2 tablespoons olive oil
1 onion, finely chopped
4 garlic cloves, finely chopped
½ tablespoon ground cumin, lightly toasted
½ tablespoon ground coriander, lightly toasted
1 teaspoon ground ginger
500 g leftover lamb, minced (or you can use uncooked mince, if you prefer)
salt
freshly ground pepper

200 g spinach leaves
150 g Danish feta
¼ cup currants
¼ cup pine nuts
¼ cup chopped coriander leaves
1 tablespoon chopped mint leaves

1 packet filo pastry
150 g melted butter
1 tablespoon icing sugar
1 teaspoon ground cinnamon

Heat the oil in a large heavy-based frying pan. Add the onion, garlic and spices and sweat gently for 5 minutes, until soft and translucent. Add the minced lamb and season with salt and pepper. Sauté for 3 minutes, stirring well so the flavours mingle. Remove from the heat, tip into a large mixing bowl and leave to cool.

Bring a large pan of salted water to the boil. Add the spinach and blanch for 1 minute before tipping into a colander to drain. When the spinach is cool enough to handle, use your hands to squeeze out as much liquid as you can, then chop it finely.

Add the spinach to the lamb mixture, together with the remaining ingredients and use your hands to mix everything together well. Divide the mixture into 10 even portions.

When ready to cook the pies, preheat the oven to 220°C.

Make the pies one at a time, keeping the rest of the filo sheets covered with a damp tea towel until you need them. They dry out very quickly. Brush a sheet of filo with melted butter and fold it in half. Butter it again, and fold in half again. Arrange a portion of filling in the centre of the pastry, then wrap the sides up and over the top, brushing with melted butter to help seal the pastry over the filling. Invert the pie so that the wrapped side is underneath. Cover with a tea towel while you make the remaining pies in the same way.

Brush the tops of all the pies with melted butter and bake in the oven for 6–8 minutes, or until the pastry is crisp and golden brown.

Mix the icing sugar and cinnamon together and sift over the pies. Serve straight away.

Makes 10 small pies

Pheasant pie

I am always surprised by pheasant meat, which is much lighter than duck or squab, yet more complex than chicken. I think its delicate flavour goes really well with the richness of suet pastry that bakes to a melting, golden crispness. This pie is a great way of using up pheasant legs after roasting a crown (page 160). But if you can't find pheasant, then by all means use chicken marylands.

4 pheasant legs
salt
freshly ground black pepper
3 tablespoons olive oil
½ onion, finely diced
2 garlic cloves, thinly sliced
½ stick celery, thinly sliced
½ carrot, thinly sliced
½ cup red wine
¼ cup port
2 cups good-quality chicken stock
1 tablespoon chopped thyme

400 g Suet Pastry (page 277)
2 egg yolks, lightly beaten with
    4 tablespoons milk

Preheat the oven to 160°C.

Season the pheasant legs generously with salt and pepper. Heat the oil in a heavy-based casserole dish and seal the pheasant in batches, until browned all over. Transfer to a warm plate.

Add the onion, garlic, celery and carrot to the casserole and sweat over a low heat until they soften. Add the wine and port and bubble vigorously for 5 minutes so that it reduces slightly. Return the pheasant legs to the pan and add the stock. Bring to the boil, then cover, and bake in the oven for 1 hour. Leave to cool completely, then pick the meat from the bones and break it up into bite-sized pieces. Return the meat to the sauce and discard the skin and bones.

When ready to make the pie, preheat the oven to 200°C and lightly grease 4 x 8 cm pie tins. Roll the pastry out on a lightly floured work surface. Cut out 4 x 8 cm circles for the lids. Cut larger circles to line the pie tins, leaving an overhang. Divide the filling between the 4 pie tins. Lightly brush the rims of the pies with egg wash and place the lids on top. Press the edges firmly to seal, then roll with a rolling pin to trim off any surplus pastry. Make small cuts in the pastry lids so that the steam can escape as the pies bake. Brush with a little more egg wash and bake for 10–12 minutes, or until the pastry is cooked on the underside and the top is a lovely golden brown.

Serves 4

Shepherd's pie

This is home cooking at its best, and a great way of using up leftovers from your Sunday roast. If you have any leftover vegies or gravy, then throw them in as well. If you don't have any leftovers – and to be honest, in my house we usually eat up every morsel – then shepherd's pie can easily be made from scratch using raw minced lamb.

The most important thing, in my opinion, is to use a shallow baking dish with a large surface area, so you get lots of crunchy potato topping. Serve with buttered Minted Peas (page 308) and tomato sauce.

1 kg leftover lamb
  (or lean minced raw lamb)
100 g butter
2 large onions, diced
2 large carrots, diced
2 sticks celery, diced
4 garlic cloves, chopped
1 bay leaf
3 sprigs thyme
1 cup port
3 cups good quality beef stock
2 teaspoons salt
2 teaspoons freshly ground black
  pepper
2 tablespoons cornflour mixed to a
  paste with a little water
¼ cup chopped parsley

Potato topping
1 kg potatoes, peeled
100 g butter, plus 1 tablespoon
  melted butter
1 teaspoon salt

Mince or chop the leftover lamb.

Heat the butter in a heavy-based saucepan. Add the onion, carrots, celery and garlic and sauté over a low heat until the vegetables soften. Add the lamb – cooked or raw – to the pan with the bay leaf and thyme.

Add the port and stock, together with the salt and pepper. Bring to the boil, then lower the heat and simmer gently for 20 minutes. Taste and adjust the seasonings if necessary. Stir in the cornflour paste and simmer for a further 5 minutes until the sauce thickens. Remove the pan from the heat and stir in the parsley.

To make the mashed potatoes, bring them to a boil in a large saucepan of salted water. Simmer until tender, then drain. Add the butter and salt and mash until smooth. For this dish, you don't need the potatoes to be super-smooth, so don't worry about using a mouli or potato ricer; a masher or even a fork will do.

When ready to bake the pie, preheat the oven to 200°C. Spoon the meat mixture into a large baking dish. Spoon the mashed potato on top and use a fork to roughen up the surface. If you're feeling fancy, you can pipe the potato on. Either way, brush the surface with melted butter and bake for 25–35 minutes, or until the filling is hot and bubbling and the potato topping is golden brown and crunchy. Serve straight away with buttered peas and tomato sauce.

Serves 6

SIDE DISHES

12

Side dishes

This is a book dedicated to the enjoyment of meat, and to my way of thinking that extends to the things that accompany it on the plate. Way back at the start of the book I talked a bit about how important I think it is for us to shift our focus from quantity to quality. It is a big ask, I realise, because inevitably, better quality meat costs more than the mass-produced stuff. But without banging you over the head with my 'message', I *really* hope that I've been able to persuade you to at least give a bit of thought to these issues. If you do make the shift – which I hope you will – it is probably going to mean you'll be eating smaller portions of meat or better quality meat, less often.

And that's why side dishes are so important!

Throughout the recipe chapters in this book you'll see that I've made suggestions about the accompaniments that I think bring out the best in each meat dish. I don't expect you to follow these ideas to the letter of course; they are just suggestions. What I do hope, is that you'll spend a bit of time browsing through this chapter, and that you'll have as much fun trying out the side dishes as the meat recipes themselves.

Here are some of my all-time favourite side dishes, grouped together as starch, vegetable dishes, and salads and dressings. I hope you'll enjoy trying them.

Top: Watercress Salad
with Red Onions
(page 315)

Bottom: Warm Autumn
Vegetable Salad
(page 319)

Starch

Creamy, buttery mash

There must be a hundred different ways of making mashed potatoes – nearly all of them good. This is my way. I always peel the potatoes before cooking them whole. I find if you cut them smaller they tend to absorb more water. One thing that's certain is that really good mash is not diet food. It needs lots of cream and butter. I can never make enough of this mash for my customers at La Luna Bistro.

750 g nicola potatoes (or another yellow, waxy variety)
150 ml cream (or more)

150 g butter (or more)
salt
pepper

Peel the potatoes and put them in a large saucepan of cold, salted water. Bring to the boil, then lower the heat and simmer until tender. This will take up to 50 minutes, depending on the size of the potato. When the potatoes are cooked, tip them into a colander to drain.

Add the cream and butter to the hot saucepan. Push the hot potatoes through a mouli or potato ricer, straight onto the cream and butter. Beat with a wooden spoon, then season to taste.

Serves 4

Garlic- and rosemary- roasted potatoes

I like to use yellow, waxy potatoes, for this dish. Nicola are my favourite, but desiree and bintje are also good. These roast potatoes are the ideal accompaniment for just about any roast, but I particularly like them with lamb or pork.

1 kg large waxy potatoes washed, but unpeeled
¼ cup olive oil
1 tablespoon salt flakes
15 garlic cloves, peeled and lightly crushed

¼ cup rosemary leaves
1 tablespoon freshly ground black pepper
½ cup chopped parsley leaves

Preheat the oven to 200°C.

Place the potatoes in a large pot of salted water. Bring to the boil, then lower the heat and simmer, uncovered, for 5 minutes. Tip into a colander to strain, and when they are just cool enough to handle, cut them into uneven chunks.

Scatter the potatoes into a heavy-based roasting tin. Drizzle with olive oil and season generously with salt. Bake for 30 minutes, shaking the tin once or twice so they brown evenly. Add the garlic cloves to the pan and scatter on the rosemary. Return to the oven for a further 20 minutes until the potatoes and garlic are both tender, crisp and golden.

Serve sprinkled with pepper and parsley.

Serves 4–6

When my eldest son was four years old, I took him out to the country to visit Dobson's farm, who supply my restaurant with potatoes. That day he rode on a tractor, a motorbike and in a four-wheel-drive truck. He's never forgotten it and has been crazy about potatoes ever since. I'm happy to say that to date, these chips are the closest my boys have come to eating 'junk' food. The slightly strange preparation method makes the chips lovely and fluffy inside. It is brilliantly useful for dinner parties as most of the preparation (which involves leaving the potatoes alone in their cooking water) can be done several hours ahead of time.

Starch
Oven-baked organic potato chips

1 kg large nicola potatoes (organic if possible), washed, but unpeeled

olive oil
salt

Place the potatoes in a large pot of salted water. Bring to the boil, then lower the heat and simmer, uncovered, for 2 minutes. Turn off the heat, cover the pan and leave the potatoes for around 2 hours until they are cool enough to handle.

When ready to cook, preheat the oven to 200°C and lightly oil a roasting tin. Drain the potatoes thoroughly and cut them into chunky chips. Scatter onto the prepared tray and drizzle with a little more oil.

Roast the potatoes for 15 minutes, or until golden brown and crunchy. Season liberally with salt and serve straight away.

Serves 4–6

I can't think of any potato dish that goes better with roast lamb. The main thing to remember is that this dish is best cooked very slowly so that the potatoes become lovely and creamy inside and have a golden crunchy crust on top.

Creamy pommes Dauphinoise

50 g butter
1 kg waxy potatoes
600 ml cream
4 garlic cloves, finely sliced

1 sprig rosemary
salt
freshly ground black pepper

Preheat the oven to 150°C and grease a deep gratin dish with half the butter.

Peel the potatoes and cut them into slices 0.5–1 cm thick. Arrange the potato slices in the gratin dish in overlapping rows.

Combine the cream, garlic, rosemary and seasonings in a heavy-based saucepan. Bring to the boil then carefully pour over the potatoes. Dot the remaining butter over the surface and bake for 1 hour. Check from time to time to ensure the surface isn't browning too quickly, and cover with aluminium foil if necessary.

You can make the Dauphinoise potatoes ahead of time and reheat them slowly in a 150°C oven for 20–30 minutes.

Serves 6

Starch

Potato salad

My favourite salad to serve at barbecues – especially when there are sticky spare ribs involved! I like to use heaps of mustard in the dressing, but feel free to use less if you prefer.

Dressing
¼ cup sherry vinegar
salt
freshly ground black pepper
3–4 tablespoons Dijon mustard
⅓ cup extra-virgin olive oil

1 kg nicola potatoes, washed but
   not peeled
mint leaves
½ cup pickled gherkins, chopped
6 spring onions, sliced
¼ cup parsley leaves, chopped
6 hard-boiled eggs, peeled and
   chopped

To make the dressing, whisk all the ingredients together in a large mixing bowl then taste and adjust the seasoning to your liking.

Put the potatoes into a large saucepan of cold, salted water. Throw in a few mint leaves and bring to the boil. Lower the heat and simmer until tender. This will take up to 50 minutes, depending on the size of the potato. When the potatoes are cooked, tip them into a colander to drain.

Peel the potatoes as soon as they are cool enough to handle. Cut the potatoes into 3–4 cm cubes and toss in the dressing while still warm. Add the remaining salad ingredients to the mixing bowl. Toss gently so that everything is evenly coated with the dressing. Serve warm or chilled.

Serves 6–8

My brother and I have vivid childhood memories of times spent in our grandparents' kitchen, and especially of my grandfather's polenta, which we used to call 'Nonno's cake'. My nonno was from a small mountain village in the far north of Italy. When he was a boy, his mother couldn't afford to buy wheat for bread, so instead she used to make sandwiches from two slices of polenta.

Nonno learned to make polenta from his mother, and my brother and I loved watching him make it for us. He had seemingly endless patience, and used to stir and stir the polenta in a large copper pot until it thickened and stuck to the bottom and sides. After Nonno tipped the polenta out, my brother and I would fight over the crusty bits that stuck to the pot. To this day I still love the smoky flavour that is so distinctive of traditionally cooked polenta.

Nonno used to pour the cooked polenta into a shallow bowl lined with a tea towel. After it had cooled and set, he would invert the polenta onto a plate and carefully peel away the tea towel. Then came our favourite bit: watching Nonno cut the polenta into wedges using a piece of string! We all adored Nonno, and a meal of polenta was always a really special occasion. To go with his polenta, my nonna always made a ragu from diced pork and small Italian sausages. She served it with grated cheese on top and a salad from her garden dressed with vinegar and Italian olive oil. I can't think of a better way of doing it.

Starch

Nonno's cake

---

1 litre of water or stock
½ tablespoon salt
250 g coarse polenta

Bring the liquid and salt to a boil in a large, heavy-based saucepan. Pour in the polenta in a slow, steady stream, whisking all the while. Keep whisking vigorously until the mixture begins to boil. As it thickens, switch to a wooden spoon – thick polenta can ruin a good whisk!

Continue cooking over a medium–high heat, stirring all the time. This is fairly hard work, and not without its dangers. You may find the bubbling polenta spits at you, so be careful…it hurts. You will also find that the polenta forms a thin crusty layer on the bottom and sides of the pan, but after 20 minutes or so, the bulk of it will form a solid mass, and come away from the sides of the pan. At this point, carefully taste a little bit of the polenta and season with more salt, to taste. Some people like to add a big knob of butter, too, but I prefer the truer taste of the cornmeal.

Pour the polenta into a shallow bowl lined with a cloth and leave it to cool and set. Invert onto a plate and cut into wedges with a sharp knife or a piece of string.

Serves 4

Starch

Soft, herby, cheesy polenta

This creamy wet polenta is quite different to firm polenta. It's fairly rich – especially if you make it with milk – but I find most people love the addition of herbs and cheese. It's certainly tasty, and I think it goes brilliantly with grilled lamb.

This style of polenta is easy to make as it doesn't require constant whisking and stirring. You can make it as firm or runny as you like by varying the ratio of liquid to polenta. Add different herbs and cheese to vary the flavour.

3 tablespoons olive oil or 75 g butter
1 onion, finely diced
2 garlic cloves, finely chopped
1 litre good-quality chicken stock or milk
150 g fine polenta ('instant' polenta is also acceptable)
1 tablespoon chopped thyme

1 tablespoon chopped parsley
1 tablespoon chopped sage
150 g grated parmesan (or use your favourite blue cheese for a stronger flavour)
salt
pinch of freshly ground black pepper

Heat the oil or butter in a large, heavy-based saucepan. Add the onion and garlic and sweat gently for 5 minutes, until they are soft, but not coloured. Add the stock to the pan and bring it to the boil. Pour in the polenta in a slow, steady stream, whisking all the while. Keep whisking vigorously until the mixture begins to boil, then lower the heat to a brisk simmer. Cook for 5–10 minutes, stirring with a wooden spoon from time to time, until the mixture thickens and becomes smooth and creamy. Remove the pan from the heat and stir in the chopped herbs and cheese. Taste and adjust the seasoning if necessary – you may find the cheese is salty enough. Serve straight away.

Serves 4

I just love these soft pillows of potato. They are equally delicious with butter and cheese, a tasty tomato sauce, a rich Lamb Sugo (page 100) or even a classic Bolognese Sauce (page 45).

The gnocchi may be prepared and cooked ahead of time. As they rise to the surface, lift them out with a slotted spoon and transfer to a bowl of iced water. Drain very well and arrange in a shallow tray. Cover with plastic wrap and refrigerate for up to three days. Reheat in your choice of hot sauce and top with a knob of butter before serving.

Starch
Potato gnocchi

1 kg nicola potatoes, washed but not
  peeled
1 egg

250 g plain flour
a pinch of salt

Place the potatoes in a large saucepan of cold, salted water. Bring to the boil, then lower the heat and simmer until tender. This will take up to 50 minutes, depending on the size of the potato. When the potatoes are just cooked, tip them into a colander to drain. Peel the potatoes as soon as they are just cool enough to handle.

Push the potatoes through a mouli or potato ricer directly onto your work surface. Break the egg onto the potato, then add the flour and salt. Use your hands to work the egg and flour into the potato as gently as you can. The idea is to work as quickly as you can so the gnocchi dough is light and a bit springy.

Divide the dough into 6 portions and roll each into a long cigar shape. Cut into 3 cm lengths. Traditionally, gnocchi are pressed onto a special patterned board or rolled across the back of a fork, to form the characteristic ridges.

Bring a large saucepan of salted water to the boil. Lower the heat to a simmer and drop in the gnocchi, around 4–5 at a time. Stir very gently to keep the water moving. As the gnocchi rise to the surface, lift them out with a slotted spoon and transfer them to a warm, lightly buttered dish. Cook the remaining gnocchi and serve with your choice of sauce and lots of grated parmesan cheese.

Serves 4–6

Starch

Bread and bacon dumplings

My little boys love these dumplings, and I often serve them just on their own, moistened with a little of the cooking liquid. They are also brilliant served with Roast Pheasant (page 160) or The Perfect Roast Chicken (page 172).

400 g fresh sourdough or
   casalinga-style bread
100 g butter
1 onion, finely diced
2 garlic cloves, finely chopped

100 g chopped bacon
2 eggs, lightly beaten
2 tablespoons chopped sage leaves
salt
freshly ground black pepper
1 cup good quality chicken stock

Preheat the oven to 150°C.

Chop the bread roughly and scatter on a baking tray. Place in the oven for 10 minutes until the bread dries out a little. Transfer to a food processor and blitz to form coarse crumbs.

Heat the butter in a heavy-based frying pan and sweat the onion and garlic for 5 minutes, or until soft but not coloured.

Combine all the ingredients, except the stock, in a large mixing bowl and use your fingers to work the mixture together until thoroughly combined. Take walnut-sized pieces of the mixture and roll into dumplings; you should be able to make about 20.

Increase the oven temperature to 180°C and arrange the dumplings on a lightly oiled baking tray. Pour in the stock and bake in the oven for 10 minutes until the dumplings are golden brown.

Makes 20

I find these dumplings are indispensable for jazzing up soups (see page 181). The dumpling wrappers can be purchased at specialty Asian stores, but they are simplicity itself to make.

Starch

Asian chicken dumplings

Chicken filling
500 g chicken breast, minced twice
   to make a smooth paste
1 tablespoon hoisin sauce
1 tablespoon low-sodium soy
1 tablespoon ketjap manis
½ teaspoon salt
1 teaspoon freshly ground white
   pepper
3 garlic cloves, finely chopped
1 tablespoon grated ginger
2 tablespoons chopped coriander
   leaves
1 teaspoon chilli paste (optional)

Dumpling wrappers
2½ cups plain flour
1½ teaspoons salt
1 cup cold water
4 drops sesame oil

To make the chicken filling, place all the ingredients into a large mixing bowl. Use your fingers to scrunch everything together well. Cover and refrigerate until ready to use.

To make the dumpling wrappers, combine the flour and salt in a large mixing bowl. Stir in the cold water and sesame oil and use your hands to work everything together to a dough. Cover the bowl with plastic wrap and leave to rest for 20 minutes.

Tip the dough out onto a lightly floured work surface and knead for 5–10 minutes until smooth and shiny. Cut the dough in half and roll each portion into 30 cm lengths. Cut each length into 22 portions.

Working with one portion at a time, roll each ball into a 7 cm pancake. Spoon a teaspoon of stuffing into the centre. Moisten the edges with a little water then press together to seal. Keep the dumplings covered with a tea towel until you are ready to cook them, or transfer to the freezer. They will keep for up to 3 months.

Makes 44

Starch
Buttery rice pilaf

I learned to make this dish when I was about twelve years old, by copying my aunty, who was a terrific cook. I've been making it regularly ever since. Rice pilaf is a really useful dish to have in your repertoire and you can vary the basic recipe endlessly by adding different herbs and vegetables. If you use good-quality chicken stock instead of water, you'll end up with a really flavoursome pilaf. This is a good thing for those who are watching their weight, as you can add less butter – although it never stops me!

1 litre chicken stock or water
2 tablespoons olive oil
1 onion, finely diced
1 garlic clove, sliced
1 small stick celery

1 bay leaf
3 cups long grain rice
1 teaspoon salt
pinch of freshly ground black pepper
50 g butter

Bring the stock to the boil (or boil the kettle), then lower the heat and keep it at a simmer.

Heat the oil in a heavy-based saucepan. Add the onion, garlic, celery and bay leaf and sweat over a low heat for 5 minutes, or until they soften. Add the rice to the pan and increase the heat. Cook for 3–4 minutes, stirring continuously. Season well then add the simmering stock or water. Bring to the boil, then stir the rice briefly and cover with a tight-fitting lid. Lower the temperature so the liquid is barely simmering and cook for 16–18 minutes.

At the end of the cooking time, turn off the heat and leave the rice to stand for 5 minutes without lifting the lid. Add the butter to the rice and use a fork to mix it through and to fluff up the grains. Remove the bay leaf and celery stick then taste and adjust the seasoning. To serve, tip the pilaf onto a platter and fluff the grains up once more.

Serves 6

I love this rich, tasty risotto as it is so easy to make. All the stock is poured in at the same time – instead of laboriously adding it, a ladleful at a time – and all you need to do is give it a stir from time to time.

Starch

Red wine risotto

2 cups red wine
50 g sugar
2 bay leaves
1½ cups good-quality chicken stock
3 tablespoons olive oil
1 small onion, finely diced
2 garlic cloves, crushed

1 cup arborio rice
salt
freshly ground black pepper
1 tablespoon butter
1 tablespoon grated parmesan
1 tablespoon snipped chives
1 tablespoon chopped parsley

Place the red wine, sugar and 1 bay leaf in a medium saucepan. Heat gently until the sugar dissolves then bring to the boil. Boil vigorously until reduced by half. Stir in the stock and bring to a simmer.

Heat the oil in a heavy-based saucepan. Add the onion, garlic and the other bay leaf and sauté gently until soft and translucent. Add the rice and stir well for 2 minutes to ensure it is coated with oil. Season well, then add the hot stock-wine mixture and bring to the boil. Lower the heat to a gentle simmer and cook for 18–20 minutes, stirring from time to time. Towards the end of the cooking time stir more frequently, to make sure the risotto doesn't catch and burn.

Remove the risotto from the heat and stir in the butter, cheese and herbs before serving.

Serves 4

Starch
Coconut rice

This rice is especially good with curries, such as Curried Pork Casserole with Sweet Spices (page 129) and Malaysian Goat Curry (page 101).

2 cups long grain rice
2 tablespoons vegetable oil
a good pinch of salt
2 cups water

1 cup coconut cream
1 kaffir lime leaf
1 teaspoon grated palm sugar
fresh coriander sprigs to garnish

Put the rice in a sieve and rinse it well under cold running water until the water runs clear.

Heat the oil in a heavy-based saucepan. Add the rice and stir over the heat for 3–4 minutes, stirring continuously. Season well then add the water and coconut cream. Bring to the boil then add the lime leaf and the sugar. Cover the pan with a tight-fitting lid then lower the temperature so the liquid is barely simmering and cook for 18 minutes.

At the end of the cooking time, turn off the heat and leave the rice to stand for 5 minutes without lifting the lid. Remove the kaffir lime leaf then taste and adjust the seasoning. To serve, tip the coconut rice onto a platter and fluff the grains up once more. Garnish with coriander and serve with your choice of curry.

Serves 6

Michael's Yorkshire pudding

Michael Slade, who runs the kitchen at La Luna Bistro, is a Yorkshire man and he makes the best Yorkshire puds I've tasted. Here is his recipe. You can make one large pudding in a baking tray or individual ones in a muffin tin. Small 'Yorkies' will take less cooking time – about 10–12 minutes.

250 g plain flour
250 ml milk

5 eggs, well beaten
3 tablespoons vegetable oil or lard

Sift the flour into a large mixing bowl. Make a well in the centre and gradually whisk in the milk. Slowly pour in the beaten eggs, whisking continuously to form a smooth, thickish batter. Set aside for 30 minutes to rest.

Preheat the oven to 200°C. Heat a baking tin or muffin pan for a few minutes. Add the oil or lard to the hot tin and return to the oven for 5–10 minutes, or until the oil is sizzling. Remove the tin from the oven and quickly pour in the batter then return the tin to the oven. Bake for 15 minutes, or until the pudding rises up in a great puffy golden mound. Serve straight away with your roast beef.

Serves 4–6

There are heaps of different vegetables that can be roasted well together. Try to get a good combination of root vegies with some onions or shallots, and then chuck in anything else that you fancy. Cut your vegies to a similar size, but remember that soft-textured vegetables such as zucchini, squash or strips of peppers, will roast more quickly than dense, firm-textured ones; so add them to the tin towards the end of the cooking time.

This dish is as pretty as a picture and I think makes a great meal on its own. It is also fantastic served as an accompaniment to grills and roasts. You can easily turn it into a Warm Autumn Vegetable Salad (page 319), by serving the vegies at room temperature, tossed with a tangy dressing.

Vegetables
Chunky-cut roasted vegetables

2 large carrots, peeled and cut into chunks
2 parsnips, peeled and cut into chunks
2 onions, peeled and quartered
2 fennel bulbs, trimmed and cut into sixths
250 g pumpkin, cut into chunks

2 medium beetroots, cut into sixths
1 head garlic, cloves separated but unpeeled
olive oil
salt
freshly ground black pepper
¼ cup chopped parsley

Preheat the oven to 190°C and lightly oil a large roasting tin.

Prepare the vegetables and transfer to a large mixing bowl. Drizzle with oil and season generously with salt and pepper. Tip the vegetables into the roasting tin and cook for 20–30 minutes until they are golden brown and tender, but not mushy.

Scatter with parsley just before serving with your favourite roast.

Serves 6

Nonna tells me that she often made this sweet pepper stew for my mum while she was pregnant with me, so that I would have red hair...and it worked!

Peperonata

2 red peppers
2 green peppers
2 tablespoons olive oil
I garlic clove, peeled and sliced
salt

freshly ground black pepper
2 tablespoons extra-virgin olive oil
¼ cup basil leaves, roughly torn
¼ cup roughly chopped parsley

Preheat the oven to 220°C. Rub the peppers all over with the olive oil and place them in a roasting tin with the garlic. Season generously and cover with aluminium foil. Roast for 15–20 minutes until the skins are blistered.

Transfer the peppers to a bowl and cover with plastic wrap. Reserve the roasting juices and garlic from the pan. When the peppers are cool enough to handle, peel off the skin and slice away the seeds and pith. Cut them into strips, about 1 cm wide, and transfer to a mixing bowl. Add the reserved roasting juices and garlic to the bowl, together with the extra-virgin olive oil. Scatter on the fresh herbs, and toss gently to combine. Taste and adjust the seasoning before you serve.

Serves 6

Vegetables
Minted peas

This is my favourite way of cooking peas. To turn them into mushy peas, simply mash them as coarsely or smoothly as you like with a fork, or blitz them in a food processor.

100 g butter
1 onion, finely diced
8 garlic cloves, crushed
600 g fresh or frozen peas

1 cup water
¼ cup mint leaves, roughly torn
1 teaspoon salt
1 teaspoon freshly ground black pepper

Melt the butter in a saucepan over a medium heat. Add the onion and garlic and sweat gently for about 10 minutes, or until the onion is soft and translucent. Add the peas to the pan and pour on the water. Bring to the boil, then lower the heat and simmer for 5–8 minutes, or until the peas are cooked the way you like them (I like them well-cooked). There should still be a little buttery liquid in the pan, but boil for a bit longer if the peas look too wet. Stir in the mint and season with salt and pepper.

Serves 6

Garlicky green beans

Beans and garlic go fantastically well together and sometimes I throw in a little chilli and freshly grated ginger too.

500 g green beans
3 tablespoons olive oil
4 garlic cloves, crushed

¼ cup roughly chopped parsley leaves
salt
freshly ground black pepper

Trim the little stalky ends off the beans and the little tails, too, if you want.

Blanch the beans in a large saucepan of boiling, salted water for 3–4 minutes then tip into iced water to cool. Lift them onto a tea towel and pat thoroughly dry.

Heat the oil in a heavy-based saucepan. Add the beans and garlic and sauté over a low heat for 3 minutes, stirring frequently, or until the beans are tender and the garlic has softened and begun to colour.

Stir in the parsley and season with salt and pepper.

Serves 6

Vegetables
Tomato-braised beans

This is a very traditional peasant-style summer dish that you'll find all around the Mediterranean. You can use skinny French beans or flat green beans.

600 g green beans
3 tablespoons extra-virgin olive oil
1 onion, finely diced
4 garlic cloves, finely diced

1½ cups tomato passata
10 basil leaves
1 teaspoon salt
a pinch of freshly ground black pepper

Trim the little stalky ends off the beans and cut them in half.

Heat the oil in a heavy-based saucepan and sweat the onion and garlic for about 5 minutes, until soft, but not coloured. Add the beans to the pan and stir well. Add the tomato passata and bring to the boil. Lower the heat and simmer for 20 minutes until the beans are very tender and the sauce is thick and rich. Stir in the basil leaves and season to taste.

Serve hot or at room temperature.

Serves 6–8

Cauliflower with currants, toasted pine nuts and parsley

1 kg cauliflower, broken into
  bite-sized florettes
salt
3 tablespoons olive oil

100 g currants
100 g pine nuts
¼ cup chopped parsley
freshly ground black pepper

Put the cauliflower into a large saucepan with plenty of cold water. Bring to the boil, then add 1 teaspoon of salt and lower the heat. Simmer for 5 minutes, or until the cauliflower is just tender. Strain.

Heat the olive oil in a large frying pan. Add the cauliflower and sauté for 3–4 minutes, or until it begins to colour a lovely golden brown. Remove the pan from the heat and stir in the currants, pine nuts and parsley. Season to taste and serve straight away.

Serves 6–8

Vegetables

Red cabbage with apple and caraway

This cabbage is a lovely blend of sweet and sour, which makes it the perfect winter accompaniment to roast pork. I also like to serve it with Roasted Duck or Seared Duck Breasts (page 193, 194).

3 tablespoons extra-virgin olive oil
1 red onion, thinly sliced
2 garlic cloves, finely chopped
1 tablespoon caraway seeds
600 g red cabbage, thinly sliced

2 Granny Smith apples, peeled, cored and grated
2 tablespoons sherry vinegar
salt
freshly ground pepper

Heat the olive oil in a heavy-based saucepan. Add the onion, garlic and caraway seeds and sweat until soft and translucent, about 8–10 minutes. Add the cabbage, apple and vinegar to the pan and season generously. Cook over a low heat until soft, which will take a further 15–20 minutes.

Serves 6

Braised Savoy cabbage with smoky bacon

There's something about cabbage and smoky bacon that works brilliantly well. Serve with grilled pork sausages and some boiled new potatoes for a hearty winter meal.

3 tablespoons olive oil
150 g thick-cut rashers smoky bacon or pancetta, cut into batons
100 g butter
1 onion, sliced
4 garlic cloves, sliced
2 sticks celery, sliced

1 large carrot, sliced
½ tablespoon caraway seeds
600 g Savoy cabbage, thickly sliced
¼ cup chopped parsley leaves
salt
freshly ground pepper

Heat the olive oil in a large heavy-based saucepan and fry the bacon until crisp. Lift the bacon out of the pan onto paper towels to drain.

Lower the heat and add the butter to the pan. Add the onion, garlic, celery, carrot and caraway seeds and sweat for 5 minutes, or until the vegetables are soft, but not coloured. Add the cabbage to the pan and season generously. Stir well and sweat for 2 minutes until the cabbage begins to soften, then increase the heat and cook, stirring frequently, until the pan juices have evaporated.

Stir in the fried bacon and parsley and serve straight away.

Serves 8

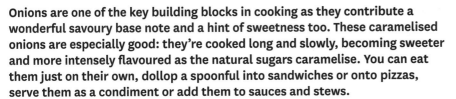

Onions are one of the key building blocks in cooking as they contribute a wonderful savoury base note and a hint of sweetness too. These caramelised onions are especially good: they're cooked long and slowly, becoming sweeter and more intensely flavoured as the natural sugars caramelise. You can eat them just on their own, dollop a spoonful into sandwiches or onto pizzas, serve them as a condiment or add them to sauces and stews.

Vegetables

Caramelised onions

¼ cup olive oil
1 kg onions, thinly sliced, as evenly as possible

a pinch of salt

Heat the oil in a heavy-based saucepan or lidded frying pan over a moderate heat. Add the onions and season. Lower the heat and cover the pan. Cook for around 15 minutes, stirring frequently, until the onions have softened and collapsed down to a soft tangle.

Remove the lid from the pan and increase the heat to medium. Continue cooking for a further 5–10 minutes, stirring frequently, until the onions deepen in colour to a deep golden brown. Take care not to burn them, as it is a fine line between deep caramel and burnt bitterness.

Serve the caramelised onions straight away, or tip them into a sealable container with all the pan juices and store in the refrigerator for up to 7 days.

Serves 6

Although most people steam or blanch asparagus, it's actually a fantastic vegetable to grill on the barbecue. The pencil-thin spears are best for this, as they cook fairly quickly without burning. You could also use thick asparagus, but blanch it briefly before finishing off on the barbecue.

Serve as an accompaniment, or on its own as a starter.

Char-grilled asparagus with pesto and parmesan

500 g thin asparagus spears
2 tablespoons olive oil
1 teaspoon salt
a generous pinch of freshly ground black pepper

100 ml Basil Pesto (page 344)
30 g parmesan, shaved

Preheat a barbecue or griddle to high.

Snap the woody ends off the asparagus and discard them. Toss the asparagus spears with the olive oil and season with salt and pepper. Cook over a medium–high heat, turning occasionally, until tender and lightly charred with golden stripes from the grill.

Transfer the asparagus onto a serving platter, drizzle with pesto and scatter with parmesan shavings.

Serves 6

Vegetables

Sautéed spinach and chilli

This is such a popular side dish at La Luna Bistro that I can never take it off the menu. The secret is to use top-quality olive oil and to heat it from cold, very slowly, with the aromatics. This allows the oil to become infused with their flavour, which won't happen as successfully if they are cooked too quickly over too high a heat.

For an Asian-inspired variation, add half a tablespoon of chopped ginger to the oil with the garlic and chilli. Once the spinach has wilted, stir through two tablespoons of ketjap manis.

3 tablespoons extra-virgin olive oil
3 garlic cloves, finely chopped
1 long red chilli, seeded and finely
   sliced

500 g baby spinach leaves
salt
freshly ground black pepper

Pour the oil into a large heavy-based frying pan and add the garlic and chilli. Heat very gently, so the garlic and chilli slowly release their flavours into the oil. Once the garlic begins to turn a pale gold, add the spinach leaves to the pan. Use tongs to turn the leaves around in the oil until completely wilted. Season to taste and serve straight away.

Serves 4

Creamed spinach

When I was a young commis chef working in a big 5-star hotel kitchen, I spent endless hours picking through great mounds of English spinach, which had to have all the stalks neatly removed. The next step was to wash it over and over again in cold water, before blanching and refreshing it in iced water. The spinach was then squeezed very dry and spread out on trays ready for service. If the sous chef found even a tiny speck of grit or dirt in the spinach I would end up with it thrown at my head!

Life is much easier these days as you can buy pre-washed spinach with the stalks already removed. And a chef friend of mine even has a wonderful creamed spinach dish that she makes using the frozen stuff. Oh how times have changed!

1 kg spinach, washed and stalks
   removed
50 g butter
½ onion, finely chopped

2 garlic cloves, finely chopped
1 cup cream
salt
freshly ground black pepper

Bring a large saucepan of water to the boil and blanch the spinach in batches. Transfer it immediately to a sink of iced water, then drain it well and squeeze out as much water as you can. Chop it roughly.

Heat the butter in a heavy-based saucepan. Add the onion and garlic and sweat for about 5 minutes over a low heat, until soft but not coloured. Add the cream to the pan and bring to the boil. Allow it to bubble for 1 minute then stir in the spinach. Stir well and season to taste.

Tip into a food processor and blend to a purée.

Serves 6

You can use any variety of mushrooms or, indeed, any combination of different varieties – the more the better. I like to keep the mushrooms fairly large and chunky, and as close to their original shape as possible. Tear or roughly chop larger varieties; keep small ones whole.

Serve as a side dish with sausages or grilled lamb. I like to add a spoonful of the reduced cooking liquid to sauces and gravies, where it adds an extra earthy depth.

500 g mixed mushrooms, roughly chopped
50 g butter
4 garlic cloves, crushed

1½ cups water
1 teaspoon salt
¼ cup thyme leaves
3 tablespoons chopped parsley

Combine all the ingredients, except for the parsley, in a large saucepan. Bring to the boil, then lower the heat to a lively simmer and cook for 15 minutes, or until most of the liquid has evaporated. The mushrooms should be tender and the liquid reduced to a thick sauce. Stir in the parsley and serve straight away. Otherwise, leave to cool before refrigerating; they'll keep for up to 7 days.

Serves 6

Vegetables

Thyme- and garlic-scented mushrooms

Salads & dressings

Fresh herb salad

When it comes to salads, it can be all too easy to think of the usual suspects – lettuce, tomatoes, cucumbers and so on. Fresh herbs make a wonderful lively change and you can mix them up in your own favourite combinations. Add an avocado and roughly crumbled goat's cheese and you've got a lovely summer starter.

1 cup parsley leaves
½ cup basil leaves
½ cup coriander leaves
½ cup chives, cut into 4 cm lengths
1 cup watercress sprigs
1 cup lettuce leaves, torn roughly

1 tablespoon lilliput capers
juice of 1 lemon
3 tablespoons extra-virgin olive oil
sea salt
freshly ground black pepper

Put all the herb and salad leaves and the capers into a large mixing bowl and toss them together gently. Whisk together the lemon juice and oil to make a dressing and pour it onto the salad. Season to taste and toss gently so that the leaves are evenly coated.

Serves 4

Green bean salad with feta dressing

This is a great tasting and very healthy salad. To make the dressing I use one of my favourite cheeses, Danish feta, which is soft and creamy with a mild flavour.

500 g green beans
1 red onion, very finely sliced
½ teaspoon salt
3 tablespoons white wine vinegar
1 garlic clove

100 g Danish feta
juice of 1 lemon
3 tablespoons extra-virgin olive oil
¼ cup chopped parsley

Trim the little stalky ends off the beans and the little tails, too, if you want.

Blanch the beans in a large saucepan of boiling, salted water for 3–4 minutes then tip into iced water to cool. Lift them onto a tea towel and pat thoroughly dry.

Toss the onion with ½ teaspoon of the salt and the vinegar and set aside for 5 minutes to reduce some of the sharp flavour. Rinse well and pat thoroughly dry.

Use the back of a knife to crush the garlic with ½ teaspoon salt until you have a smooth paste. Combine with the feta, lemon juice and oil in a food processor and blend to make a creamy dressing.

Place the beans, onion and parsley in a large mixing bowl and pour on the dressing. Toss to combine and serve straight away.

Serves 6

This chunky salad is wonderful with all sorts of grilled and barbecued meats, but I think it's especially good with lamb. Try to find smooth, creamy Danish feta, if you can. Add a big handful of roughly chopped rocket leaves and it becomes a Big Italian Salad!

Salads & dressings

Big Greek salad

1 Lebanese cucumber, cut into
  2 cm cubes
2 roma tomatoes, cut into 2 cm cubes
1 red onion, cut into 2 cm cubes
¼ cup kalamata olives, pitted
10 basil leaves, roughly torn
1 tablespoon roughly chopped parsley

1 teaspoon dried oregano
130 g Danish feta, roughly crumbled
juice of 1 lemon
¼ cup extra-virgin olive oil
½ teaspoon salt
1 teaspoon freshly ground black
  pepper

To make the salad, combine all the ingredients in a large mixing bowl and toss together gently.

Serves 6

Watercress salad

Dressing
3 tablespoons extra-virgin olive oil
2 tablespoons tarragon vinegar
1 tablespoon grainy mustard
salt
freshly ground black pepper

1 bunch watercress, washed and
  leaves picked
1 small bunch frisee (curly endive),
  inner pale leaves only
a big handful rocket leaves
1 cup parsley leaves
2 spring onions, finely sliced into rings

In a large mixing bowl, combine the dressing ingredients and whisk together well.

Combine all the salad ingredients in a large mixing bowl. Pour on the dressing and toss everything together gently.

Serves 6

Salads & dressings

Asian slaw

I think this coleslaw goes really well with Asian-style Sticky Spare Ribs (page 116), but it's also good with satays and other barbecued meats.

500 g Chinese cabbage, very thinly sliced
6 spring onions, thinly sliced into 3 cm lengths
1 small red onion, very thinly sliced
75 g oyster mushrooms, roughly torn
2 long red chillies, seeded and thinly sliced
1 tablespoon chopped ginger
½ cup coriander leaves, roughly chopped
salt
freshly ground pepper
2 tablespoons deep-fried shallots (available from Asian stores)

Dressing
½ cup thick mayonnaise
juice of 1 lime
2 tablespoons soy sauce
2 tablespoons mirin
2 tablespoons ketjap manis
½ teaspoon sesame oil

In a large mixing bowl, combine all the salad ingredients except for the salt, pepper and shallots. Toss together gently.

Whisk the dressing ingredients together and pour onto the slaw. Toss together well, then tatse and season if need be. Garnish with the deep-fried shallots.

Serves 6

American slaw

There are a million versions of this classic barbecue salad. It's best if you can make it a few hours ahead of time, which softens the cabbage a little and allows the flavours to develop.

500 g white cabbage or Savoy cabbage, very thinly sliced
2 carrots, peeled and grated
1 small red onion, very thinly sliced
2 Granny Smith apples, finely sliced into matchsticks
⅓ cup parsley leaves
salt
freshly ground black pepper

Dressing
¼ cup cider vinegar
1 tablespoon soft brown sugar
1 cup thick mayonnaise
1 teaspoon celery seeds
1 tablespoon Dijon mustard

In a large mixing bowl, combine the cabbage, carrots and onion and toss gently.

To make the dressing, combine the vinegar and sugar in a small saucepan and heat gently until the sugar has dissolved. Remove from the heat and leave to cool. When cold, whisk into the mayonnaise, then stir in the celery seeds and mustard.

Pour the dressing onto the slaw and toss well. Leave to stand for a minimum of 2 hours, or overnight if possible, for the flavours to combine. Just before serving, stir in the apple and parsley and season to taste.

Serves 6

Heirloom tomatoes are very popular among chefs and foodies for their good old-fashioned tomato flavour – it's a million miles away from the tasteless chilled supermarket varieties. They are increasingly available in a range of colours, shapes and sizes so you can have a bit of fun when choosing them.

At La Luna Bistro we preserve boxes of artichokes when they are in season, to keep us going through the autumn and winter. But they are widely available in delicatessens, as is provolone, a semi-hard cow's milk cheese, which tastes a bit like a mild parmesan.

Heirloom tomato, artichoke and basil salad with provolone

500 g heirloom tomatoes
250 g preserved artichoke hearts
    (available from good delicatessens)
½ cup basil leaves
¼ cup parsley leaves
2 tablespoons snipped chives

juice of 2 lemons
4 tablespoons extra-virgin olive oil
salt
freshly ground pepper
75 g shaved provolone

Slice the tomatoes and artichoke hearts thickly and place in a large mixing bowl with the fresh herbs. Add the lemon juice and olive oil and toss everything together gently. Season to taste. To serve, tip the salad onto a serving platter or shallow bowl and scatter with shavings of provolone.

Serves 6

Beetroot, lemon and coriander salad with extra-virgin olive oil

3 large beetroots
3 tablespoons extra-virgin olive oil
juice of 2 lemons
zest of ½ lemon

1 cup coriander leaves
salt
freshly ground black pepper

Wash the beetroots thoroughly and cut off the leaves. Place in a large saucepan of cold water and bring to the boil. Lower the heat and simmer for 1–2 hours (it will vary, depending on the size), until the beetroots are tender.

Drain the beetroots and when cool enough to handle, peel away the skins. Cut into large dice and place in a large mixing bowl. Add the oil, lemon juice and zest and coriander leaves and season to taste. Toss gently and serve straight away.

Serves 4–6

Salads & dressings

Cabbage, apple and tarragon salad

This is a great salad in its own right, but serve it topped with slices of roast pork and crunchy crackling, and it really shines.

At La Luna Bistro, we salt the cabbage overnight to take away the rawness and soften it a little bit. The end result is a bit like fresh sauerkraut.

1 kg white cabbage, hard core removed and very finely shredded
75 g salt
1 Granny Smith apple, skin on, cored and sliced into thin matchsticks
½ cup roughly chopped parsley leaves

1 cup watercress sprigs
2 tablespoons snipped chives
3 tablespoons tarragon vinegar
3 tablespoons extra-virgin olive oil
salt
freshly ground black pepper

Toss the cabbage with the salt in a large container. Cover with a damp tea towel and leave for 1–2 hours. You can leave it overnight, which will soften the cabbage even more.

Tip the cabbage into a colander and wash very thoroughly to remove the salt. Pat the cabbage dry and transfer to a large mixing bowl. Add the apple and fresh herbs and toss gently. In a separate bowl, whisk together the vinegar and oil. Pour onto the salad and toss to combine. Season to taste and serve with hot roast pork.

Serves 6

White bean, blood orange and watercress salad

The creamy blandness of white beans goes brilliantly with the tang of oranges and peppery watercress. Do feel free to use other beans or pulses if you prefer. I love borlotti beans and even chickpeas or lentils. Blood oranges have a limited season, so substitute other citrus fruits, to taste. This salad is especially good with roast duck and grilled pork chops.

3 blood oranges (or navel oranges)
400 g cooked white beans (or 1 x 400 g tin white beans, well rinsed and drained)
3 roma tomatoes, skinned, seeded and roughly chopped
2 cups roughly chopped watercress sprigs
¼ cup snipped chives
¼ cup chopped parsley

Dressing
¼ cup blood orange juice (see above)
¼ cup extra-virgin olive oil
salt
freshly ground black pepper

Use a small sharp knife to peel the oranges. Carefully cut out the segments, making sure there is no membrane or pith still attached. Reserve as much juice as you can to make the dressing.

Put the orange segments into a mixing bowl and add the remaining salad ingredients.

In another bowl, whisk together the dressing ingredients. Pour onto the salad and toss together gently.

Serves 4

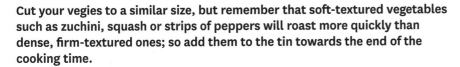

Cut your vegies to a similar size, but remember that soft-textured vegetables such as zuchini, squash or strips of peppers will roast more quickly than dense, firm-textured ones; so add them to the tin towards the end of the cooking time.

Salads & dressings

Warm autumn vegetable salad

2 large carrots, peeled and cut into chunks
2 parsnips, peeled and cut into chunks
2 onions, peeled and quartered
2 fennel bulbs, trimmed and cut into sixths
250 g pumpkin cut into chunks
2 medium beetroots, cut into sixths
2 heads garlic, halved crosswise (reserve 1 for the dressing)
olive oil
salt
freshly ground black pepper
¼ cup chopped parsley

Dressing
1 head roasted garlic (see method below)
1 tablespoon grain mustard
3 tablespoons sherry vinegar
¼ cup extra-virgin olive oil
salt
freshly ground black pepper

Preheat the oven to 190°C and lightly oil a large roasting tin.

Prepare the vegetables and transfer to a large mixing bowl. Drizzle with oil and season generously with salt and pepper. Tip the vegetables into the roasting tin and cook for 20–30 minutes until they are golden brown and tender, but not mushy.

To make the dressing, squeeze the roasted garlic out of its skins and put in a blender with the mustard and vinegar. Blend until smooth and creamy. With the motor running, add the olive oil, a few drops at a time, until the dressing thickens and emulsifies. Increase to a slow, steady stream until all has been incorporated.

When ready to serve, warm the vegetables for 10 minutes in an oven preheated to 190°C. Tumble them out onto a large serving platter and drizzle with the dressing. Scatter on the parsley and serve straight away while still warm.

Serves 6

STOCKS AND SAUCES

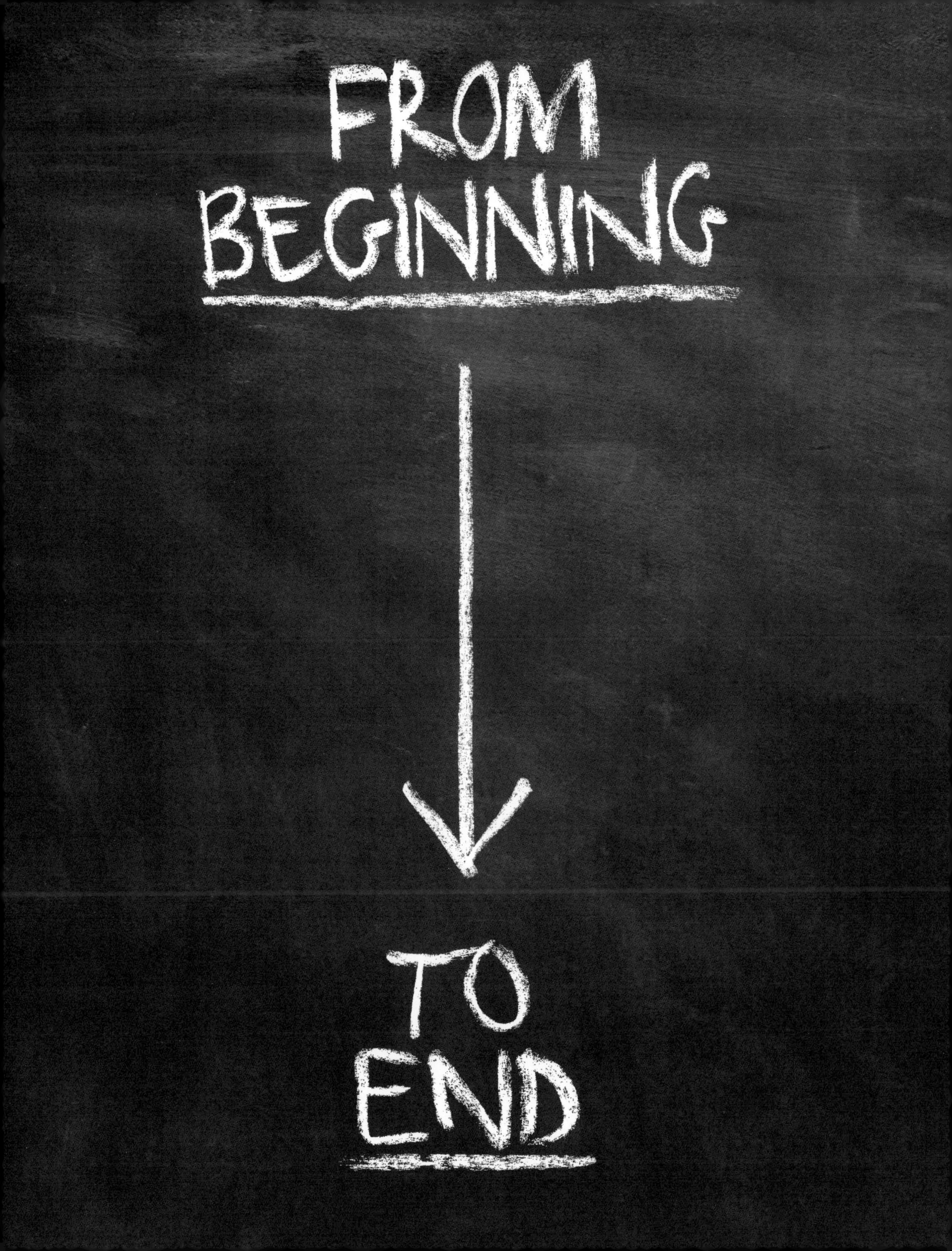
FROM
BEGINNING
TO
END

Stocks & sauces

STOCKS

Stocks are the building blocks of good cooking. They form the basis of loads of sauces, as well as soups, stews and braises. Stocks are probably the most important items that are made in good restaurant kitchens, and yet most of us just can't be bothered to make them at home.

It's hard to fathom, really, because stocks are so incredibly easy to make. And a good homemade stock will really transform a dish – they're certainly in a different universe to the commercially available cubes, powders and liquids that you find on supermarket shelves.

Stocks are also really cheap to make as they need so few ingredients. Apart from water, all you need are some vegetables, a few aromatics, such as peppercorns and herbs, and some fresh meaty bones. And at a pinch, the bones can even be left over from your dinner, which makes for a very economical stock indeed. In fact to make a good stock the only thing that you need in abundance, is time – up to three or four hours to extract the maximum taste and goodness. But it doesn't have to be *your* time, because for the most part, stocks make themselves.

Realistically, though, because of the time required, it's probably not a good idea to start off a recipe by making a stock. I suggest you cook up a large amount of stock and then freeze it in sensible batches (say 500 ml, or 1 litre) so you've always got some on hand for immediate use. If possible, try to have one white stock and one brown stock in your freezer.

White stocks and brown stocks are made from the same ingredients and in more or less the same way. The difference is that with brown stocks, the bones and vegetables are thoroughly browned in the oven before you add water. This browning makes for a fuller-flavoured and richer stock.

Here are a few tips for making great stocks:
- Use good-quality ingredients – not the rotting carrots and mouldy old onion that you scrape up from the bottom of your fridge.
- Fresh herbs are better than dried – with the possible exception of bay leaves.
- Be generous with the ratio of vegies and bones to water. You want to really pack vegies and bones into your stockpot before you add any water.
- Use the biggest stockpot you can fit in your kitchen cupboard. There's no point in making stock in tiny quantities.
- Bring the water to the boil slowly, skimming away any foam and scummy bits that rise to the surface.
- Once it reaches boiling point, lower the temperature so the water barely simmers. If you allow it to boil for any length of time, your stock will become cloudy and taste bitter.
- Skim your stock regularly to keep it clear of the fat and scum that rises to the surface.

Finally, remember that not all stocks are equally rich and tasty. If you use your leftover chicken carcass or beef bones to make a stock, then the result will not be as flavoursome as if you use raw meaty bones, chicken wings and even pig's trotters. In fact some top-notch and really intense stocks even use another lighter stock as the liquid instead of water.

SAUCES

If stocks are the starting point for many dishes, then sauces are the finishing touch. Who doesn't love to slosh generous amounts of tasty gravy over the Sunday roast, or to liven up a grilled chicken breast or lamb chop with an elegant sauce? Sometimes meat just seems a bit naked without a bit of sauce.

Many old-fashioned sauces are thickened with flour, using a roux. But these days more chefs and home cooks prefer lighter and fresher tasting sauces, which are based on stock reductions. It's true that I often whisk in a knob of butter to add a shine, or a spoonful of cream to add richness, but I think both of these are preferable to the slightly dull flavour you get with flour-based sauces. The only exceptions I make are with gravy (pages 330 and 331), which I steadfastly believe is the ultimate comfort sauce.

I've included some of my favourite sauces in this chapter. Some of them are incredibly simple, like Nanna's Gravy (page 330), which uses the flavour you get for free from the bottom of the roasting tin. Others are more sophisticated and 'cheffy', such as Jus (page 331) and Red Wine Reduction (page 332). I encourage you to have a go at a making a variety of different sauces. Your taste buds will thank you for it.

Stocks
Beef stock

This is the big one! It's a rich, deep brown in colour, and full of beefy flavour. When reduced to make Jus (page 331), it becomes thick and syrupy – the perfect base for a full-flavoured sauce.

When I'm making beef stock at home, I use water as the base, but at the restaurant we usually use chicken or veal stock, which give a more intense flavour. Most chefs use a combination of beef and veal bones to make a good beef stock, as the veal bones are rich in gelatine and give the stock body. Another good 'cheffy' trick is to add a split pig's trotter to the stockpot with the beef bones. Trotters are especially full of gelatine, which enriches your stock and then gives your sauces a nice sheen. Alternatively, add 500 g chicken wing tips to the stock for the last 1½ hours, which will also add richness to the stock. And make sure you ask your butcher to find you good meaty bones, and get him to chop them up as much as he can.

It does take a long time to make a good beef stock, so it's worth making a decent amount. You can always divide it into 500 ml batches and freeze it.

2 kg chopped meaty beef bones
2 kg chopped meaty veal bones
2 medium carrots, roughly chopped
2 sticks celery, roughly chopped
2 onions, roughly chopped
4 garlic cloves, peeled and halved
1 pig's trotter, split in half lengthwise (optional)

2 bay leaves
1 tablespoon black peppercorns
handful mushroom stalks (optional)
handful bacon rinds (optional)
pinch of salt
½ cup parsley leaves
3 sprigs thyme

Preheat the oven to 220°C.

Arrange the bones in a large roasting tin and roast for 5–10 minutes, or until a rich golden brown. Turn the bones around and scatter in the chopped carrots, celery, onion and garlic. Cook for a further 5–10 minutes, until it smells like Sunday dinner! You want everything to be a deep golden brown, but not black and burnt.

Remove the roasting tin from the oven and tip the contents into a large stockpot or saucepan. Deglaze the roasting tin with a little water and add to the stockpot. Add the pig's trotter and pour on enough cold water to cover. Bring to the boil slowly and use a ladle to skim away the foam or other impurities that rise to the surface. When the stock boils, lower the heat and add all the remaining ingredients, except for the parsley and thyme. Simmer very gently for 6–8 hours, skimming away any foam from time to time. Top up with more cold water as necessary; the bones should always be completely covered with water.

Remove the pan from the heat and throw in the parsley and thyme. Leave it to sit for 20 minutes or so, to allow the sediment to settle and to freshen the flavour.

Once the stock has cooled down a bit, there are two ways to strain it. For a more rustic style, simply pour it through a fine sieve into a jug or bowl. For a clearer, more refined stock, or if you're making clear broths or consommés, carefully ladle the stock out of the pot into a fine sieve. Leave to cool completely, then remove any fat that sets on the surface.

Divide the stock into batches and refrigerate or freeze. It keeps well in the fridge for up to 7 days and in the freezer for up to 3 months.

Makes 4–5 litres

Veal stock

Veal stock has a reputation for being a bit of a restaurant stock. And it's true; chefs love veal stock, because it is rich in gelatine which makes for lovely shiny sauces, and helps maintain body in a stock or sauce when you reduce it down. Second, veal stock has a much lighter flavour than a big beef stock, so it doesn't overpower other ingredients. Both of these qualities mean that veal stock is often used in combination with other stocks in restaurant kitchens.

As with other stocks, you can make white veal stock, which is lighter and more delicate, or brown veal stock, which is fuller-flavoured.

This is one dish where it really helps to know your butcher, as it has been known for some less scrupulous butchers to fob off cheaper pork bones on unsuspecting customers, rather than the more costly veal bones. Ask your butcher to cut the bones to the size of a small fist, and to split the trotter for you.

2 kg chopped veal bones
2 medium carrots, roughly chopped
2 sticks celery, roughly chopped
2 onions, roughly chopped
4 garlic cloves, halved
1 veal or pig's trotter, split in half
   lengthwise

2 bay leaves
1 teaspoon black peppercorns
1 teaspoon salt
½ cup parsley leaves
3 sprigs thyme

Preheat the oven to 220°C.

Follow the same procedure as for the beef stock, described on page 324.

Makes 3–4 litres

Lamb stock

Lamb stock is not used very much in restaurant kitchens as it has a rather strong and overpowering flavour that dominates other meats. I think it does work well with lamb dishes, though, as the flavour underpins and intensifies the natural lamb flavour. Personally, I love lamb stock and I use it as a base for all sorts of lamb soups and stews and for gravy or sauce for a roast lamb dinner.

2 kg chopped lamb bones
2 medium carrots, roughly chopped
2 sticks celery, roughly chopped
2 onions, roughly chopped
1 fennel bulb, roughly chopped or
   1 tablespoon fennel seed

4 garlic cloves, halved
2 bay leaves
1 teaspoon black peppercorns
1 teaspoon salt
½ cup parsley leaves
3 sprigs thyme

Follow the same procedure as for the beef stock, described on page 324.

Makes 3–4 litres

Stocks

Chicken stock

There's nothing like a pot of chicken stock on the stove to fill the house with mouth-watering aromas. There's something wonderfully reassuring and comforting about it, and it always makes me feel right at home.

Chicken stock is a great 'use-it-for-anything-and-everything' kind of stock. When I worked in a seafood restaurant, we even used chicken stock for making seafood risottos, because it adds a satisfying depth of flavour, without being overpowering. A good chicken stock provides you with the basis for all manner of dishes, from risottos and braises to soups and sauces. And as we all know, a steaming bowl of chicken broth (with a little fresh ginger and garlic) is a cure for all kinds of ailments.

As with stocks made from other meats, I make both white and brown chicken stocks. Although they are made from the same basic ingredients, with brown stocks, the bones and vegetables are thoroughly browned – usually by roasting in the oven – before adding water. As a result, brown stocks are darker in colour and have a richer, fuller flavour than white stocks. They have different uses, too: white stocks are perfect for delicate sauces and soups, whereas brown stocks are better for robust stews and braises or for strong, intense sauces.

Many recipes ask you to skim away all the fat that rises to the surface of your stock as it cooks and to scrape off the solid fat that settles after it's chilled. I'm not one for doing much skimming or scraping. I do scoop off any scummy bits and foam that come to the surface, as they can cook back into the stock and make it bitter, but I tend to leave the fat as I think it really adds to the flavour of the stock.

Once the stock has cooled down a bit, there are two ways to strain it. For a more rustic style, simply pour it through a fine sieve into a jug or bowl. For a clearer, more refined stock, or if you're making clear broths or consommés, carefully ladle the stock out of the pot into a fine sieve. Leave to cool completely, then divide into batches and refrigerate or freeze. It keeps well in the fridge for up to 4 days and in the freezer for up to 3 months.

Use the same quantities and method to make white and brown turkey stock.

White chicken stock
1 kg raw chicken bones or 1 x 1 kg boiling chicken
200 g chicken wing tips (I trim these off whole chooks before roasting, and collect them in bags in the freezer just for making stock)
1 onion, roughly chopped
1 stick celery, roughly chopped

1 leek, white part only, roughly chopped
2 garlic cloves, halved
1 bay leaf
1 teaspoon salt
4 black peppercorns
6 sprigs parsley
3 sprigs thyme
¼ cup parsley leaves

If using raw chicken bones, wash them briefly in cold water to remove any bloody bits.

Place all the chicken pieces in a stockpot or large saucepan and pour on enough cold water to cover. Bring to the boil slowly. Use a ladle to skim away the foam or other impurities that rise to the surface. When the stock boils, lower the heat and add all the remaining ingredients, reserving half the thyme and the parsley leaves. Simmer very gently for 2 hours, skimming away any foam from time to time. Top up with more cold water as necessary; the chicken pieces should always be completely covered with water.

Remove the pan from the heat and throw in the rest of the thyme and the parsley leaves. Leave it to sit for 20 minutes or so to allow the sediment to settle and to freshen the flavour. Strain and, when completely cold, divide into batches and rerigerate or freeze.

Makes 3–4 litres

Chicken stock

Brown chicken stock

1 kg raw chicken bones
200 g chicken wing tips (I trim these off whole chooks before roasting, and collect them in bags in the freezer just for making stock)
olive oil
2 carrots, roughly chopped
1 onion, roughly chopped
1 stick celery, roughly chopped

1 leek, white part only, roughly chopped
2 garlic cloves, halved
1 bay leaf
1 teaspoon black peppercorns
1 teaspoon salt
6 sprigs parsley
3 sprigs thyme
¼ cup parsley leaves

Although you can make this stock using water, I often use white chicken stock (see previous recipe) to make a brown stock, as you end up with a much deeper and more robust flavour. Similarly, deglazing the roasting tin after cooking the bones and vegetables makes the stock darker in colour and richer in flavour.

Preheat the oven to 220°C. Toss the chicken bones and wing tips in a little olive oil and arrange them in a large roasting tin. Scatter the chopped vegetables and garlic among the bones and roast for 5–10 minutes, or until a light golden brown. Turn the bones and cook for a further 5–10 minutes. You want everything to be a deep golden brown, but not black and burnt.

Remove the roasting tin from the oven and tip the contents into a large stockpot or saucepan. Tip out any remaining fat from the roasting tin and place over a medium heat. Add a few big splashes of water and stir to scrape up any caramelised sediment. Scrape the deglazed liquid into the stockpot with the roasted bones and vegetables and then pour on enough cold water to cover.

Continue, following the same procedure as for the White Chicken Stock, above.

Makes 3–4 litres

Stocks

Peking duck stock

Like many people, I love Peking duck, and this recipe is a great way to make an expensive treat go a long way. Not only do you get a great meal from the duck itself (enjoyed with all the traditional accompaniments, of course), but if you turn the carcass into a stock, you can add that authentic flavour to all sorts of Asian soups and noodle dishes – I've even used it to make a shiitake mushroom and duck risotto.

Buy a roast Peking duck from Chinatown, and ask for the cavity juices to be put in a separate container for you.

1 x roast Peking duck carcass
the juices and aromatics from the duck's cavity (star anise, ginger, garlic etc)
5 spring onions, roughly chopped
2 tablespoons chopped ginger
2 sticks celery, roughly chopped
6 garlic cloves, chopped
¼ cup light soy sauce

3 tablespoons hoisin sauce
¼ cup ketjap manis
2 tablespoons plum sauce
1 stalk lemongrass, bruised with the back of a knife
1 long red chilli, seeded
juice of 2 limes
1 cup fresh coriander leaves (keep the stalks and roots for the stock)

Put the duck in a stockpot or heavy-based saucepan and pour on enough cold water to cover. Bring to the boil slowly. Use a ladle to skim away the foam or other impurities that rise to the surface. When the stock boils, lower the heat and add all the remaining ingredients, except for the lime juice and coriander leaves (but do add the coriander stalks and roots). Simmer very gently for 1½ hours, skimming away any foam from time to time. Top up with more cold water as necessary; the duck should always be covered with water.

Remove the pan from the heat and throw in the coriander leaves. Leave it to sit for 20 minutes or so to allow the sediment to settle and to freshen the flavour.

Once the stock has cooled down a bit, there are two ways to strain it. For a more rustic style, simply pour it through a fine sieve into a jug of bowl. For a clearer, more refined stock, or if you're making clear broths or consommés, carefully ladle the stock out of the pot into a fine sieve. Leave to cool completely, then divide into batches and refrigerate or freeze. It keeps well in the fridge for up to 4 days and in the freezer for up to 3 months.

Makes 2 litres

I wasn't sure about including a recipe for vegetable stock in such an unashamedly meat-focused book, but it's such a simple process that it seems silly to leave it out. Vegetable stocks are quick to make and they are a good way of adding flavour, albeit without a meaty depth.

Vegetable stock

2 large carrots, roughly chopped
3 sticks celery, roughly chopped
2 medium onions, roughly chopped
2 leeks, roughly chopped
1 fennel bulb, roughly chopped
1 cup chopped parsley, stalks and leaves

2 bay leaves
1 teaspoon black peppercorns
2 teaspoons salt
2 cups white wine
3 sprigs thyme

Put the chopped vegetables, parsley stalks, bay leaves, peppercorns and salt into a tight-fitting saucepan. Pour on enough water to cover. Bring to the boil slowly. Use a ladle to skim away the foam or other impurities that rise to the surface. When the stock boils, lower the heat and simmer very gently and add all the remaining ingredients, except for the parsley leaves. Simmer very gently for 45 minutes, skimming away any foam from time to time.

Remove the pan from the heat and add the wine, parsley leaves and thyme. Once the stock has cooled completely, refrigerate overnight.

Strain through a fine sieve then divide into batches and refrigerate or freeze. It keeps well in the fridge for up to 4 days and in the freezer for up to 3 months.

Makes 3–4 litres

Sauces

Nanna's gravy

When it comes to real comfort food, you can keep your fancy jus and your restaurant-inspired reductions: nothing beats nanna's gravy. And no matter how much she's overcooked the vegies, somehow her gravy always makes up for it. Let's be clear from the start; this isn't a thin, refined sort of gravy at all. It's thick and tasty and you need lots of it to pour over your roast potatoes and meat.

Much of the flavour for nanna's gravy comes for free, from all the stuff that's left in the bottom of the roasting tin. The body of the gravy comes from flour, or from squishing some of the vegies through a sieve – and damn it all, sometimes from both!

The best thing about Nanna's gravy is that you can knock it up pretty easily while the meat is resting in a warm place. Here's how it's done.

First, pour away most of the fat, leaving just a little in the bottom of the tin with the roasting juices. If you're going with the flour-thickened version, sprinkle in a generous teaspoon of flour, and stir over a medium heat to make a gunky brown paste. Alternatively, chuck in a cup of mixed diced vegies – carrot, celery, onion and garlic – and stir well.

Whichever method you're using, at this point you need to put the roasting tin back into a very hot oven for about 10 minutes, until the paste darkens, or the vegies colour.

Next, return the tin to the stovetop and slosh in a cup of wine, stock or water. With a wooden spoon, stir everything about vigorously, reaching right into the corners and making sure you scrape up all the crisp bits of goodness that are stuck to the bottom of the tin. Cook over a medium heat, stirring continuously, until the mixture thickens.

Add more stock, or the cooking water from your vegies, until the gravy reaches a consistency you like. You do need to let it bubble away for a good 5 minutes or so – especially if you're using flour. And don't forget to taste the gravy to see whether it needs a bit more wine, a pinch of salt or pepper, or even a touch of mustard or a spoonful of redcurrant jelly (this is especially good with roast lamb).

When you're happy with your gravy you can pour it through a fine sieve, using your wooden spoon to squish through as many of the vegetables as you can. Alternatively, for an authentic 'nanna' touch, don't strain your gravy at all – a few chunky bits won't worry anyone, and they'll taste delicious.

Sauces

Classic thick gravy

This is really just another way of making a good, thick gravy. You make it the same way as a white sauce, but using stock instead of milk. In some ways it's actually easier than making a gravy in the roasting pan, as you can make it ahead of time, rather than at the last minute. But you do need to have a good, full-flavoured beef stock to hand.

1 tablespoon butter
1 tablespoon plain flour
1½ cups good beef stock

2 tablespoons cream
salt
freshly ground pepper

Heat the butter in a small saucepan until it begins to foam. Add the flour and stir over a low heat for about 5 minutes, until the flour is cooked and the roux begins to colour. Add the stock a little at a time, stirring continuously. You may find you want to add more or less liquid; just add enough to make a thick, smooth gravy that's the thickness you like best. Lower the heat and cook for around 5 minutes at a very low simmer. Remove the pan from the heat and stir in the cream; it will give your gravy a lovely sheen.

Taste and adjust seasoning to your liking.

Makes 1½ cups

Jus (the chef's friend)

All chefs love a good jus because it is so richly flavoured and adds a brilliant intensity to any dish. Jus is versatile, too, as you can use it as an easy gravy, or, reduced somewhat, to create a thick, slightly sweet glaze.

I admit that it is a bit time-consuming to prepare a good jus, (although it's not at all difficult), so I suggest you make it in this large amount. Luckily it keeps very well in the freezer. You absolutely must use a good gelatinous stock, as this is what gives the jus body and shine. In an ideal world, make your jus using a combination of beef stock and veal stock.

3 tablespoons olive oil
2 carrots, roughly chopped
2 sticks celery, roughly chopped
2 onions, roughly chopped

4 garlic cloves, roughly chopped
4 sprigs thyme, plus a few extra
4 litres of good-quality gelatinous beef stock (see page 324)

Heat the olive oil in a large stockpot. Add the chopped vegetables and thyme and stir well. Sauté for 5 minutes, or until the vegies colour a lovely golden brown.

Add the stock and bring to the boil slowly, skimming away the foam or other impurities that rise to the surface. When the stock boils, lower the heat and simmer until the liquid reduces by half. This will take 1–2 hours. Taste it frequently to make sure it doesn't reduce too far and become bitter.

Once reduced, the stock will take on a rich, shiny quality and will have the consistency of runny cream. At the end of the cooking time throw in a few more sprigs of thyme to freshen the flavour.

Freeze the stock in batches and use as an instant sauce or as a sauce base.

Makes 2 litres

Sauces
Red wine reduction

This red wine reduction is a great way to add an intense flavour boost to meat sauces and gravies. It adds richness and sweetness, both of which complement meat dishes brilliantly. It will keep in a sealable container in the fridge for 1–2 weeks. Alternatively, freeze it in an ice tray. That way you can pop out a few blocks and slip them into your gravies to add a last-minute flavour hit.

2 litres well-flavoured beef or veal stock
2 cups red wine
2 cups port

1 tablespoon chopped thyme
salt
freshly ground pepper

Bring the stock to a boil over a high heat. Simmer until reduced by half. Add the red wine and port and return to the boil. Lower the heat and simmer until reduced by half. Stir in the chopped thyme and season to taste. Leave to cool, then transfer to a sealable container and refrigerate or freeze.

Makes 600ml

Green peppercorn and brandy sauce

This is a wonderful sauce to serve with any steak. Sure it's a bit of an old retro-classic, but I love it! Just be careful when you add the brandy in case it flames up. If you're feeling brave, then by all means do the cheffy flambé thing – but it's not absolutely essential.

1 cup veal or chicken stock
¼ cup brandy
¼ cup green peppercorns

¼ cup cream
salt
freshly ground black pepper

Bring the stock to a boil in a small saucepan. Allow it to bubble vigorously, until reduced by half.

Once the steaks are cooked and rested add the brandy to the frying pan, and flambé it if you wish. Add the stock to the pan and use a wooden spoon to scrape up all the residual cooking juices. Allow it to bubble for 5 minutes, until reduced by half. Stir in the peppercorns and cream and season to taste. Pour over steaks and serve.

Makes 1 cup

Sauces

Caramelised cherry and brandy glaze

This sauce is especially wonderful with dark gamey meats, such as duck or goose and I really like it with roast pork. When cherries are not in season you can use tinned cherries, in which case add the juice to the sauce as well. If you prefer a thicker sauce you could thicken it with one tablespoon of cornflour, or tip the lot into a liquidiser and whiz it to a purée.

100 g sugar
1 cup warm water
400 g pitted cherries (fresh or tinned)

1 cup good-quality chicken stock
½ cup brandy
salt

Combine the sugar and water in a small saucepan. Heat gently, stirring from time to time, until the sugar has dissolved. Bring to the boil, then lower the heat and simmer to form a light golden caramel.

Carefully add the cherries – the caramel may splutter and spit – then stir in the stock. Simmer for 15 minutes over a low heat. (If using tinned cherries, they'll only take about 4 minutes.) Add the brandy and simmer for a further 8 minutes. Season to taste before serving.

Makes 2 cups

Caramelised apple and calvados sauce

The apple flavours in this sauce work brilliantly with all sorts of pork dishes. For an extra depth of flavour you can add half a cup of Jus (page 331) with the calvados, or if you like your sauces creamy, stir in two tablespoons of cream just before serving.

Calvados is an apple brandy from Normandy in France. It adds a lovely warmth and a bit of a kick to this sauce.

5 Granny Smith apples
300 g castor sugar
250 ml warm water

¼ vanilla bean
½ cup calvados

Peel and core the apples and cut them into sixths.

Combine the sugar and water in a medium saucepan. Heat gently, stirring occasionally, until the sugar dissolves. Increase the heat and bring to the boil. Simmer until the syrup becomes a light golden caramel. Transfer the pan straight away to a sink of iced water, which will stop the caramel cooking further.

Carefully add the apples to the caramel, then scrape in the seeds from the vanilla pod and stir gently to combine. Return the pan to the heat and bring to the boil. Lower the heat and simmer gently until the apples are tender, but still firm. You don't want them mushy. Stir in the calvados and simmer for 2 minutes, then serve straight away.

Makes 2 cups

Sauces

Creamy mushroom sauce

This mushroom sauce has a lighter flavour than the recipe that follows it. I like to serve it with pan-fried chicken breasts, grilled pork chops, or even as a pasta sauce.

1 cup good-quality chicken stock
50 g butter
¼ small onion, finely diced
1 garlic clove, crushed
400 g mixed mushrooms, thinly sliced

¼ cup white wine
2 tablespoons chopped thyme
300 ml cream
salt
freshly ground black pepper

In a medium saucepan, bring the chicken stock to a boil, then lower the heat and simmer for 5 minutes until reduced by a third.

In another saucepan, melt the butter, then add the onion and garlic. Sweat gently for 5 minutes until soft and translucent. Add the mushrooms to the pan and cook for 2–3 minutes until they soften. Add the wine and simmer for 5 minutes. Add the reduced chicken stock and simmer for another 5 minutes. Finally, stir in the thyme and the cream and simmer for 5 minutes. Season with salt and pepper and serve.

Makes 1½ cups

Intense mushroom sauce

This sauce doesn't include cream and it is darker and more intensely flavoured than the preceding recipe. Serve with grilled steak or lamb chops.

50 g butter
1 onion, finely diced
1 garlic clove, crushed
400 g mixed mushrooms, thinly sliced

½ cup red wine
200 ml Jus (page 331) or 1 cup
  good-quality beef stock
2 tablespoons chopped thyme

Melt the butter in a heavy-based saucepan then add the onion and garlic. Sweat gently for 5 minutes until soft and translucent. Add the mushrooms to the pan and cook for 2–3 minutes until they soften. Add the wine and simmer for 5–8 minutes, or until reduced by half. Add the jus and simmer for 2–3 minutes. Stir in the thyme and serve straight away.

Makes 1½ cups

ACCOMPANIMENTS

14

THAT LITTLE SOMETHING ON THE SIDE

Accompaniments

Okay. So you've got your meat, vegies and gravy sorted. But perhaps you feel that there's still something missing. And I would agree: I think it's always important to have a little something extra on the side of your plate.

I'm talking about condiments of course. The mustards, relishes, salsas, pickles and mayonnaises that liven everything up. They are all great ways of complementing and increasing the flavour and juiciness of meat.

The recipes that follow vary from mayonnaises and creamy dipping sauces to tangy vinegar-based preserves and pickles, which are a natural accompaniment to the rich flavours of charcuterie. I've also included a selection of quick-and-easy flavoured butters, which add instant 'sauce' to a grilled steak.

There is a wide range of these items available ready-made in good delicatessens and farmers' markets, and I would suggest you have fun buying a selection for the pantry. But remember too that many condiments are simplicity itself to throw together yourself – and nothing is quite as good or satisfying as homemade, is it?

Mayonnaise

You can make mayonnaise by hand, or in a blender or food processor. Here I give the hand-whisked method as I think it's really important to understand the process. Whichever method you use, the important thing is to add the oil very slowly to begin with, until the mixture emulsifies. Start drop by drop, then increase to a drizzle, and once the mayonnaise is glossy and thick, you can add the rest of the oil in a slow, steady stream.

Mayonnaise is fantastically versatile and you can flavour it in various ways. Some of my favourite variations follow.

2 free-range egg yolks
juice of ½ lemon
1 teaspoon Dijon mustard

1 teaspoon salt
1½ cups olive oil
a pinch of freshly ground white pepper

Place the egg yolks, lemon juice, mustard and salt in a mixing bowl and set it on a damp tea towel to keep it steady. Beat with a balloon whisk until smooth and creamy. Now start adding the oil, drop by drop, whisking all the time. Don't be tempted to rush this stage. Once a third of the oil has been added, increase the speed to a slow, steady stream, whisking continuously until it has all been incorporated.

Taste the mayonnaise and adjust the seasonings and acid level to your liking. If the mayonnaise is too thick, you can thin it with a little water.

Store in the fridge in an airtight container.

Makes 1½ cups

Aïoli (garlic mayonnaise)

This mayonnaise for garlic lovers is best made in a food processor. I suggest you pound the garlic to a smooth paste first, that way you'll avoid any lumpy bits in the finished sauce.

4 garlic cloves
½ teaspoon salt
2 free-range egg yolks

juice of ½ lemon
1½ cups olive oil
a pinch of freshly ground white pepper

In a mortar and pestle, pound the garlic to a smooth paste with the salt. Spoon the paste into a food processor with the egg yolks and lemon juice and process until smooth and creamy. With the motor running, add the olive oil a few drops at a time, until the mayonnaise emulsifies and thickens. Increase to a slow, steady stream until it has all has been incorporated.

Taste the aïoli and adjust the seasonings and acid level to your liking. If it is too thick, you can thin it with a little water.

Store in the fridge in an airtight container.

Makes 1½ cups

Chilli mayonnaise

Add more or less chilli powder, depending on how fiery you like your sauces. I like to use habaneros chillies – but they are definitely not for beginners!

2 long red chillies, seeded (or hot chillies, to taste)
2 free-range egg yolks
juice of 1 lime
¼ teaspoon salt
1½ cups olive oil

1 teaspoon smoked paprika
1 teaspoon hot chilli powder or chilli flakes
2 tablespoons chopped coriander leaves

Chop the chillies finely then transfer to a food processor with the egg yolks, lime juice and salt and process until smooth and creamy. With the motor running, add the oil a few drops at a time, until the mayonnaise emulsifies and thickens. Increase to a slow, steady stream until all has been incorporated.

Add the paprika, chilli powder and coriander, then taste and adjust the seasonings and acid level to your liking. If it is too thick, you can thin it with a little water.

Store in the fridge in an airtight container.

Makes 1⅓ cups

Thick yoghurt sauce

I like to serve yoghurt-based sauces with meat because I think the creamy texture and slight sourness complements the richness of many grills and roasts brilliantly. This recipe makes for a fairly thick and creamy sauce. If you want to make it thinner, give it a spin in a food processor.

1 garlic clove
½ teaspoon salt
250 g thick natural yoghurt

1 tablespoon chopped mint leaves
1 tablespoon chopped coriander leaves
juice of ½ lemon

Use the back of a knife to crush the garlic with the salt until you have a smooth paste. Stir into the yoghurt, and add the fresh herbs and lemon juice.

Makes just over 1 cup

Tzatziki

This well-known Greek sauce is often served with lamb dishes and as a dip with raw vegetables. I think tzatziki is especially good when you make it with new season's garlic, which is much sweeter than the stuff that's available all year round.

Hanging the yoghurt overnight to drain off some of the liquid (the whey) makes it thicker, creamier and richer.

500 g natural yoghurt
1 Lebanese cucumber, peeled
salt
1 garlic clove, crushed

1 tablespoon chopped dill
½ teaspoon freshly ground white pepper
juice of ½ lemon

Spoon the yoghurt into a clean tea towel or square of cheesecloth or muslin. Tie the four corners together and suspend the bundle from a wooden spoon set over a deep bowl. Refrigerate and leave to drain overnight, or for up to 2 days.

Split the cucumber in half lengthwise, scoop out the seeds and discard them. Grate the cucumber into a small bowl and sprinkle lightly with salt. Leave for 5 minutes then tip into a sieve and rinse. Use your hands to squeeze out as much of the liquid as you possibly can – you want the cucumber to be very dry or it will leak and make your tzatziki watery.

Tip the drained yoghurt into a large mixing bowl. Add the cucumber with all the remaining ingredients and stir well. Taste and adjust the seasoning to your liking. Chill until required, and use within 7 days.

Makes just over 1 cup

Horseradish cream

To my mind, nothing goes better with a thick slice of rare roast beef than horseradish cream. I think it's well worth buying some fresh horseradish root to make your own. The flavour is so much better than the shop-bought, ready-made stuff, and you can tailor the heat level to your liking. Another handy trick is to soften the heat by stirring a few drops of vinegar into the grated horseradish before adding the cream.

100 g fresh horseradish root
200 ml cream

salt
a pinch of freshly ground white pepper

Peel the horseradish root and grate it finely. Whip the cream to soft peaks. Fold the horseradish and seasonings into the cream then taste it and adjust to your liking.

Store in a sealed container in the fridge for up to 2 days.

Makes just over 1 cup

Adrian's one-size-fits-all mustard

This is a great-tasting mustard blend that goes with most grilled and barbecued meats and sausages.

¼ cup good Dijon mustard
¼ cup good French grain mustard
1 tablespoon freshly ground black
   pepper

2 tablespoons chopped thyme
3 tablespoons cognac

Combine all the ingredients in a small bowl and stir well. Transfer to a sealable container and store in the fridge indefinitely.

Makes ½ cup

Homemade tomato sauce

In the summer you can make this sauce using fresh roma tomatoes. Good-quality passata will do just as well when tomatoes are not in season.

1 litre good-quality tomato passata
¼ cup white wine or cider vinegar
¼ cup soft brown sugar
1 tablespoon salt

2 teaspoons freshly ground white
   pepper
¼ cup Worcestershire sauce

Combine all the ingredients in a large saucepan. Bring to the boil, then lower the heat and simmer gently for 20 minutes, stirring from time to time.

Allow to cool a little, then decant into 2 x 500 ml sterilised jars. Seal and keep refrigerated for up to 1 month.

Makes 1 litre

Beetroot jam

Beetroot has a lovely earthy sweetness that makes it ideal to serve with strong gamey flavours, such as duck, venison and kangaroo. But it's also pretty good served with cold ham and salad and crusty white bread.

1 kg raw beetroot, grated
1 onion, grated
200 g soft brown sugar
2 tablespoons red wine vinegar
1 tablespoon finely grated ginger
1 tablespoon caraway seeds

1 stick cinnamon
2 cardamom pods
½ cup coriander leaves
a pinch of salt
1 teaspoon freshly ground white
   pepper

Combine all the ingredients in a large saucepan. Bring to the boil, then lower the heat and simmer gently for 20 minutes, stirring from time to time.

Allow to cool a little, then decant into 2 x 500 ml sterilised jars. Seal and keep refrigerated for up to 1 month.

Makes 1 litre

Mint sauce

The classic accompaniment for roast lamb. When you make it yourself, it tastes so much better than any shop-bought stuff.

1 cup fresh mint leaves
2 tablespoons white sugar
¼ cup boiling water

¼ cup sherry vinegar
salt
freshly ground black pepper

Put the mint leaves and sugar into a mortar and pound to a coarse, gritty paste. Pour in the boiling water and stir to dissolve the sugar completely. Stir in the vinegar then season to taste. Leave to cool and serve with roast lamb.

Makes just over ½ cup

Basil pesto

This classic Italian sauce is not just for spaghetti! I think it's brilliant with grilled lamb and barbecued chicken or quail.

3 cups well-packed basil leaves
2 garlic cloves, crushed
½ cup toasted pine nuts
½ cup extra-virgin olive oil, plus more
  to cover

¼ cup freshly grated parmesan
salt
freshly ground black pepper

Combine the basil, garlic, pine nuts and oil in a liquidiser or food processor and whiz to a smooth paste. When evenly blended, stir in the cheese and season to taste with salt and pepper. Tip the pesto into an airtight container and pour in enough oil to cover the surface; this helps prevent the pesto discolouring. Store in the fridge for up to 7 days or freeze for up to 3 months.

Makes 1½ cups

Salsa verde

This is a vibrant green sauce, chock-full of gutsy flavours. It's traditionally served with poached or grilled meats and also fish. I also love to serve it with Classic Veal Schnitzel (page 60) or with pork terrines.

½ cup green olives, pitted and
  chopped
½ cup gherkins, chopped
¼ cup chopped parsley
juice of 1 lemon

3 tablespoons extra-virgin olive oil
salt
freshly ground black pepper
1 garlic clove, finely chopped (optional)

Chop the olives, gherkins and parsley separately. Place them all in a large mixing bowl with the lemon juice and oil. Stir well, then season to taste and stir in the garlic, if using. Leave the salsa to sit for 30 minutes at room temperature, so the flavours can develop. Stir briefly before serving.

Makes just over 1 cup

Eggplant salsa

This chunky salsa also works really well as a side dish. It's wonderfully summery and goes brilliantly with all sorts of grilled meats and poultry.

1 medium eggplant
olive oil
3 roma tomatoes, cut into 1 cm dice
2 tablespoons chopped coriander
1 fresh long red chilli, seeded and
  chopped
2 tablespoons chopped parsley

1 teaspoon sesame seeds
2 spring onions, sliced
juice ½ lemon
3 tablespoons extra-virgin olive oil
1 teaspoon salt
1 teaspoon freshly ground
  black pepper

Cut the eggplant into 1.5 cm slices. Sprinkle them with salt and layer them in a colander. Leave for 30 minutes then rinse them well. Pat the eggplant thoroughly dry.

Preheat the grill or barbecue to medium–high. Brush the eggplant slices with oil and grill for 5 minutes on each side, or until golden brown and tender. Allow the eggplant to cool then chop into 1.5 cm dice.

Place the diced eggplant and tomato in a large mixing bowl. Add all the remaining ingredients and toss together well.

Makes 2 cups

Tapenade

This Mediterranean paste can be made with green or black olives, although each version will taste slightly different. Either way, the better the quality of olives you use, the better the end result.

Tapenade is brilliantly versatile: you can use it as a topping for crostini, dollop it onto tomatoes and eggplant before baking them in the oven or drizzle it over roast lamb.

1½ cup good-quality olives, pitted
2 anchovy fillets
1 tablespoon capers

1 teaspoon freshly ground black pepper
2 tablespoons extra-virgin olive oil,
  plus more to cover

Roughly chop the olives and anchovies then place them in a food processor with the remaining ingredients. Blitz to a fairly smooth paste, being careful not to overwork it.

Tip the tapenade into a sealable container and cover with a thin layer of oil. Store in the fridge for up to 2 weeks.

Makes 1 cup

Onion jam

This jam is brilliantly useful. You can serve it up with sausages or grilled chops and steaks, or even with cold ham or cold meat sandwiches.

¼ cup extra-virgin olive oil
1 kg onions, thinly sliced
100 g soft brown sugar
2 tablespoons sherry vinegar

1 teaspoon salt
½ teaspoon freshly ground
 black pepper

Heat the oil in a large heavy-based saucepan. Add the onion and cook, stirring frequently, for 2–3 minutes. Lower the heat and cook covered, for 30 minutes, stirring from time to time to ensure the onions don't stick to the bottom of the pan and burn.

When the onions are very soft, remove the lid and increase the heat. Cook over a high heat, stirring constantly, until the onions are evenly coloured a lovely golden brown. Add the sugar and vinegar to the pan and stir until dissolved. Stir in the salt and pepper, remove the pan from the heat and leave to cool.

The onion jam can be kept in a sealed container in the fridge for up to 7 days.

Makes 1 cup

Quick pickled onions

This is a quick-and-easy sort of pickle, which is more about softening the harshness of the raw onions than preserving them for any length of time. I like to serve it with all sorts of smallgoods and terrines, and I also scatter them in salads for a piquant surprise.

¼ cup red wine vinegar
1 teaspoon salt
3 red onions, thinly sliced
3 tablespoons extra-virgin olive oil
1 cup parsley leaves

½ cup coriander leaves
1 tablespoon ground sumac
½ teaspoon freshly ground black
 pepper

Combine the vinegar and salt in a large mixing bowl and stir until dissolved. Add the onions and stir so that they are covered with the pickling mixture. Cover with plastic wrap and leave to soak for 2 hours.

In another small bowl, mix the olive oil with the fresh herbs, sumac and pepper. Remove the onions from the pickling mixture and stir into the oil. Serve straight away or refrigerate for up to 1 week.

Makes around ¾ cup

Pickled cherries

You can use this pickling liquid to make all sorts of pickled fruits. In the autumn I like to substitute quinces, which should be peeled, cored and cut into 1 cm slices.

Serve with a selection of smallgoods and terrines. They are especially good with Spanish jamon and prosciutto.

700 g white sugar
24 black peppercorns
12 cloves
6 bay leaves

1 garlic clove, unpeeled (optional)
1 litre white wine vinegar
1 kg cherries (left whole)

Combine the sugar, peppercorns, cloves, bay leaves and garlic, if using, in a medium saucepan. Add the vinegar and heat gently, stirring from time to time, until the sugar dissolves. Increase the heat and bring to the boil, then lower the heat and simmer for 10 minutes. Remove the pan from the heat and leave to cool.

Spoon the cherries into a 2 litre sterilised jar and pour on the cooled pickling liquid – make sure the fruit is completely covered. Seal the jar and store in the fridge for 2 days before using. Keep up to 1 month.

Makes 2 litres

Balsamic syrup

This intense sweet-sour syrup is brilliantly versatile. It is thick and syrupy, which makes it perfect fro drizzling. I use it on grilled and roasted meats and will often add a splash to salad dressings, and it is brilliant for livening up frittatas (page 190). Sometimes I serve a little bowl of this syrup with extra-virgin olive oil, and bread, for dipping.

1 cup sugar

1 cup balsamic vinegar
  (less expensive brand is fine)

To make the balsamic syrup, put the sugar and vinegar into a small saucepan and heat gently until the sugar has dissolved. Increase the heat and bring to the boil, then simmer until reduced by half. Remove the pan from the heat and leave to cool. Tip into a sealable jar. The syrup will keep for several months in the fridge.

Makes ½ cup

Flavoured butters

Flavoured butters – or compound butters, to give them their fancy name – are a wonderful way to add an instant tasty 'sauce' to your grills and roasts. You can add all sorts of ingredients to the butter before rolling it into a log shape, wrapping in plastic wrap and storing in the fridge or freezer. All you do then is cut off a slice as you need it. The following are some of my favourite combinations.

Garlic butter

Is this everyone's favourite butter? You can use it to make garlic bread, dollop it into baked potatoes or let it melt over the top of a perfectly cooked steak (pages 29, 31).

250 g unsalted butter, at room temperature
10 garlic cloves, crushed
2 tablespoons finely chopped parsley

1 teaspoon salt
½ teaspoon freshly ground black pepper

Put the butter into the bowl of an electric mixer and beat with the 'k' paddle until very pale and fluffy. Add the remaining ingredients and mix in well. Tip the flavoured butter out onto a large square of plastic wrap, aluminium foil or greaseproof paper and roll to form a log shape. Twist the ends securely and chill until required.

The butter will keep in the refrigerator for 2 weeks or up to 3 months in the freezer.

Makes 300 g

Porcini butter

This has a wonderful earthy flavour from the porcini mushrooms and goes especially well with grilled steak or mushrooms. You can buy porcini mushroom powder from specialty food stores, but it's also easy to make your own at home. All you do is slice some porcini mushrooms thinly, leave them to dry out in a cool, airy spot, then blitz them to a powder in a food processor. The powder will store for several months in an airtight container and can be used in sauces, stuffings or to sprinkle on meats before and after grilling.

250 g unsalted butter, at room temperature
4 tablespoons porcini powder
1 tablespoon chopped thyme

1 teaspoon salt
½ teaspoon freshly ground black pepper

Put the butter into the bowl of an electric mixer and beat with the 'k' paddle until very pale and fluffy. Add the remaining ingredients and mix in well. Tip the flavoured butter out onto a large square of plastic wrap, aluminium foil or greaseproof paper and roll to form a log shape. Twist the ends securely and chill until required.

The butter will keep in the refrigerator for 2 weeks or up to 3 months in the freezer.

Makes 300 g

Fancy butter

Although I love to use this fancy butter as a topping for grills, sometimes I just spread it thickly on fresh crusty bread and give it a few seconds on the barbie.

250 g unsalted butter, at room
  temperature
1 tablespoon smoked paprika
1 teaspoon cayenne pepper
1 tablespoon chopped coriander leaves

1 tablespoon chopped parsley
1 teaspoon salt
½ teaspoon freshly ground
  black pepper

Put the butter into the bowl of an electric mixer and beat with the 'k' paddle until very pale and fluffy. Add the remaining ingredients and mix in well. Tip the flavoured butter out onto a large square of plastic wrap, aluminium foil or greaseproof paper and roll to form a log shape. Twist the ends securely and chill until required.

The butter will keep in the refrigerator for 2 weeks or up to 3 months in the freezer.

Makes 300 g

Herby butter

This butter goes especially well with white meats, such as grilled chicken or pork chops.

200 g softened butter
¼ cup chopped parsley
1 tablespoon fresh thyme

1 teaspoon fresh rosemary
1 teaspoon salt
1 teaspoon freshly ground black pepper

Put the butter into the bowl of an electric mixer and beat with the 'k' paddle until very pale and fluffy. Add the remaining ingredients and mix in well. Tip the flavoured butter out onto a large square of plastic wrap, aluminium foil or greaseproof paper and roll to form a log shape. Twist the ends securely and chill until required.

The butter will keep in the refrigerator for 2 weeks or up to 3 months in the freezer.

Makes 300 g

Index

Thanks

First and foremost, thanks to my family:
To Michelle my loving, gorgeous, glamorous wife for 14 years of devotion, support and love and for never (almost never) saying no! To my beautiful three boys Rex, Rudi and Roman, for climbing over, under, and on top of me, while I was trying to write – there was a tickle for every page. To mum and John, thanks for believing, for giving me the chance to live my dream, and for always being there for your children. Dad, thanks for teaching me to fly, and for giving me a good work ethic. You were right, I *could* do anything I wanted to. And to my brothers, Mark and Andrew, thanks for the non-stop late night eating! To my greatly missed nonno, Armenio Ferrai, thanks for everything: for the polenta cooking lessons, the mixed 'eggy' and for teaching me to make coffee at the age of five – two sugars, no milk, I still drink it that way today. (There was never too much salt in Nonna's cooking, and you knew it!) To my Nonna Yole Ferrai, for being the best cook in the world, for the Saturday arvos spent cooking, talking and watching Elvis movies, for opening my eyes to food from around the world, for love and for family. I still cook the way you taught me. To Peter and Cathy my other grandparents: vegetarians, gardeners and lovers of the good life! You're the other best cooks in the world! Thanks for the brawn recipe.

A huge thanks to the crew at La Luna Bistro, both past and present:
To Lynda for her smile, and for eight years of dedication, devotion, and loyalty – you are the best luv! To Slade for keeping it sweet in the kitchen, for hard work, organisation, and loyalty. To Kristy, Osher and Liz for early mornings, late nights, and extra-long hours testing, testing and testing. To all the chefs, waiters and staff who have worked at La Luna over the years for their endless enthusiasm in keeping a very busy restaurant running, and for keeping the bar well stocked with gin and pinot. Thanks for making our restaurant the success it is today.

And to Justine May, my agent (the other tasty red head!), thanks for believing in me. We've come a long way and here's to an even brighter future.

A massive thanks to all the people who worked so hard in putting this book together:
To my publishers Hardie Grant, thanks for giving me the opportunity – what a great team! To Mary Small, for letting me double the size of the book (and barely flinching), and being so one hundred percent positive all the time. To Ellie Smith, my special taste tester, thanks for working so damn hard on this book, we barely knew you were stressed. To designer Dom, you got it right from the start – fantastic work! To Lucy Malouf, for advice, spelling, grammar, and for holding my hand through the entire process. You are the best! (And not forgetting George and Molly, for all the slobber, and Big George for the sideshow!) To the very stylish Caroline Velik , thank you for making the photos look great. And to Dean Cambray, after so many years of talking about doing a book together, we finally did it! Thanks for your encouragement, advice, and the best photos. It was, still is, and will always be a pleasure.

My unending gratitude goes to the brilliant people who make it possible for me to put such amazing meat on my customers' plates:
To Bob and Karen Webster for being so hospitable and for having the best-looking chickens and the tastiest scones. To Joerg, Janet, Kate, Kyle and Emma Henne, without whose help the front cover would not look so fab! (And thanks to Calgary, the bull, for standing still for so long in the field.) To Judy Croagh for the delicious little suckling pigs and for the big fat chestnut-fed sows. To Mick, Joe and John at Westside meats, you are the best slaughtermen in Australia. Thanks for always working so hard to give me the very best meat and guts in the country – now we just have to work on getting the pig's blood! To Ross and Damien at R & A Meats in Carlton. You are the best 'old-school', Continental butchers and *salumiere* around! Thanks for teaching me so much. (Yes Ross, you did teach me everything I know!)

And to all my chef friends, where would I be without you? First and foremost, to Kurt Sampson, Michael Dijon and Manu Feildel for being beautiful cooks and letting me rip off their best dishes. And thanks, too, to the other great people I have worked with over the years: to Cliff 'flem grill' Gertsits, Ian 'it's only a sock' Cameron, and Martin 'I hope it's cold in Ireland' O'Connor. To Michael Bacash, the best fish cook ever, for teaching me to be an owner chef, and helping me understand what not to do. To Greg 'hairy face' Malouf, thanks for the mention in your book (now it's one all), and for the knife that appears in many of the photos (Yes, I was the one who pinched it!). And to Kate 'ace' Daziel, thanks for being the ace-est.

And finally, to the people who kept me going during the hard work putting the book together:
To Steve Jess and the crew at Deco Bar, for making it so easy to relax. To Rob 'it's bigger than you think' Martin, for keeping me in touch with my other love, surfing. To Kurt (again), for late night down-hill skateboard bombing runs, to Todd Beckinsale and Andrew Jones, and to my snow-boarding buddy Pat, thanks for the pizzas!